Children and Counselling

Samotny Król – Lonely King

I found this picture in a flat in Warsaw in a collection of several paintings by children suffering from a variety of serious illnesses. My friend, whose wall houses this collection, asked which had in my view been painted by a dying child. I had no hesitation in choosing Samotny Król.

This pen sketch is based on a painting by an 8-year-old Polish boy who was suffering from leukaemia, not very long before his death at 9.

The painting is in heavy black on a background of intermingling blues and browns. The castle (zamek) is slightly larger in the original and is, perhaps, echoed by the "ghostly" zamek in the bottom left-hand corner.

Permission to use this copy has been given by my friend Zbigniew Sendułka, for which I record my thanks.

Children and Counselling

Margaret Crompton

Edward Arnold
A division of Hodder & Stoughton
LONDON   MELBOURNE   AUCKLAND

© 1992 Margaret Crompton

First published in Great Britain 1992

British Library Cataloguing in Publication Data

Crompton, Margaret
 Children and Counselling
 I. Title
 362.7

 ISBN 0-340-55435-5

Whilst the advice and information in this book is believed to be true and accurate at the date of going to press, neither the author nor the publisher can accept any legal responsibility or liability for any errors or omissions that may be made.

Typeset in Great Britain by Saxon Printing Ltd, Derby
Printed and bound in Great Britain for Edward Arnold, a division of Hodder and Stoughton Limited, Mill Road, Dunton Green, Sevenoaks, Kent TN13 2YA by Biddles Ltd, Guildford & King's Lynn

Contents

Preface   vii

Acknowledgements   xi

1   A childist approach to counselling   1

2   An idea of counselling   15

3   On empathy   27

4   Tips, dumps and privacy   45

5   A few feet of silence   69

6   A house with four rooms   82

7   Enter these enchanted tales   120

8   A story of life   143

9   Roses, pagodas and owls   163

10 A sound of their own   181

Conclusion   Good enough being   203

Appendix   ChildLine: An example of child-focused counselling   208

Bibliography   218

Subject Index   228

Authors Index   240

Preface

I think that the faith of the counsellors has implicitly retained the notion of an unanalysable proclivity and need to love and to be loved (Halmos, 1965, p. 194).

Shortly before publication of *Attending to Children* (1990) I was invited to offer a proposal for a book on counselling children. The resulting *Children and Counselling* bears little resemblance to that proposal for, in the 16 months of preparation, I have read many books, met many people, thought many thoughts and written many words, a few thousand of which follow this *Introduction*.

This is not a guidebook to either counselling or children. It is a series of linked papers on aspects of the topic which particularly interest me and which seem to receive relatively little, or no, attention in other counselling literature.

Interpretation of *children* and *counselling* is very broad and I have drawn on material from, for example, *therapy* and *casework*.

As counselling is about every individual's story, so this book is a chapter in my own story. As we are all 'tall children' so this reveals the author as a child in woman.

As with my other books (1980, 1982, 1990) I have chosen to refer to a wide range of literature, using autobiography, fiction, writing for and by children, and professional texts from such disciplines as counselling, cultural history, education, nursing and psychology.

I am convinced that familiarity with literature, in many covers, is essential to developing understanding of oneself and other people. Read attentively, *Jane Eyre* (Brontë) or *The Secret Garden* (Hodgson-Burnett) reveal infinitely more about unhappy childhood than the most scientific and elegant textbook. Far from relying on literature, I revel in and reveal it, recognizing the truth of contemporary literary criticism which proposes that all literature is intertextual; in other words, it is impossible to write one book without, however unintentionally, resonating with many others.

I have decided to speak more with my own voice in the present book, including claiming my own work. In *Attending to Children* I used pseudonyms and disguised case examples heavily. But I later thought that this became obfuscating and have, with the permission of children's regular social workers, written in my own name. Where pseudonyms are used, they are in inverted commas at first appearance in any chapter.

Since this topic is immense I have limited study to work with individuals only; any references to family, group or residential work are incidental. However, I hope that workers in those fields will find interest and relevance in these pages.

Because *Attending to Children* was published so recently (1990) I have deliberately not discussed again main topics from that text, for example, truth, fear, trust, love, meaning, beginning and ending contacts. I have also avoided discussion of such means of communication as non-verbal and environmental messages. Some authors referred to in that book appear again in the following pages. Although I cannot expect readers of *Children and Counselling* to have read *Attending to Children*, I do regard this as in many ways a companion volume.

Chapters on art, music, silence and story/myth develop rather than repeat my work in *Respecting Children* (1980). The chapters on empathy and spiritual aspects of counselling are my first attempts to study these topics.

Children and Counselling begins with some ideas about approaches to counselling, with particular reference to working with children and young people.

The Appendix, a brief study of ChildLine, illustrates some of the main themes.

I have not tried to cover or even refer to every kind of agency or problem, or to discuss every kind of counselling approach and method. This is a book about individuals, inwardness and connections. I hope that my individual inwardness will connect with readers whom I can meet only in print and who will make their own further connections, illuminating their own inwardness.

Many people have helped me.

Richard Holloway, formerly of Edward Arnold, gave me the initial idea for the book.

Gary Hornby, Lecturer in Education in the University of Hull gave generous informal tutorials and encouragement and lent books.

Practitioners in a number of agencies gave time and shared experience. A letter in a magazine *(The Friend)* attracted many responses, including long letters, articles (published and unpublished), a dissertation and books. I have used directly only a fraction of this material but it has all been very valuable in developing the idea of counselling which forms the basis of the present text.

Several authors (for example, Jocelyn Chaplin and Ann Gillespie) have been particularly generous in responding to draft sections quoting their work and in encouraging my work. Robert Holman read the entire text and his understanding, encouragement, and last minute suggestions have been of the greatest help.

The greatest headache has been contact with publishers for permission to quote from books. I have learnt almost as much about the immense (and bewildering) changes in the world of publishing as I have about counselling. Moves and amalgamations rendered attempts at contact slow and tortuous. Permissions editors have been very helpful and detailed acknowledgements appear after this Preface.

It has not of course been possible to read more than a tiny sample of the ever-growing literature of counselling. Without the Brynmor Jones Library of the University of Hull, I could not even have started.

Writing this Preface, just before Christmas 1991, I long to begin the whole work again. Ideas developed throughout the 16 months of preparation and writing are coming together in new ways and I have to resist the temptation to disturb my almost flawless typescript and add an idea here, a thought there. Fortunately my husband John, always my aid and tutor, holds me to common sense. Enough is enough.

I have written this book with all these people in mind and in gratitude. But, above all, with thanks to the children in whose lives I have been, however briefly, involved. This book is dedicated to 'Luke' and 'Mark' and all the children I have loved, and to John.

December 1991   Apley MC

Reference

Halmos, P. (1965). *The Faith of the Counsellors*. Constable, London.

Acknowledgements

I am grateful for permission to quote from the following publications:

Counseling Children, 2nd edition, by C. L. Thompson and L. B. Rudolph (c1988, 1983). By Wadsworth, Inc., by permission of Brooks/Cole Publishing Company, Pacific Grove, CA 93950 USA.

The Skilled Helper, 4th edition, by Gerard Egan. (c1990, 1985, 1972, 1975). By Wadsworth, Inc. By permission of Brooks/Cole Publishing Company, Pacific Grove, CA 93950 USA.

Empathy and its Development, by N. Eisenberg and J. Strayer. (1987). By permission of Cambridge University Press.

The Spiritual Needs of Children, ed. J. A. Shelley. By permission of Scripture Union.

The Spiritual Rights of the Child. By permission of the author John Bradford. (1979). The Children's Society.

The Collected Stories of Elizabeth Bowen, ed. Angus Wilson. (1983). The Estate of Elizabeth Bowen. By permission of Jonathan Cape (Random Century Group).

Discovering Music with Young Children by E. Bailey (1958). By permission of Methuen.

An Introduction to Counselling Skills by B. Mallon (1987). By permission of Manchester University Press.

Music for the Handicapped Child by J. Alvin (1965). By permission of Oxford University Press.

Special Needs in Ordinary Schools by P. Lowe (1988). By permission of Cassell.

Children as Writers: 20th year (1979). Heinemann. By permission of W. H. Smith.

The Scrake of Dawn. ed. P. Muldoon (1979). By permission of the Blackstaff Press.

Counselling as a Spiritual Process by permission of the author, D. G. Benner (1991). Clinical Theology Association.

One Small Plot by Elise Boulding (1989). By permission of Pendle Hill Publications. Wallingford, Pennsylvania 19086.

Beyond Fear by Dorothy Rowe (1987). Collins. By permission of Harper Collins.

The Reality Therapy Reader. eds Bassin, A., Bratter, T. E. and Rachin, R. L. (1976). By permission of Harper Collins.

Inscapes of the Child's World by John Allan, including Foreword by James Hillman (1988). By permission of Spring Publications Inc. Dallas.

The New Short-term Therapies for Children by Lawrence E. Shapiro (1984). By permission of Prentice Hall. A division of Simon and Schuster. Englewood Cliffs, New Jersey.

Material from ChildLine, by permission of ChildLine, 2nd Floor, Royal Mail Building, Studd Street, London N1 0QW.

Childhood in the Middle Ages by permission of the author Jeffrey Richards. 1991.

Feminist Counselling in Action by permission of the author Jocelyn Chaplin. 1988.

Music: a Way of Life for the Young Child by Bayless K. M. and Ramsay M. E. (1982). By Permission of C. V. Mosby and Co, by permission of Macmillan, New York.

Individual Therapy in Britain. ed. W. Dryden (1984). By permission of Harper Collins.

Courage to Grow by Ruth Fawell (1987) QHS. By permission of the author.

A Minority of One, A Journey with Friends by Harvey Gillman (1988). By permission of the author.

Art Therapy At the Family-Makers Project by Anne Gillespie (1986). By permission of the author.

How Do We Treat Our Children? Keith Redfern (1991). By permission of the author.

1 A childist approach to counselling

Acting lessons on being a person

Children who seek contact with, or are referred to, counsellors usually have some presenting problem connected with, for example, impaired health, offending behaviour, poor educational performance, or bereavement. If such contact is to be effective, it should lead to some development of the whole person. Mind and body, emotion and spirit are one. Distress or fulfilment in one part of life affects the rest.

At times of difficulty it may seem impossible to feel like a real person. Lennie, eponymous hero of *The TV Kid* (Byars, 1976), has some trouble in school. The teacher asks him a question:

> 'let me think'. Lennie had put his hand to his chin at this point to give the impression of deep thought. Lennie always had a hard time arranging his face in the right expression. Looking interested or studious was especially hard for him. He sometimes thought he needed acting lessons on being a person (p. 64).

Lennie lives in a fantasy world of TV games and serials, compensating for the instability of life with his mother who is continually seeking to make a safe and successful home but constantly having to move on. Then she inherits a motel. '"Now we can live like other people", she had said. She had begun to hum. Her favourite songs were about home and going home...They looked like people who moved around, Lennie thought' (p. 32).

> All Lennie's life his own feelings had been as hard to get at as the meat in a walnut. His feelings were there - Lennie was sure of that - somewhere inside the hull, probably just as perfectly formed as the rest of the things nature put in a shell (p. 66).

Although he wants 'to be a success', Lennie breaks into an empty house, is bitten by a rattlesnake and nearly dies. Real-life drama saves him since he is brought face-to-face with real feelings and fears, with the consequence of his own action, and with sensible adult assistance for his mother and himself. Gaining contact with his feelings helps him to feel like a real person. He learns that his life (aided, it must be acknowledged, by some pretty high drama) is 'In a lot of ways...better than the stuff you see on television...It's *realler*' (p. 111).

A central activity of counselling is discovering what is 'realler' and helping gently to crack the walnut shell surrounding the meat of feeling; for many people, Lennie's fear that it is necessary to act being a person, that there may be no one and nothing inside the shell, itself inhibits the attempt to live fully.

When I was asked to work with children who were, it was feared, at risk of being 'frozen' I felt that their internal meteorological problem was fog rather than frost. In a variety of ways, I tried to help them learn more about themselves, to find safety in an increased range of feelings - letting sadness and anger become acceptable and smiles less fixed - and to gain a sense of self-esteem and thus of self.

Richard Gardner (1970) in *The Boys and Girls Book about Divorce* addresses the problem of bewilderment about feelings:

> When something happens that's sad and painful usually the best thing for you to do is to try to find out exactly what the trouble is. Then it is easier for you to decide what to do to help yourself feel better. Some children don't do this. Instead, they make believe that nothing's wrong or they try to hide their sadness. When they do this, they are not trying to help themselves, and so their problems usually are not solved, and they may even get worse. It's much better to know the truth about your problems than to hide from them, even though the truth can often be frightening or painful. When you know the truth, you can often do something about your troubles. If you hide from the truth, you can do nothing about your problems, and so things usually get worse (pp. 25-8).

He writes reassuringly that

> Most children who see therapists don't look or behave any differently than other people. They're children who have special problems in a few parts of their lives but who do quite well in most things. Not everything is wrong with them, just a few things (p. 151).

This is a useful addition to the concept of wholeness, of the whole person. Obtaining help for one symptom, one anxiety, one problem, does not imply that everything is wrong, that the child is sick or unusual. Many children (and adults) fear to be thought odd; we like to be unique individuals but not *different*.

Whatever the context of counselling, whatever the reason for contact, it is crucial and fundamental that both child and counsellor regard themselves as ordinary and equal. They are both special and unique, too, but as individual people, not victim and helper.

A childist approach

When considering a title for the present book I thought of *Child-*

Centred Counselling. This I rejected lest it suggest that I was writing exclusively about the Rogerian approach, but the spirit and meaning of child-centredness remain.

The Feminist approach to counselling follows no single model of human development and behaviour but draws on a world of experience, philosophy, religion, myth and analysis within a feminist framework. The symbol of the gently curving serpent, representing natural swing between happiness and sadness, energy and tiredness, activity and rest, is preferred to the pyramid of upward progression where success sits on failure (Chaplin, 1988b).

What would characterize a child-centred approach? Semantic considerations reveal a good deal about our approach to children: the parallel to *feminist* would be *childist*, but no such word exists. If it did, what would it mean?

Is the *Children Act, 1989* a piece of *childist* legislation? It is designed to promote the best interests of the child, taking into account the child's own view of her/his life, past, present and future. What part have children taken in formulating and implementing the new law?

Feminism implies ways of regarding womanhood and the lives of women as individuals and corporately. It is not necessary to be a woman to be a feminist but it is necessary to value the female in terms of, for example, women, womanhood, the feminine aspect of every personality.

Childism should be easy; everyone has been a child and has experience of childhood. To be a *childist* would not imply regarding children as superior to all other beings but would suggest regarding the world from the point of view of people other than adults. But *childist* is very close to *childish* – with perjorative associations of foolishness and immaturity. We even tell children not to be childish, although a dictionary defines this (Old English) word as 'of or proper to a child', continuing, 'puerile, unsuitable for a grown person' (The Concise Oxford Dictionary, 1982).

Puerile (from Latin) is 'boyish, childish; suitable only for children, trivial'.

Words based on *infant* (Latin) – *infantilist, infantilism* – have even worse resonances; *infantile* has taken the meaning of 'behaving inappropriately as a young child'. *Infantilism* is given as 'state of being mentally or physically undeveloped though of adult age' (but an *infant prodigy* is 'a very precocious child': it is apparently laudable to be adult-like in childhood).

Greek derivation offers no more help in the search for positive descriptions of the nature of *child. Paedophilia* is tied indissolubly to 'sexual love directed towards children', with connotations of illegality and disgust. But *philia* has only the sense of 'love of, fondness for', from '*philos* dear, loving'.

A glossary of good, potentially positive words gone to waste; what does contemporary English usage reveal about contemporary British attitudes towards children and childhood? Chaplin draws attention to the study of Dale Spender (1980) which shows how 'our very language is constructed in a way that implies woman's second-class status. The norm is seen as masculine' (Chaplin, 1988b, p. 47). What would a study of language demonstrate about the status of children?

Even the lovely *childlike* has detracting associations in everyday usage, although the dictionary offers 'having good qualities of a child, as innocence, frankness, etc.'

A childlike approach to counselling? Characterized by innocence and frankness? An attractive idea. But I wish my dictionary proposed further good qualities of a child. What adjectives are commonly used to evoke the positive qualities of childhood? What do they suggest about the speaker/writer and our corporate view?

I return to *childist*. But here are aural associations with *ageist, racist, sexist* – terms usually indicating that the subject is prejudiced by consideration of age, race or sex. Does anyone claim, in anything but jest, to be *ageist*?

Just as the philosophy and practice of counsellors adopting a feminist approach are extended not only to women but also to men and children, a childist or child-centred approach would, by implication, extend to adults; particularly important since there is no point at which we cease to be the selves of our chronological childhood.

> The psychologically 'healthy' person is rhythmic not stuck and rigidly split. She recognizes and understands all the opposites within herself. She is reasonably comfortable with *both* her strong and weak sides, her 'masculine' and 'feminine' sides, her rational and emotional sides, and her 'parent' and 'child' sides. There may be conflict between them. But at least there is a dialogue. They can respect each other. Neither side is completely denied.
>
> Sometimes they fight and sometimes they dance together. Everyone has her own dance, her own rhythms. One day she may be strong and bossy and another day gentle and vulnerable. She alternates between them, when it is appropriate (Chaplin, 1988b, p. 45) (re-paragraphed).

The idea of *vulnerability* as a positive quality is important:

> In our society weakness is seen as inferior to strength, failure is seen as inferior to success. We do not recognize that weakness and vulnerability are a vital part of us...we feel we must be *totally* successful, almost perfect *or* else we must be *completely* useless (p. 44).

Albert van den Heuvel (a theologian) speaking at a conference on telephone counselling, offered 'as a blueprint for being human his "ten words"' of which number three is 'You shall overcome fear for your own vulnerability', elaborated as 'Blessed are they who discover the strength of their own"' (Salisbury, 1991, p. 1346).

Chaplin (1988b) proposes that

> We grow and change in more of a spiral than in a straight line. We go
> backwards as well as forwards. Perhaps we can only go forwards if we
> go backwards and regress into childlike feelings first. Growth is
> working with the rhythms, not proceeding from some depressing
> reality to a perfect harmonious self in the future (p. 45).

Many models of human growth and development reflect an onwards
and upwards rather than a *spiral* movement. The Erikson (1965) eight-
stage model, for example, proposes opportunities for success and
failure at age-related crises throughout life and particularly in early
childhood. Failure successfully to complete the task appropriate to the
chronological age impairs ability to proceed to the next task and thus
all future emotional development.

In so far as this reflects the necessary sequence of physical growth –
you cannot become four feet tall if you have never been three foot
eleven – it has value. But the value laden connotations of consistent,
one way emotional progress, success and failure, are questionable.

The study of childhood

A childist approach to counselling requires respect for the idea of
childhood as well as for every individual child. If *feminism* involves the
study of the feminine in all aspects of culture – for example, religion,
politics, dress, art, literature, power, oppression – *childism* would
involve equivalent study about childhood.

Adults training to work with children in health and social care and
welfare would be expected to undertake an holistic study of childhood
– physical, cognitive, emotional, spiritual. Attention would be given to
attitudes towards childhood in other times and cultures, and the
religious beliefs and practices and political preoccupations which
inform and influence whatever are the current attitudes.

A childist counsellor would begin with the idea of a child of whatever
age being a complete person rather than an immature version of the
adult s/he would become. An acorn is not an immature oak tree; an
acorn is perfectly an acorn. It contains everything necessary for growth
into an oak tree but neither acorn nor tree contains greater or lesser
value and virtue. Each is entire unto itself, both are of use to other
forms of life.

But an acorn cannot remain as an acorn forever. In order to become
a tree it requires certain nurturing conditions. John Westerhoff (1980)
writes of the tree, perfect at every moment of growth: 'a one-year-old
tree is truly and completely a tree. As it develops, it doesn't become
more truly a tree; it only becomes more complex' (p. 24).

A tree surgeon, hoping to help a poorly growing oak, would need to
know about the nature and needs of the tree. To understand the

problems of one oak, would require knowledge of soil and weather, plants and creatures living on, in, under and near the tree – perhaps human behaviour in the locality; (oak abuse – sawing off branches, carving initials, poisoning the atmosphere).

Interest might extend to studying the oak in literature, importance in religious ceremonies, legends, famous individual oaks. To heal or strengthen an oak tree demands proper understanding of and respect for the acorn as acorn, sapling as sapling, tree as tree; for oak as oak.

Really to offer a child help, whether through counselling or casework, therapy or guidance requires understanding and respect, breadth and depth of interest and study. Counsellors adopting a childist approach would read books written for, about and by children – fiction and picture books, biography and poetry. They would watch television and videos, listen to the radio, look at comics and magazines.

They would spend time in playgrounds, cinemas, discos and Sunday schools. They would have placements in schools, listening to staffroom conversation, watching classroom behaviour, attending lessons and sharing school dinners. They would identify the images of children popularized in advertising. They would study the history of politics and philosophy relating to children in the legislation of education, employment, religion, health and social welfare. They would learn to deconstruct the messages of authority.

It is essential to encourage counsellors to listen to children. But – listen to what, and in what context? And to do what with what the counsellor has 'heard'? When 'Ena's' father described his daughter, in care, as 'it' we were all shocked; a senior officer found proof in this of the man's callous and abusing attitude. Not one social worker concerned with this family thought to learn about the use of English on the Caribbean island from which first the parents, then very recently, Ena herself, had come.

Listen we might, but what was done with what we heard? We interpreted it in our own familiar, white, middle-class system and even colluded in regarding the man as 'paranoid' and the girl as 'backward'. This took place long enough ago for confession to be easy (although I have made so many other mistakes since). But similar, tragic errors occur daily. Not only may we ignore the different connections of a different racial, national or social group, we may not be concerned to identify the relevant culture and images of childhood.

Nursery nurses in some London day nurseries were found by Asrat-Girma (1986) to be insensitive to the context of the lives of some children in their care. She writes of West Indian parents who 'had often tried to explain the difficulty of getting sand out of their children's hair, yet the staff reaction typically was "Coloured parents don't like their children to get dirty...some of them even ask that their children be not allowed to play with sand or water"' and recalls 'an Asian child whose parents had put a certain type of cream on her hair which was promptly washed off by the staff when she entered the nursery, on the grounds that it was "smelly"' (p. 44).

Syble Morgan (1986) emphasized the importance of giving Afro-Caribbean foods to 'black children in social services run nurseries' who could thus be 'taught respect for the value their ancestors must have placed on this part of their culture, so that through practice and oral traditions they pass it on' (pp. 73–4).

Everything that is the child

James Hillman, in his *Foreword* to Allan's (1988) book on Jungian counselling in schools and clinics, writes that 'Today, children everywhere are worried about and need "help", from infant massage to play therapy to corrective lessons. Something is always "wrong" with them' (p. xiii).

Hillman associates what he regards as the increasing and regrettable need of children for 'help' with declining recognition of the spiritual life (p. xiii).

Westerhoff (1980) (a minister) considers that 'In our culture we both celebrate and belittle childhood'. Add *sentimentalize, possess* and *exploit*. 'We project onto it a false state of happiness and freedom from care' while feeling 'compelled to help children become serious and responsible'. Children are regarded as 'incomplete human beings in need of being shaped into adults'. Children are not treated 'as full human beings. Now they are *only* children' (p. 15).

He finds that 'children are not valued for what they *are* but only for what they can *become*. The less potential a child has, the less value he or she assumes. At best, we pity and patronize those with limited potential' (p. 16).

Keith Redfern (1991) (writer and teacher), comments on attitudes in Great Britain

> where it seems that children are thought to be lesser mortals, to be looked down upon and talked down to; to be considered unable to cope or understand; to be treated as 'different'; to feel self-consciously aware of, much as those who are physically impaired, the partially sighted, the hard of hearing and those confined to wheelchairs.
>
> A child holds a door open for an adult and the adult breezes through without a word of appreciation as if the child had done no more or less than was expected of them.
>
> Or a child stands in a shop queue and is brushed aside by a rushing adult who pushes ahead as if the child didn't exist.
>
> Or a baby is distressed and attempts are being made to provide comfort. 'Oh dear. Goo goo goo goo. Oh dear me. What's the matter? Goo goo goo goo...' I witnessed this earlier this year.
>
> Or an old lady, having lived alone with her budgies for several years, talking to my infant son in his carry cot. 'Who's a pretty boy, then?'

Or a child reports an incident that has happened involving an adult
and the adult's word is taken rather than the child's. For some reason
it is assumed that the child is making it up or that, simply for reasons
of greater age, the adult is more to be trusted.

Why is this? It appears to be a national characteristic. It is
inconsiderate and demeaning to those of lesser years; it annoys them,
sometimes embarrasses them, often distresses them and it is just plain
rude (p. 853).

These comments give us much to think about. How can we help
children develop ways of managing difficulties and grow in health if we
are not clear about the worlds in which they live, their expectations of
themselves and the expectations of other people, both individually and
institutionally and, in particular, the conflicting messages and values
with which they are bombarded from birth? With such questions I
would begin teaching a childist approach to counselling.

These writers are deeply concerned with the whole life of children as
complete individual people. They relate and develop their ideas in the
context of their own lives, beliefs and experience which is fundamental
to counselling. The opening sentence of Wittgenstein's (1921) *Tractatus Logico – Philosophicus* may translate as 'The world is everything
that is the case': an opening for the present book might be 'Counselling
is everything that is the child and the counsellor' including the
counsellor's child self.

Testing the evidence

Both Hillman and Westerhoff regard the negative attitudes towards
children in twentieth-century Western society as due to the 'new'
phenomenon of childhood.

For centuries, the state of childhood was unrecognized. Children were
simply considered to be miniature adults. Then, during the Age of
Enlightenment, in the eighteenth century, children were discovered
and placed in a class of their own. Ever since that time, children have
been excluded from the world of adults (Westerhoff, 1980, p. 15).

Only in this century of our Western history has the child been
overburdened with carrying the 'bad seed' of our civilization's disorder
(Hillman, 1988, p. xiii).

What do these statements mean? They are seductive at first glance and
should, indeed, be regarded seriously. But they should lead the reader
to ask further questions, finding a way into the image building of
childhood. If the idea and image of children has changed, what does
this mean for individual children? But also, are there other views about
childhood and if so, what can they tell us about not only childhood
itself but also the power of ideas?

Jeffrey Richards (1991) (professor of cultural history) explores the changing view of childhood in the Middle Ages developed by Shulamith Shahar and John Boswell in 'books of wide-ranging scholarship, acute perception and warmhearted humanity'. They challenge the influential thesis of Philippe Ariès (1973) that 'the Middle Ages had no concept of childhood', whose argument is based on 'the absence of visual representations of children, claiming that when they appeared it was as miniature adults'.

While the life of and attitudes towards fourteenth-century children may not greatly concern twentieth-century counsellors, it is useful to reflect on the dangers of accepting without question the opinion of authority. It may not be possible to replicate research but it should always be practice to question.

Richards notes that, far from there being no clues to a concept of childhood in the Middle Ages, 'there were many pictures of children as children...and abundant evidence that they were viewed as children and were loved as children'.

On my own advice I should question Richards too – and, indeed, I can follow the clues he offers, look at pictures and statues, read contemporary literature and do my best to apply a lively mind to his material. In this particular instance, I have looked (though super-ficially) at his two source books and can to some extent test his thesis for myself. But I could certainly not pursue the many texts quoted in Boswell and Shahar: however much I might wish to decide for myself whether or not children were valued in the Middle Ages, I should have to make an active choice either to trust or reject these scholars.

With regard to children in the twentieth century, it is considerably easier to test the evidence. A first step is to be clear about meanings and resonances of individual words. I have discussed implications and attributions of such words as *childish* and *infantile* and the importance of context. (Meanings attributed to *counselling* are discussed in Chapter 2.)

It is important to be clear about the authority of the authorities. In the literature of counselling, how have the many and various approaches been developed? Who has been influenced by whom? What views of humanity and ideas of life inform the theorist practitioners?

Ideas represented in the many counselling approaches are drawn from a variety of countries and nationalities, religions, philosophies, literatures and centuries. There are references to classical Roman texts and contemporary North American business practice, to Eastern Asian mysticism and Western work ethic, German philosophy nods to chemical engineering, scientific agriculture to hypnosis.

The attitude of individuals and groups who formulate and develop counselling approaches towards the purpose of life and the way in which people grow, experience crises, regain impaired health, and solve problems affects fundamentally the expectations of guidance given to the counsellor. If the counsellor is developing a childist approach, it is particularly important to identify the attitudes towards children and childhood inherent in the informing approach.

Attitudes given authority within legislation, too, should be identified by counsellors adopting a childist approach. The *Children Act, 1989*, received much publicity in October 1991 with commentaries and phone-ins on, for example, BBC Radio 4 programmes; but I think I heard a good deal of wheel re-invention.

The legislation may be elegant and devoted to the welfare of children. But anyone involved in the implementation should ask 'Why now? What are the real purposes and influences? What is really being said and expected?' and 'What happened to all the other attempts to improve the care and welfare of children? Where are the cracks?', even 'What will go wrong this time? Why will it be disappointing? Do the values of the law-makers coincide with those of the people with power to provide resources, with responsibility to implement the Act, and the people supposed to benefit – the children?' Why *do* the same issues constantly return?

In the week that I write this, a local authority announces an extra £1,000,000 for residential child care because of a shock report on the poor quality of this care, in respect of conditions, staffing, training – apparently every aspect. How can this have been a surprise? Why was money available for first aid but not day-to-day maintenance of the most basic standards? What service may be deprived next to pay for this failure?

As I write, the Cleveland case is still recent and the subsequent Report is an important document. Yet only a few months ago, a Scottish sheriff peremptorily returned nine children to their families on Orkney, five weeks after dramatic and traumatic removal from home (known as 'uplifting' in Scotland) on 27.2.91.

> In his judgement, Sheriff Kelbie quoted a passage from the report on the Cleveland case to which he had been referred. 'It is important to remember that children are persons too and not simply subjects of concern', and added, 'It appears to me that if the Reporter and the hearing had borne that in mind throughout, they would not have failed to appreciate the importance of sticking to the rules, and, indeed, why they are there' (Brett, 1991, p. 146).

Legislation, rules can be made and remade, millions of pounds spent on inquiries, publicity, guidelines and first aid. But this avails nothing if the spirit, the inwardness are not realized, understood, acknowledged; if those who make and those who implement legislation do not really *care* and never ask themselves why the rules and they themselves are there.

These are important questions for practitioners in every field of work with children.

A book of connections

Both student and practitioner need constantly to ask if the conclusions drawn by authorities (whether authors in print or senior officers in agencies) can be authenticated. Do the links work or are connections made where no connection can, or should, be? Umberto Eco (1989) in a *tour de force* exposing the fatal danger of devotion to connection rather than common sense writes:

> wanting connections, we found connections – always, everywhere, and between everything. The world exploded into a whirling network of kinships, where everything pointed to everything else, everything explained everything else (pp. 463–4)

and:

> The lunatic...doesn't concern himself at all with logic; he works by short circuits. For him, everything proves everything else (p. 67).

This is a definition not of a people out of contact with 'reality' (that is, the idea of reality held by the people with most power, and/or the majority) and possibly confined in a place of safety, but of individuals who become obsessed with making links and impervious to any idea of the world but their own.

Cave counsellor. Beware the false connections of approach makers, of authorities, of clients, of yourself.

This is a book of connections. The connector is the present writer. To introduce a childist approach to counselling, I offer short studies of aspects of childhood and counselling with ideas and illustrations from many sources.

> The counsellor needs to be willing to develop all of her potentialities in order to be authentic when she invites the client to develop all of the client's potentialities (Clarkson, 1989, p. 22).

Those potentialities include the ability to seek enlightenment wherever it may be found: this may not be in textbooks. Philosopher Frederick Copleston paraphrases Wittgenstein: 'if all the problems of science were answered, the problems of life wouldn't have been touched' (Magee, 1987, p. 230).

The title I eventually chose for the present book, *Children and Counselling,* deliberately and importantly puts children first. I rejected *Counselling Children,* because not only are there at least two other books of that name but also the implication is of someone doing something to someone else – presumably an adult counsellor doing something to a child client.

I note this pairing of participle and noun may imply that the subject – here the unidentified counsellor – is active and the identified people are object: the children are counselled by someone else. In other such pairings the identified people are the subjects and appear to be active; *battering husbands* would imply that the husbands do the battering, not that they are battered.

A real boy

A fundamental component of any true counselling is that both (or all) participants are fully and equally involved. The child cannot be a lesser, less important partner. In my experience, the adult counsellor has much to learn from the child. The counselling context is not organized for the benefit of the adult but, once the two people have met, who is to say which is the greater gainer?

Children too are helping one another all the time in ways which might well be described as counselling. Solicitor Mike Morris (1986) records a young girl who had received advice from him, bringing her friend to him for help.

This chapter began with Lennie, wanting 'acting lessons on being a person'. Facing death helped him to find a sense of the reality of life. In *Attending to Children* (Crompton, 1990) I referred to Julia whose struggles to become a 'real girl' are vividly described by Margaret Hunter (1987, p. 30). I have introduced Julia again in the present book because a central aim of the childist counsellor is, surely, this: to enable troubled children to recognize and embrace their own reality, the inwardness which balances being and growth, stability and change.

It is fitting to end with

> a child patient in a cancer ward giving an adult a guided tour.
> 'And this is Gerald. He's got cancer as well. All his hair has come out because he's on chemotherapy'.
> Very matter of fact. No embarrassment. No attempt to use euphemisms to hide what makes us feel uncomfortable.
> Straightforward, open, honesty. Speaking the truth in love (Redfern, 1991, p. 854).

A real boy, in need of no lessons at all on being a person.

Summary

Feeling **real** is hard for everyone. A central aim of counselling is to help people become more fully themselves. Having one problem does not mean that everything is wrong but the **whole person** is involved in counselling. The idea of a **childist approach** is discussed, including the implications of some child-related words. Ideas for a study of **childhood** essential to childist counselling are suggested. Readers are encouraged to test **authority** and while being sensitive to links, to beware seductive false **connections**. Children are real, are persons too and not simply subjects of concern.

Link

In preparation for the present book, I met, corresponded with and read books and papers by practitioners representing a number of organizations and holding many different views on counselling, although all might agree that all such work is designed to help other people focus on being a person. Continuing this brief introduction to a childist approach to counselling, Chapter 2 draws on some of these practitioners and writers to offer the beginning of 'An Idea of Counselling'.

References

Ahmed, S., Cheetham, J. and Small, J. (eds) (1986). *Social Work with Black Children and their Families*. Batsford Books, London.

Allan, J. (1988). *Inscapes of the Child's World: Jungian Counseling in Schools and Clinics*. Spring Publications, Dallas, Texas.

Ariès, P. (1973). *Centuries of Childhood*. Penguin, Harmondsworth.

Asrat-Girma, (1986). Afro Caribbean children in day care. In Ahmed, et al., pp. 40–50.

Boswell, J. (1989). *The Kindness of Strangers: the Abandonment of Children in Western Europe from Late Antiquity to the Renaissance*. Penguin, Harmondsworth.

Brett, R. (1991) Orkney: aberration or symptom? *The Journal of Child Law*, September–December 1991, 143–6.

Byars, B. (1976). *The TV Kid*. The Bodley Head, London.

Chaplin, J. (1988b). *Feminist Therapy*. In Rowan and Dryden (eds).

Clarkson, P. (1989). *Gestalt Counselling in Action*. Sage, London.

The Concise Oxford Dictionary (1982) Seventh edn, Sykes, J. B. (ed.). Clarendon Press, Oxford.

Crompton, M. (1990). *Attending to Children: Direct Work in Social and Health Care*. Edward Arnold, Dunton Green.

Department of Health. *Children Act, 1989*. HMSO, London.

Eco, U. (Weaver, W. (trans.) (1989). *Foucault's Pendulum*. Secker and Warburg, London.

Erikson, E. (1965). *Childhood and Society*. Penguin, Harmondsworth.

Gardner, R. A. (1970). *The Boys and Girls Book about Divorce: with an Introduction for Parents*. Jason Aronson, New York.

Hillman, J. (1988). Foreword. in J. Allan. above. pp. xiii–xx.

Hunter, M. (1987). Julia: a 'frozen' child. *Adoption and Fostering*, 11, (3), 26–30.

Magee, B. (1987). *The Great Philosophers: An Introduction to Western Philosophy*. Oxford University Press, Oxford.

Morgan, S. (1986). Practice in a community nursery for black children. In Ahmed, et al., pp. 69–74.

Morris, M. (1986). Communicating with adolescents. *Adoption and Fostering*, 10, (4), 54–55, 71.

Redfern, K. (1991). How do we treat our children? *The Friend*, 149, (27), 853–4.

Richards, J. (1991). *Childhood in the Middle Ages*. BBC, Radio 3.

Rowan, J. and Dryden, W. (eds). (1988). *Innovative Therapy in Britain*. Open University Press, Milton Keynes.

Salisbury, E. (1991). The ten words. *The Friend*, 149, (42), 1346.

Shahar, S. (1990). *Childhood in the Middle Ages*. Routledge, London.

Spender, D. (1980). *Man Made Language*. Routledge and Kegan Paul, London.

Westerhoff, J. H., III. (1980). *Bringing up Children in the Christian Faith*. Winston Press, Minnesota.

Wittgenstein, L. (1921). *Tractatus Logico-Philosophicus*. In Magee.

2 An idea of counselling

A long woolly muffler

From the Editor's Prospectus to the *Girls Own Paper,* 1880:

> This magazine will aim at being to the girls a Counsellor, Playmate,
> Guardian, Instructor, Companion and Friend. It will help to train
> them in moral and domestic virtues, preparing them for the
> responsibilities of womanhood and for a heavenly home (Forrester,
> 1980).

For readers of the *Girls Own Paper* (1880–1901), counselling was a
one-way activity, delivered as wholesale homilies on dress and
deportment (early social skills training). Girls who followed the
counsel contained in its weekly pages might hope to lead irreproach-
able lives on Earth, leading to spiritual reward. The content of 1990s
'teen-mag' counsel may be different but the idea is the same;
generalized wisdom transmitted through print can change the individual's life.

Margaret Moran (1968) (a nun) in her book *Pastoral Counselling for
the Deviant Girl* (deviant, presumably, from more than the *Girls' Own
Paper* description of a real, or rather, acceptable, girl) notes that until
about 1940, 'most people thought of counselling in a general way as
giving somebody advice or perhaps a reprimand' (p. 1). In 1991, I have
found that the association of *counselling* with *advice* is still widespread.
For example, a teacher said that he had counselled a boy that if he
continued to smoke on the bus he would be in trouble.

The word has had associations of power and authority. The *Messiah,*
for example, is described as 'Wonderful Counsellor' (Handel; Isaiah
9:6). Linked with attributions of godhead and government, this
counsellor is, clearly, neither advising about the pre-occupations of
girlhood nor operating a ChildLine telephone.

Counselling here is wisdom undilute, good judgement, perfectly
controlled power. Moran quotes Thomas Aquinas' *Summa Theologica:* 'in human affairs those who are unable to take counsel for
themselves, seek counsel from those who are wiser' (Moran, 1968, p.
5). Wisdom and judgement, authority and advice.

These very associations of authority and advice lead a number of the
practitioners with whom I had contact in preparation for the present
book to express dislike of the term *counselling*. Since I felt uneasy with
it myself their reservations particularly caught my attention.

A retired child psychiatrist hears that '"counselling" sounds like "I'll tell you what to do"': he emphasises the importance of love and responding to the individual child.

A senior social worker in a child guidance clinic, (closed in 1991 reorganization) finds 'connotations with work with adults, not children'. In her clinic, the psychiatrist might have 'asked a social work colleague to counsel parents' but social work contact with children would have been defined as 'child management'. 'Counselling activity' would have been focused on 'teaching better ways of behaving'.

'Ralph', a psychologist in a child and family unit, does not use such words as *therapist, counselling, healing,* disliking 'the connotations of mystique, doing something wonderful, special skills', and preferring to describe himself as 'a problem solver'. He suggests that 'all that counselling is, is conversations, talking to each other in words which children and parents can understand'.

A senior child psychologist (in a different unit) also dislikes the word and quoted a group of teachers who preferred to define such activity as 'listening to children'.

Nurses in a child and family unit attached to a hospital described counselling as 'a very mixed word' not used (or misused) in their unit in their attempt to avoid jargon and labelling: they emphasized 'look, learn, listen'.

A counsellor in a college student welfare service regards counselling as associated with education rather than social or health care.

A volunteer member of a victim support group dislikes 'the term counselling because, whatever the intention, it is often seen by clients/victims as advice. I prefer to think of my work as "comforting" in the sense of reinforcing the skills and strengths that people already have to cope with problems or disasters. However, that term has its disadvantages, not least its sense of a long woolly muffler'.

The gap between psychotherapy and friendship

Loving, listening, responding, teaching, comforting – all have their place but no one word expresses the overall idea and activity of counselling. Yet this word, popular with theorists and training courses, appears to be unpopular with a variety of practitioners because of its associations.

Ellen Noonan (1983), in *Counselling Young People,* identifies that

Counselling has its beginnings, both historically as an emerging
discipline and daily as a popular activity, in many different
professions. It fills the gap between psychotherapy and friendship, and
it has become a recognized extension of the work of almost everyone
whose business touches upon the personal, social, occupational,
medical, educational and spiritual aspects of people.

Because, like Topsy, it just grew, because it falls as much within the province of bringing on the already well-functioning as that of diminishing distress, and because it refers to people who deem counsellors and others who apply counselling skills as they deem appropriate, there is no unified concept of its work. Indeed, the literature on counselling is a rather motley and intriguing array (p. vii) (re-paragraphed).

The gap between psychotherapy and friendship is extensive and one which other words have been used to describe.

Moran in 1968 considered that 'Counselling is the main discipline of the professional social worker, so much so that in Britain the words "counselling" and "casework" are used synonymously' (Moran, 1968, p. 2). In 1991 I am not clear how much 'casework' is used; yet when I trained in social work in the 1960s, this word described the main skill and activity of my profession as a caseworker.

In 1955, Herbert H. Aptekar had published *The Dynamics of Casework and Counseling,* identifying a problem of semantics and usage, for was counselling

casework, or therapy, or a form of help *sui generis.* Whether both diagnostic and functional casework should be distinguished from or identified with counseling, whether counseling was simply an old form of help with a new name, whether counseling and therapy were one and the same thing, and above all, whether there must be two types of counseling, just as there were two types of casework, were some of the troublesome problems with which caseworkers were now confronted (Aptekar, 1955, pp. 105–106).

He defines and distinguishes between casework and counselling. Essentially, 'in social agencies, where caseworkers have traditionally practised, specific social services are administered, such as financial assistance, placement, and homemaker service'. The caseworker requires special skills, knowledge and 'understanding of what goes into help-giving and help-taking' which 'associated with specific social services, is casework' (p. 108).

Counselling, unlike casework

can be carried out privately, and without the need to call on agency resources ... all that is required is a person who has a problem and one who is willing to share that problem and bring to bear upon it whatever skill he may have, so that a solution to it may be reached (p. 109).

He regards counselling as 'geared to a problem and not to a service' and counsellors as working not 'with any and all problems, but instead with special ones toward which they are oriented' (pp. 109, 110).

Aptekar predicted that *casework* would be replaced by *counseling* (p. 115) but Anne Jones writing on *Counselling Adolescents* in 1984 considers counselling still to have 'much in common with what social workers call casework' (Jones, 1984).

Aptekar proposes that

> In counseling, it is the way a client relates to a particular worker, and the worker to him, which determines whether the client will be helped or not. The principal dynamics must be sought in personal factors rather than impersonal ones and agency function therefore plays a comparatively limited role (pp. 130–31).

'Counseling is a form of therapy' (Aptekar, p. 131). In 1991 *counselling* and *therapy* are not synonymous. The debate is a large one, doubtless arousing much feeling. I use *therapy/therapist* when quoting material which I consider relevant to my wide interpretation of *counselling/counsellor*.

For the purposes of the present book I regard counselling children as

> The purposeful interaction between adults and children/young people within the context of an agency or organization, statutory or voluntary, concerned with social, educational, occupational, spiritual and/or health care and welfare.

I regard the purpose of counselling as

> help, through the development of a professional relationship, to recognize and manage problems and difficulties connected with and/or stimulated by a range of factors including environment (for example, school), event (for example, bereavement), individual development (for example, sexual), relationship (for example, with parents), movement (for example, within care, between divorced parents), behaviour (for example, offending), and to assist with growth and development in all aspects of the individual person – cognitive, emotional, physical and spiritual.

When I asked a group of nurses in a child and family unit what they considered to be the most important focus for a discussion of counselling, they answered 'the therapeutic relationship'.

Petrūska Clarkson (1989) writing about the Gestalt approach describes the counsellor as using 'himself or herself actively and authentically in the encounter with the other person. It is more a "way of being and doing" than a set of techniques or a prescribed formula for counselling' (p. 19).

The practitioners I met were not seeking prescribed formulae; indeed, it may partly have been fear of such ideas which underlay reluctance of many to use the word *counselling* and/or claim association with any particular approach.

A teacher member of the counselling team in a comprehensive school disclaimed any particular theoretical base for the in-service training course he had attended, until recalling that Gerard Egan's Developmental Eclectic approach had been introduced.

A nurse who had recently completed a post-qualification course on direct work with children based on Carl Rogers' person-centred approach, joined colleagues in her unit in drawing on ideas and experience relevant to each individual, rather than following any one counselling model.

Social workers in a child guidance unit based their approach broadly on Family Therapy but adapted the model and undertook a great deal of individual, largely play-based work with children (very often the victims of sexual abuse).

On the other hand a college student counsellor described his approach firmly within the Freudian psycho-dynamic tradition; while a child psychologist follows Gestalt principles.

A pouch of happiness dust

Although Aptekar did not consider the agency/organizational environment/function to contribute to the process of counselling, my reading and direct contacts suggest that counselling children at least is influenced by agency, reason for referral and counsellor's individual style.

Ralph (psychologist) described himself as 'a problem solver in some respects'. He disliked any connotations of *healing* which 'implies that things get better. Rather than problems being solved, people get better at dealing with problems'.

In order to gain access to 'someone to talk to', the potential client has to identify a problem and seek immediate help and/or referral. A child whose problem is identified as causing or being caused by impaired physical or mental health may be taken to a general practitioner and thus referred to medical and/or psychiatric services. If a problem is identified in religious and/or spiritual life, the child may be taken to a minister or priest, while difficulties displayed in school may lead to referral via a school counsellor to an educational psychologist. It is possible for the same child with the same presenting problem to be referred into any one of several counselling *fora*.

In order for a child to obtain contact with adult professional assistance in problem solving, it is probable that adults rather than the child will define the problem (indeed, defining the child as *having* or *being* a problem) and thus determine the context and focus of assistance offered.

There are, however, opportunities for children to seek assistance on their own account, notably within schools, student counselling services, voluntary counselling centres and telephone schemes.

If *problem solving* implies the identification and acknowledgement of problems, *healing* suggests not only 'that things get better' but also that there is a sickness to be cured. For Ralph *healing* has unacceptable connotations linked with 'laying hands on someone, making them OK'. I suggest that *healing* should be associated with regaining full health or wholeness in an holistic context and also, with recovery from wounds for example, after desertion, physical trauma, abuse.

Clarkson (1989) writes of the important 'assumption that treating the client as a human being with intelligence, responsibility and active choices at any moment in time is most likely to invite the client into autonomy, *self-healing* and integration' (p. 20) (my italics).

The counsellor must avoid the role of miracle worker. Brenda Mallon (1987) (writing from a person-centred base but with relevance to all approaches to counselling) warns that many people define counselling as

> giving advice or problem solving, emphasising that it is the counsellor who solves the problem. It is as if the counsellor has a magic box which is full of 'answers' or 'solutions' and a pouch of happiness dust to sprinkle on the pained counsellee resulting in immediate alleviation of anxiety.
>
> Counsellors with such accoutrements do not exist. Counsellors working in the real world are ordinary people who have learned skills which they use in their work with others. They do not solve other people's problems for them. Rather they support and enable them to find their own solutions (p. 2).

Self-healing, autonomy, finding one's own solutions.

Anne Jones (1984) regards counselling as basically

> an enabling process, designed to help an individual come to terms with his life and grow to greater maturity through learning to take responsibility and to make decisions for himself (p. 29).

Donald W. Morrison (1977), writing in *Personal Problem-solving in the Classroom,* underlines the long-term, indeed life-long, significance of gaining the strength to seek such solutions:

> Failure to solve personal problems when they occur inevitably leads to a continuation of the problem and of the detrimental effects throughout the person's life. Unsolved problems persist and are capable of destroying the human spirit and the will to seek solutions (p. 16).

In the context of counselling in schools, Jones and Mallon stress both the fundamental importance of helping children to develop their own strengths and recognize the particular foci and constraints of the setting.

> In modern connotation, counselling is not meant to denote a process of advice-giving, of *telling* someone what to do, but rather of providing

the conditions with which an individual will be able to make up his mind what, if anything, he should do. Sometimes an individual needs help of a specific nature, for example objective information about a job or about his own limitations and capabilities; sometimes he needs simply to talk out in a calm, relaxed atmosphere his innermost thoughts (Jones, 1984, p. 29).

Mallon recognizes that

> Counselling happens in many settings, at many times and in many different ways. It is not restricted to a private room where a confident, fully trained counsellor receives those who wish to be helped. Rather, in most educational settings, a somewhat harried adult searches for a quiet space in which to snatch some time for a distressed child or parent to talk. The contact is often brief, unplanned and unsatisfactory for all concerned, though in many instances it is the best that is available at the time (Mallon, p. 1).

Despite such difficulties, including lack of support, 'it is still important to strive for the best. If you aim to counsel well then it is worth organizing the best possible physical setting as well as developing your own skills, (Mallon, pp. 1–2).

Some ideas of counselling appear to exclude children. Allen and Mary Ivey (1990) consider counselling to be 'a verbal occupation. Most early elementary children simply do not have the words or concepts for our traditional theories and methods' (p. 299). Judging from the millions of words written about counselling, this may be true.

But no practitioners I met shared this view. Counselling with anyone depends on a great deal more than the spoken word. I gather that some traditions forbid the use of touch but I imagine that most counsellors engaged with children would use physical as well as aural activity and/ or contact in playing, comforting, walking together. And how can any communication take place without silence? 'To hear, one must be silent' (LeGuin, 1971, p. 28).

Approaches to counselling

> In the multitude of counsellors there is safety (Proverbs, 9:14).

Before I began study in preparation for the present book I had no idea of the range and variety of theoretical bases associated with the development of counselling practice. I had planned to include an overview of them all but rapidly recognized my error; there would have been no room for anything else.

I focused on eight approaches, associating every approach with *counselling* although originators and commentators might use, for example, *therapy*.

These were chosen for a variety of reasons. Reality Therapy (Glasser) and Person-Centred Therapy (Rogers) I already knew and liked; about Freud and Jung (Psychoanalytic) I felt embarrassed at my vagueness; Developmental Eclecticism (Egan) was introduced to me by a lecturer in education as one of the most important current approaches, and Gestalt (Perls) by a child psychologist; I met the Rational Emotive (Ellis) and feminist (for example, Chaplin) approaches in books and was fascinated by the first and deeply attracted by the second. I limited terms of reference by excluding group or family-based approaches.

I became particularly interested by the range of background, (including nationality, religious belief, philosophy, personal relationships), represented by my chosen eight.

Egan is a Jesuit; Freud and Perls were Jews; Rogers prepared for Christian ministry; Jung, son of a Protestant pastor, studied many religions; the feminist approach refers to images from ancient and worldwide forms of worship. Ellis draws inspiration from philosophers of Greece and Rome.

Education and employment background differ greatly too. For example, Rogers studied scientific agriculture; Ellis graduated in business administration and worked to match new trousers with unworn-out suit jackets, then in a gift and novelty firm; Glasser trained in chemical engineering.

They were brought up in very different social and cultural settings. Freud in Vienna (where he experienced anti-Semitism); Jung in Switzerland; Rogers in the agricultural mid-West of the USA (Illinois); Ellis in East coast Pennsylvania: Perls, born in Germany, worked in South Africa before moving to the USA: Chaplin, born in West Africa, studied and practises in England.

Had I studied a different eight approaches I should have found a different eight combinations of birth, education, experience, every one producing an unique idea of human life and the ways in which one person may help another. The lives of these originators are rich and vigorous and these qualities are reflected in their approaches. Just as change occurs with time, even involuntarily, so these ideas and approaches have changed and are changing. This is very important. These approaches are all, (to use words broadly and not technically), eclectic and dynamic. The originators learned and developed and changed within their own lives and so does their work, having richness, depth and courage.

Similarly, succeeding generations of practitioners/theorists bring different individual backgrounds and interests and both practise and theorize in unique ways. This must be so. Rigid adherence to any one formulation can only be inimical to communication. The opposite danger is that disciples diffuse and devalue the original idea.

Doris Lessing (1979) identifies these twin problems in *Shikasta*. Lessing, like my approach originators, combines a rich background of upbringing and experience, education and philosophy in her wide-ranging and deeply considered work. *Shikasta* is Earth, visited constantly by *agents* and *envoys* of the planet Canopus in perpetual efforts to return the lives of the Shikastans 'to Canopean requirements and thus save the future of Shikasta' (p. 111). It is not too far-fetched to think of the envoys as counsellors and Shikasta as the theory of human emotions, development, relations, and the practice of helping.

> Shikasta was an *olla podrida* of cults, beliefs, religious creeds, convictions; there was no end to them, and each of our envoys had to take into account the fact that before he, she, was dead, his instructions would have already taken flight into fantasy, or been hardened into dogma: each knew that this newly minted, fresh, flexible method, adapted for that particular phase, would, before he had finished his work, have been captured by the Shikastan Law, and become mechanical, useless. She, he, would be working against not only a thousand past frozen formulations, but his own . . . An envoy put it like this: it was as if he were running a race at the top of his speed, to keep ahead of his own words and actions springing up just behind him, and turned into enemies – what had been alive and functional a few minutes ago was already dead and used by the dead (p. 111–12).

Any theory, any formulation, may take flight into fantasy or harden into dogma, but any communication between individuals depends on sense and flexibility. A third response may be rejection of the idea of theory. The counsellor espousing *any* approach must beware of both rigidity and woolliness. Flexibility and attention to individuality is no excuse for lack of discipline and rigour.

The single commentary I have found most useful is *Counseling Children* (Thompson and Rudolph), partly because a short biography of each originator is given. A central thesis of the present book is that, as novelist/poet Margaret Atwood says, 'People think of their own lives as narratives and rewrite them constantly', quoting a psychiatrist who described his work as 'helping people tell their stories' (Atwood, 1991). It is as important to know the context of the inception and development of theoretical approaches to counselling, as it is to learn the background of individual clients engaged in counselling.

It is impossible for counsellors not to be influenced by the work of predecessors, famous or unknown. In the interpretation of other people's words, whether uttered as teachers or clients, *beware*. The attribution of false meaning is all too easy. Casaubon, first person narrator of Umberto Eco's novel of tragic obsession with interpreta-tion, ends with a warning: 'It makes no difference whether I write or not. They will look for other meanings, even in my silence. That's how They are. Blind to revelation' (Eco, 1989, p. 641). In approaching the writings of both originators and commentators, there is a necessary question. What is and what is not, revelation?

Good counsel

During this year of study, I have read much guidance for counsellors and learnt a great deal. But the most useful single sentence is before me as I write, in a report of a recent international conference of telephone counsellors.

Albert van den Heuvel (a theologian) offered 'as a blueprint for being human his "ten words"'. While all 10 might be discussed as a blueprint for counselling, number two encapsulates both the hope of the counsellor for the client and, for the counsellor herself, good counsel: 'You shall be yourself' (Salisbury, 1991, p. 1346).

Summary

Counselling has many associations and changes its meaning according to where, when and by whom the word is used. The responses of a number of practitioners in a variety of fields are quoted to illustrate the variety of connotations. Described by one writer as filling **the gap between psychotherapy and friendship,** brief consideration of such concepts as **casework** and **therapy** has been offered. Associations with **problem solving** and **healing** have been identified, together with points about **advice, guidance** and **realistic expectations.** Eight **approaches** to counselling have been mentioned, with a warning about approaching approaches with either rigidity or woolliness.

Link

A word/concept often popular with people engaged in counselling and, increasingly, in many other activities, has attributed to it a wide range of meanings and is, at the same time, very difficult to define. Chapter 3 focuses 'On Empathy'.

References and Further Reading

Allan, J. (1988). *Inscapes of the Child's World: Jungian Counseling in Schools and Clinics.* Spring Publications, Dallas, Texas.
Allan, J. and Nairne, J. L. (1984). *Class Discussions for Teachers and Counselors in Elementary School.* Guidance Centre, Faculty of Education, University of Toronto.
Aptekar, H. H. (1955). *The Dynamics of Casework and Counseling.* Houghton Mifflin, Boston.
Aquinas, T. *Summa Theologica.* Quoted in Moran.
Atwood, M. (1991). *Bookshelf.* BBC Radio 4 Interview, 13.10.91.
Axline, V. (1971). *Dibs: in Search of Self.* Penguin, Harmondsworth.

Bassin, A., Bratter, T. E. and Rachin, R. L. (eds). (1976). *The Reality Therapy Reader: a Survey of the Work of William Glasser.* Harper and Row, New York.

Chaplin, J. (1988a). *Feminist Counselling in Action.* Sage, London.

Chaplin, J. (1988b). Feminist therapy. In Rowan and Dryden, pp. 39–60.

Chaplin, J. (1989). Counselling and Gender. In Dryden, et al. (eds), pp. 223–36.

Cupitt, D. (1985). *The Sea of Faith: Christianity and Change.* BBC, London.

Clarkson, P. (1989). *Gestalt Counselling in Action.* Sage, London.

Dorfman, E. (1951). Play therapy. In Rogers.

Dryden, W. (ed.) (1984). *Individual Therapy in Britain.* Harper and Row, London.

Eco, U. [Weaver, W. (trans)]. (1989) *Foucaulti's Pendulum.* Secker & Warsburg, London.

Egan, G. (1990). *The Skilled Helper: a Systematic Approach to Effective Helping.* Brooks/Cole, California.

Ernst, S. and Maguire, M. (eds) (1987). *Living with the Sphinx.* The Women's Press, London.

Forrester, W. (ed.) (1980). *Great Grandmama's Weekly: a celebration of the Girls' Own Paper, 1880–1901.* Lutterworth Press, Guildford.

Glasser, W. (1975). *Reality Therapy: a New Approach to Psychiatry.* Harper and Row, New York.

Glasser, W. (1976). In Bassin, et al.

Hillman, J. (1988). Foreword. In Allan, J (1988). *Inscapes of the Child's World: Jungian Counseling in Schools and Clinics.* Springer Publications, Dallas, Texas.

Houston, G. (1990). *The Red Book of Gestalt.* The Rochester Foundation, London.

Inskipp, F. with Johns, H. (1984). Developmental eclecticism: Egan's skills model of helping. In Dryden, pp. 364–88.

Ivey, A. and Ivey, M. B. (1990). Assessment and facilitating children's cognitive development: developmental counseling and therapy in a case of child abuse. *Journal of Counseling and Development,* 68, (2), 299–305.

Jacobs, M. (1984). Psychodynamic therapy: the Freudian approach. In Dryden, pp. 23–46.

Jacobs, M. (1988). *Psychodynamic Counselling in Action.* Sage, London.

Jones, A. (1984). *Counselling Adolescents: School and After.* Kogan Page, London.

Lambert, K. (1984). Psychodynamic therapy: the Jungian approach. In Dryden, pp. 76–101.

Le Guin, U. (1971). *A Wizard of Earthsea.* Penguin, Harmondsworth.

Lessing, D. (1979). *Shikasta.* Jonathan Cape, London.

Lowe, P. (1988). *Special Needs in Ordinary Schools: Responding to Adolescent Needs: a Pastoral Care Approach.* Cassell, London.

Mallon, B. (1987). *An Introduction to Counselling Skills for Special Educational Needs: participants' manual.* Manchester University Press, Manchester.

Mearns, D. and Thorne, B. (1984). *Person-centred Counselling in Action.* Sage, London.

Moran, M. (1968). *Pastoral Counselling for the Deviant Girl.* Geoffrey Chapman, London.

Morrison, D. W. (1977). *Personal Problem Solving in the Classroom: the Reality Technique*. Wiley, New York.

Murgatroyd, S. (1985). *Counselling and Helping*. The British Psychological Society/Methuen, London.

Noonan, E. (1983). *Counselling Young People*. Methuen, London.

Oaklander, V. (1978). *Windows to our Children: a Gestalt Therapy Approach to Children and Adolescents*. Real People Press, Utah.

Page, F. (1984). Gestalt therapy. In Dryden, pp. 180–204.

Rogers, C. R. (1961). *On Becoming a Person: a Therapist's View of Psychotherapy*. Constable, London.

Rogers, C. R. (1951). *Client Centered Therapy: its Current Practice, Implications, and Theory*. Constable, London.

Royal College of Nursing. (1978). *Counselling in Nursing. The report of a working party held under the auspices of the Royal College of Nursing Institute of Advanced Nursing Education*. Royal College of Nursing, London.

Salisbury, E. (1991). The ten words. *The Friend*, 149, (42), 1346.

Shapiro, L. (1984). *The New Short-term Therapies for Children: a Guide for the Helping Professions and Parents*. Prentice-Hall, New Jersey.

Thompson, C.L. and Rudolph, L. B. (1988). *Counseling Children*. Brooks/Cole, Pacific Grove, California.

Thorne, B. (1954). Person-centred therapy. In Dryden, pp. 102–28.

Wilson, K., Kendrick, P. and Ryan, V. (1992). *Play Therapy: a Non-directive Approach with Children and Adolescents*. Baillière-Tindall, London.

3　On Empathy

Tea and sympathy?

'Counselling' wrote Michael Jacobs (1988) 'consists of much more than attentive listening and empathic responses. The "tea and sympathy" image...' (p. 77).

Murgatroyd (1985) defines sympathy as 'offering another person support and emotional comfort because they are in some distress or pain' (p. 15).

Mearns and Thorne (1988) offer, 'sympathy arises from feeling compassionately moved by the experience of another, and to some extent sharing in it' (p. 26).

Three members of nursing staff in a child and adolescent psychiatric unit offered comments. 'Sam' suggested an image: 'If a man has a foot stuck in a ditch, don't stand on the edge and encourage him – that's sympathy.

'Jill' considers that 'sympathy can cripple. You can't *share* the feeling of, for example, abused children. You need to understand but not collude'.

'Kay' recalled her feeling for 'Pam' during a holiday spent together by staff and patients. As a young woman, Kay felt that she was sympathizing with the teenage girl whose dilemma in part reflected her own experiences. She recognized, 'The need to take care not to share in problems in a collusive way'.

Jacobs, writing on psychodynamic counselling, considers that 'The ability to sympathize often forms a good starting point for empathy (as long as we do not confuse our own feeling with the other person's). Yet it is not necessary to be sympathetic to a person in order to be empathetic' (p. 30).

Anne Jones (1984) finds sympathy to be 'a self-centred emotion: the counsellor knows how he would feel if his mother didn't love him, but how does that help John?' (p. 43).

Gerard Egan (1990) finds that sympathy 'has much more in common with pity, compassion, commiseration, and condolence than with empathy. While these are fully human traits, they are not particularly useful in counselling'. He quotes Boole (1988): 'Empathy is often confused with sympathy, kindness, and approval. Thus it may come to mean behaving compliantly in response to the patient's behavior' so that 'the therapist runs the risk of only identifying and colluding with the patient's experience (p. 422)'. Egan suggests that sympathy 'denotes agreement, whereas empathy denotes understanding and acceptance of the *person* of the client'. He refers to those clients who 'fail to manage their lives better because they take an "Isn't it awful!" attitude towards their problems. Sympathy makes this worse' (Egan, 1990, p. 139).

'Empathy' said one child psychologist, meaning the word rather than the phenomenon, 'can be very overused'. It certainly appears in surprising places.

Film critic Barry Norman (1991) described his father's response to a film. Mr Norman senior was not 'criticising it as a piece of film-making;...his argument was that he couldn't empathise with it. The Second World War, he said, simply wasn't like that' (p. 32). Surely the writer means that his father did not find his own experience reflected within the film. *Empathy* would imply that he felt 'as if' he shared the experience of the characters in the film. I do not think it is possible to empathize with a whole war.

In a biography of Arbella Stuart, cousin to James I, I learnt that 'The improvement in her finances may have come about through her own influence with the king.' She had 'built up an empathy with her royal cousin which was paying off' (Durant, 1978, p. 147). While I 'feel' that this is not correct usage the 'right' word will not come to mind: I am, it seems, unable to empathize with the author (although I enjoyed the book).

The idea, though not the word, pervades the fictionalized biography of Alexander the Great and his lifelong empathic relationship with Hephaistion who 'was used to reading Alexander's thoughts in the back of his head'. No tea and sympathy here. Alexander's father has just been murdered and the thoughts Hephaistion reads are not about warm beverages (Renault, 1970, p. 403).

But is thought reading empathy, any more than sympathy? I decided to write this chapter when I realized how often and variously this word was used, how difficult people find it to define and how confused I was becoming.

Some definitions

Just as I thought I had grasped the concept I found *Empathy and its Development*, (Eisenberg and Strayer, 1987). As a non-psychologist I could hardly do justice to the many papers and ideas. However therein are answers to questions I had not yet thought of asking and more questions awaiting exploration. I am indebted to several of the contributors for material included in this chapter (Eisenberg, Hoffman, Strayer, Wispé).

One question I had expected never to have answered was, where does the concept of empathy come from? Lauren Wispé's essay (1987) reveals that 'empathy' is the translation by early twentieth-century American experimental psychologists of *Einfuhlung*, from the vocabulary of late nineteenth-century German aesthetics, in connection with 'the psychology of aesthetics and form perception' (p. 18).

He summarizes:

> The concept was utilized by many personality theorists of the 1930s; was borrowed, cherished, and revitalized, especially by Rogerian psychotherapists, during the 1950s; had a brief encounter with conditioning theorists during the 1960s; and most recently has been called into service by social and developmental psychologists as an explanation for altruistic behaviour (p. 17).

Strayer and Eisenberg note that in the mid-1980s some Canadian psychology students were asked to interview people in their community, their parents and others about 'the word *empathy* and what it meant. Many persons outside the university had not heard of it, and most responded that it meant sympathy' (Strayer and Eisenberg, 1987, p. 390).

Soon after this an unexpected encounter with 'a famous English actor' led to discussion of the same subject. He 'knew precisely that empathy entailed feeling in oneself the feelings of others...a crucial process...not only in his rendering of character, but also in his reading of plays' (pp. 390–91).

'Feeling in oneself the feelings of others' raises the central question of whether this is possible. An actor portraying or even 'becoming' another person for a limited time and with a script and role, may 'feel' the emotions of a betrayed wife, a dying man, a superstar child. But the acting person is not the acted person, even if the actor is in 'real' life betrayed, dying or Shirley Temple.

Context is crucial.

Eisenberg and Strayer (1987) 'define empathy as an emotional response that stems from another's emotional state or condition and that is congruent with the other's emotional state or situation' (p. 5). The feeling I presently experience began with and is owned by you; my feeling is like yours.

Carl Rogers defines it as 'the ability to experience another person's world as if it were one's own without ever losing that "as if" quality' (Murgatroyd, 1985, p. 15). At no time must I get lost in your world, particularly if it is 'frightening and confusing'. Indeed 'empathic understanding can only be accomplished by a person who is secure enough in his own identity to be able to move into another's world without the fear of being overwhelmed by it' (Thorne, 1984, p. 119).

Mearns and Thorne (1988) describe the Rogers model of empathy as the 'complex and delicate process of stepping into another person's shoes and seeing the world through his or her eyes without, however, losing touch with one's own reality' (pp. 26–7).

Brenda Mallon (1987) advises 'Try to get into the skin of the client: see the world through his eyes; feel what it must be like to be in his shoes. It is of little value to a client if you have no empathetic understanding of his life for he will only feel further distanced and isolated' (pp. 6–7).

References to this point have been taken from texts relating to working with adults. Polly Lowe (1988) writing on 'Adolescent needs: counselling and problem-solving' describes 'Empathic understanding' as 'walking in another person's shoes, attempting to feel what it is like to be that person. Through the reflection of conveyed feelings, the helper reassures the youngster that she is not alone, and that a genuine attempt is being made to share feelings. It can only be an approximation, however, when we say that we understand'. It is crucial always to remember that 'One person's experience is unique to that person. We can only speculate and share facets of that experience' (p. 73).

This popular image of stepping into or walking in another person's shoes is less appropriate than it may look. Someone else's shoes are the last items of clothing easily to be assumed. Worn down and bulged out, they have been moulded perfectly to fit particular feet. High heels or heavy boots, sloppy espadrilles or sculpted trainers, they are chosen for function as well as fit. Familiar to their owner's feet another walker in your shoes may teeter or trip.

Actor Beryl Reid is famous for developing character portrayals from the feet, learning first to walk in appropriate footwear. Having walked for a while in another person's shoes she, surely, gladly, returns to her own slippers.

Just as 'It can only be an approximation...when we say that we understand', the actor wears the shoes, literally and figuratively, as an approximation. Her feet, her corns, her blisters are not those of Mrs Malaprop. The actor is portraying, representing, even for a while being the other person. The counsellor is being *with* the other.

The counsellor may experience feelings 'as if' but cannot have the exact experiences and feelings of the client.

Lowe continues that 'From the client's viewpoint the exhilaration is in knowing that someone is at least making a genuine effort to understand, and is focusing totally upon you. It can be an enriching experience for both client and counsellor' (Lowe, 1988, p. 73). Here is the positive balance to Brenda Mallon's warning that lack of empathic understanding may lead to further distancing and isolation.

Egan's discussion of empathy (and non-empathy) is very detailed, comprising a chapter entitled *Communication Skills 2: Empathy and Probing* and a section on *Advanced Empathy*. Empathy is described as both a way of being and a communication skill. Egan considers that 'However deep one person's empathic understanding of another, it needs to be communicated to the other'. Communication need not always be verbal: 'People with empathic relationships often express empathy in actions' (Egan, 1990, p. 125).

'Mary' (a university student counsellor) describes empathy as 'giving attention, understanding, giving space, *giving*, listening.'

Thompson and Rudolph (1988) (summarizing Rogers) describe empathy as 'the attitude that holds the counseling process together. By attempting to understand, the counselor is helping to convince people that they are worth hearing and understanding' (Thompson and Rudolph, 1988, p. 19).

The very concentration needed to attend to other people must indicate the counsellor's belief in their worth. Without such belief the attending can only be flawed and empathy, however defined, impossible.

This is a reminder too that the recipients of counselling are often in their own and/or other people's estimation unworthy of regard, respect, attention, even help. Chaplin (1988a) writes that 'Most children of either sex are not taken seriously and are frequently humiliated, for example, by being laughed at when they are serious, or by being patronized' (p. 32). It is easy to humiliate and patronize children even within a counselling relationship and to withhold empathy or mistake for it some other such response as sympathy.

Chaplin proposes that since women, like children, are frequently 'dismissed and devalued', so are such traditionally 'feminine skills' as 'empathy, warmth and unconditional positive regard' (p. 16). It may be of significance that an adult male of good status but well in touch with his own apparently rigid and restricted childhood and with the humility to recognize his own errors and growth, identified empathy as so crucial a component of counselling (see Rogers, 1961; Thompson and Rudolph, 1988, pp. 65–6).

Mearns and Thorne (1988) define empathy as 'a continuing process whereby the counsellor lays aside her own way of experiencing and perceiving reality, preferring to sense and respond to the experiences and perceptions of her client. This sensing may be intense and enduring with the counsellor actually experiencing her client's thoughts and feelings as powerfully as if they had originated in herself' (p. 39).

They regard the 'communication of accurate understanding' as 'a vital part of the empathic response: the client must *feel* understood'. Crucially it

> is not a 'technique' of responding to the client, but a way-of-being-in relation to the client. Empathy often feels like being on the same train, or camel, as the client! It is the client's journey which the counsellor is joining and staying with, no matter how bumpy it is.

Such journeys are characterized by

> the same qualities of immediacy and intensity whether they are in the play-room with the six-year-old, in the locked ward with the

schizophrenic, or in the student counselling office with the student who cannot decide whether or not to leave the university (p. 4).

Thorne considers that 'Empathic understanding of the kind that the person-centred therapist seeks to offer is the result of the most intense concentration and requires a form of attentive listening which is remarkably rare'. He finds himself 'startled and saddened when a client says to me, "You are the first person who has ever really listened to me" or "You really do understand what I feel and nobody else ever has". He regards empathic understanding of this kind as 'the most reliable force for creative change in the whole of the therapeutic process' (Thorne, 1984, pp. 119, 120).

The main differences within these definitions of empathy are, I think, the intensity of the immediacy and of the encounter between client and counsellor.

Two-way communication

An aspect of empathy for which I looked almost in vain is reciprocation. Mearns and Thorne note the importance of the 'communication of accurate understanding...the client must *feel* understood for the empathy to have its impact' (p. 41). But here the empathy seems still to be one way; the counsellor actively understands the client; the client's task is passive, to feel understood.

The client, however, is a whole real person. The appellation 'client' applies only within the particular relationship with the counsellor. Children and young people are counsellors' clients for only an hour or so a week. For most of the time they are daughters or sons, sisters or brothers, students or pupils, friends or foes, patients or prisoners.

Communication between individuals may include more or less understanding of feelings, may be more or less empathic. The counsellor's client may in other circumstances be the receptive listener, the initiator of the empathy. 'Mothers and wives', for example, 'are expected to be good at listening' (Chaplin, 1988a, p. 16).

The purpose of counselling contact is not for clients to listen to and understand the problems and feelings of their counsellors. But since counsellors are whole people too and spend most of their lives within a wide range of relationships, they inevitably bring feelings from outside into counselling sessions.

Physical illness will probably be obvious; if the counsellor has a cold the client may feel at least sympathy and possibly fear (of catching it). But there may at another level be communication of impaired concentration (fuzzy head), frustration (blocked nose) and misery (misery).

Menstrual pain and pre-menstrual tension may communicate to the client (of either sex) low energy and misery.

Anxiety about the counsellor's own health, emotional, social or spiritual situation may be put out of consciousness during working contacts but cannot be expelled altogether.

However much the counselling time belongs to the client the counsellor is present, physically, emotionally, mentally and spiritually. If this is not so, the client is being sold short; but if it is, the counsellor in a truly empathic interaction is communicating far more than understanding alone.

Only once in all my reading and listening have I found an example of this, in the work of psychologist and writer Dorothy Rowe (1987). Finding the book in itself had the quality of empathy. During an emotional crisis and lengthy depression while I was preparing the present book, I tackled myself in the light of lessons from the counselling models I was studying. Finding William Glasser's astringent sense helpful and hard I faced the uncomfortable realization that my life was considerably influenced by fear. What, said Glasser in my head, are you going to do about it?

Other silent helpers assured me that I could not and need not get free in one great leap but should seek one step at a time – an exercise, a task which I could accomplish without too much effort, a good chance of success, a beginning. Needing some form of action I went to the university bookshop and browsed. If only there was a book about fear. Comfortable in my certainty that no such book existed I was safe from actually doing anything. Idly I gazed at a stand with which I do not usually engage. *Beyond Fear* leapt to my eye and hand. Even the price was acceptable. I knew of the author's fine reputation. The book spoke to me.

The mobilization of energy which took me to the bookshop at all and permitted me to spend the money on an 'unnecessary' book was the beginning of recovery. The book continued to speak to me, a kind of long-range empathy: 'How does she know so much about me when she's never met me?'

And it is Dorothy Rowe who writes of a client's understanding. Harry was a young man whose 'life had been spent at home and at school and nowhere else...going to university far away from home had been...an unsettling shock to him'. His contact with her was as a 'schizophrenic client'.

During his second session Harry said suddenly:
'This room is your haven'. This hit straight home at me. My office was not a particularly attractive or comfortable room, but it was my own territory. At that time I was feeling under great threat from some powerful people outside my office, so I was often glad to retreat to its safety.

Moreover, the threat and anxiety concerned Harry, for in previous years I would have been able to give Harry a great deal of time and perhaps would have been able to work with the counsellors at his university so he could continue his career, but the threats to the future of our psychology service meant that we could not give Harry the help he needed.

All the time I was listening to Harry and trying to understand what he was telling me I was angry and grieving that this gentle young man had entered upon a path which, without adequate intervention, would mean that he would either die by his own hand or spend his days like those strange automatons which every day I saw walking past my window. He saw that this room was my haven, and he tried to comfort me (p. 361) (re-paragraphed).

Because the client is so likely to be open to the unspoken feelings of the counsellor, it is very important for the counsellor to be aware of and clear about those feelings. It might be more honest and useful to postpone or cancel a contact, than to expose an already troubled client to an invisible barrage of confusion, grief or anger which do not even belong to the counsellor's response to the client.

I had a very strong empathic relationship with 'Bet'. I did not see her often but we seemed to make contact when she had some crisis. Shortly after the death of her mother I found myself impelled to cross a crowded room and sit beside her during a Meeting, through which I then wept. I had not known her mother and we had not met in order to talk about her. I simply had an overwhelming sense of a sadness I knew was not my own and I wept for and with my friend. This was completely different from sympathy.

Some time later Bet endured another major crisis. After we had met I experienced immense anger. Since I had been feeling calm and happy and although, once I felt the anger, I could find plenty to be angry about, I knew that it was not my own. I telephoned Bet to ask her to have her own anger, which she could not herself own and express. My experience of her anger was different from the anger I felt myself about people who had, in my view, hurt and harmed her.

Within a few weeks I entered the depression of which I have already written. Since most of this was my own and none hers, I knew it would be almost literally fatal for us to meet; our individual depressions would have bounced to and fro, not because I should have told her my own miseries but because, however brightly I might have chatted, my feelings would have been communicated. I felt guilty at apparently withdrawing friendship but, recognizing that empathy can work two ways, considered my absence to be the kindest service I could offer.

The need to recognize and order the counsellor's own feelings, to become centred before a session, and the possible intensity of empathic contact, is vividly evoked in an encounter between a North American war veteran (I assume from Vietnam) who has become mute and a counsellor. The whole extract is quoted to retain the full impact;

Tonight Bob and I had our most powerful session to date. When I went into his room he had 'American Pie' playing on the record player. As usual he was lying, fully dressed, on his bed. I sat precisely where I had finished the day before, which was just close enough to touch him. Before I had come to him, I had spent some time in the car, getting myself relaxed and centred. That was important because right away he looked into my eyes. His look was so fundamental – right away it shook my very being but I was centred enough to meet it and to return it. He kept looking at me and I kept receiving it and sending back my own warmth.

I lost track of time, as always, but it must have been about half-an-hour later because we had turned the record back to the 'A' side when I found myself crying, inside. I could feel it so strong – I was really choked and yet not a sound came out of my mouth. Everything flashed before me – I knew that I wasn't crying for *me* – I knew that my history had some similarities, but it wasn't with me then. It wasn't *me* crying – it was more *like he was crying inside me.* And that crying was very strong and *mute.*

As I looked at him and he looked at me it felt like love passed between us, from one to the other. I remember *Vincent* was playing. I reached out to Bob with both my hands, and he put one of his own between them. It was as though the touch had 'earthed' all the sensing that was so strong within us. I cried. Not that gentle tear that often is a response to the sadness in a client, but a deep deep sobbing.

I remember being amazed at the strength of this feeling within me, yet, at another level, I knew that it was OK. Slowly, Bob cried too, and eventually his sobbing became screaming. He reached out and held me tight. (I later found my back was bleeding from cuts made by his nails). He let his desperation and his fear meet the light of our day. And I cried with him more and more.

As I write these notes some hours later I know that we have begun. I also am aware that I am still trembling (Mearns and Thorne, 1988, p. 89) (re-paragraphed).

The empathy of children

While these examples are not about work with children I suggest that counsellors need to be even more careful to recognize, acknowledge and manage their own feelings when meeting such particularly vulnerable clients.

Laurence E. Shapiro (1984) writes that in 'the slow unravelling of the Gordian Knot of the psyche that characterizes the analytic mode of therapy' he 'had learned the rewards of patience and empathic caring built on an unhurried acceptance of the way children reveal themselves' (p. v). An important revelation is the empathy of the children themselves.

Teachers in particular will be familiar with this from children's writing. In an essay about God, Nicola McDowell (1976) considers that in Heaven

I shall meet my Nana and we shall shake hands and go off talking
about things. I always talk to my Nana whose dead and I always think
she's listening. I tell her what happened today and may tell her jokes. I
always think they can hear what you think. I get the feeling that
somebody is listening or watching me but I never know how (p. 36).

The empathic relationship between Nicola and her Nana has, it seems,
been so strong that the girl can hold the feeling in her mind and
continue to experience communication.

In *Thursday* (1974) Catherine Storr describes the relationship
between Bee (15) and her friend Thursday. Her understanding of his
feelings at the deepest level leads her to seek him when he disappears
from school and home. She must employ the age old method of holding
him in whatever transformation to bring him back to full life, from a
'breakdown', or from enchantment.

To rescue Thursday, Bee endures a number of ordeals, some in
conversations which challenge her so far clear view of life. Her mother,
with whom she has a happy loving relationship and whom she assumes
to be nothing but content, reveals that the good home life she provides
and maintains is not without cost to herself. Bee grows in experience
and understanding which strengthen her love and channel her empathy
into appropriate action.

Martin L. Hoffman (1987) summarizes the development of empathy
in children in four stages.

1. *'Global empathy'* During the first year of life 'witnessing someone in
distress may result in a global empathic distress response' so that
'infants may at times act as though what happened to the other
happened to themselves'. He cites as example a girl (11 months) who
'on seeing a child fall and cry, looked as though she was about to cry
herself, then put her thumb in her mouth and buried her head in her
mother's lap, as she does when she herself is hurt' (p. 51).

2. *'Egocentric empathy'*. As the child becomes 'aware that another
person and not the self is in distress...the other's internal states remain
unknown and may be assumed to be the same as one's own'. Here the
example is of a boy (18 months) who 'fetched his own mother to
comfort a crying friend although the friend's mother was also present',
which behaviour is regarded as 'responding with appropriate empathic
affect'.

3. *'Empathy for another's feelings'*. Two or three year old children
become 'aware that other people's feelings may differ from one's own
and are based on their own needs and interpretation of events'. With
the acquisition of language they may empathize 'with a wide range of
increasingly complex emotions'. These may include 'a victim's distress'
and 'the victim's anxiety about the loss of self-esteem, hence with the
desire *not* to be helped'. Children may also 'be empathically aroused
by information about someone's distress even in that person's
absence'.

4. *'Empathy for another's life condition'*. By late childhood (not

defined) awareness has developed 'that others feel pleasure and pain, not only in the immediate situation but also in their larger life experience' so that the 'empathic response may be intensified when one realizes that the other's distress is not transitory but chronic'.

Hoffman concludes that 'the most advanced empathic level involves some distancing – responding partly to one's mental image of the other rather than only to the other's immediate stimulus value'. He presents his definition of empathy 'not as an exact match of another's feelings, but as an affective response that is more appropriate to the other's situation than to one's own' (pp. 51, 52, 53).

I cannot discuss this analysis and can offer it only in support of the belief that children from a very early age are capable of empathy. Dorothy Rowe explains this succinctly:

> Just as we were born with the ability to breathe so we were born with the ability to experience our emotions fully and to be aware of other people's emotion. We can keep our capacity to experience the full range and totality of our feelings and our capacity to empathize with other people. We can use these capacities to know ourselves, to know other people and to let them be themselves. We can do this. But we rarely do. Society, the group we belong to, will not let us (Rowe, 1987, p. 82).

She develops the idea of empathy as innate: 'We are all born with a capacity to hate and destroy. We are also born with the capacity to know our inner world and to empathize with others. A child brought up in love and acceptance develops all these capacities and can balance one against the other. The empathy balances the hate and keeps the destructiveness in check.' Failure to have these experiences may leave the child 'at the mercy of his hate and destructiveness' with potentially appalling consequences (p. 343).

Healthy development of the whole person may lead to the strength to stand away from the hateful, hating and destructive behaviour of the group we belong to. Under the sub-heading *Empathic injustice* Hoffman illustrates this with the story of a boy (14) living in a Southern state of the USA who joined his friends in harrassing black children. However he began to recognize one of the children as 'a kid, not a nigger' and eventually broke up an assault on him. To his own surprise and in front of the other white youths, he said to the black boy, 'I'm sorry'.

In due course he 'became the black youth's friend and began advocating "an end to the whole lousy business of segregation"'. He attributed his change of attitude and behaviour to 'seeing that "kid behave himself, no matter what we called him, and seeing him insulted so bad, so real bad. Something in me just drew the line, and something in me began to change, I think"' (Coles, in Hoffman, 1987, pp. 56–7).

It may be significant that the white boy was a popular athlete so had status among his peers. He had, we may suppose, the confidence to stand apart from his fellows, attending to what Hoffman regards as an empathic response. Yet this very standing and confidence might have led to denial of his feeling for and understanding of the black boy.

The incident allows a glimpse of a young person deciding which voice in his life is stronger, the approval of the group – society – or attention to the feelings and needs of another individual, risking rejection for himself.

The white boys had of course feelings and needs too and we are shown how the empathic response both requires and develops the concept of justice and injustice. Children are capable of a very strong sense of justice and become confused when that sense is challenged by obvious injustice by powerful adults.

'Mark' (10) was deeply puzzled when the court, which he would be expected to regard as comprising powerful adults interested in his welfare and worthy of his respect, made apparently unjust decisions, separating him from his parents although they had been guilty of no assault against him and he had committed no crime against them, or anyone else. The decisions of the adults were made despite the feelings of the child. However empathic the social workers, consideration of reason and reasons dominated.

The weeping child

The confused grief consequent on injustice towards and experienced by children is delicately portrayed in a story by Jane Gardam (1987). The narrator has been walking in a garden where, 'I heard a child crying and saw that there was a little boy standing near the tap in the corner. He was sobbing and weeping dreadfully. As if his heart was quite broken...the more I spoke to him the more he wept and turned away from me'.

She tells the gardener about 'the boy crying in the greenhouse' and he says 'Oh aye. It's me...I'm often there. People are often seeing me'. He had been wrongfully accused of 'something I never did. I'm very often there'.

A friend asks, 'What was it he'd done?' and the narrator answers, 'Oh, he hadn't done it. I rather think he'd forgotten what it was all about. I had that feeling.' She describes the weeping as 'not remorse or anger' but 'tremendous disappointment and bitterness and sorrow. A sort of ... essence of sorrow. Like a scent. A smell. Something very heavy and thick in the air' (pp. 185–6).

The narrator is empathic, receiving the sense of that long ago sorrow through sight, (the boy), sound (crying), smell ('a scent') and touch ('something very heavy and thick in the air'). 'I had that feeling' she says, referring to the old man, empathic to the difference between his unassuaged sorrow and his cleansed memory – 'I rather think he'd forgotten what it was all about.' But can we be sure that the old man is not himself a haunting, an evocation of feeling?

His crying child self, says the gardener, is 'often there. People are often seeing me.' The seeing, the conversing, even the conscious remembrance of long past experience do not, it seems, free the old man. Or has he become free by splitting off his sad child self or, conversely, by accepting that self as an ordinary part of life, as a full grown tree shows its whole history in the scars of lost limbs, the configuration of rings, the parasitic plants, and birds and insects to which it is host?

So the child is present constantly in the adult who cannot be mature if not tolerant of and learning from the immature. Indeed the present book, while focusing on chronological children is inevitably about anyone, of whatever apparent age, for the child is always present, always in need – not of rejection and humiliation but of joyful recognition. 'Except ye be as a little child' recommends the adult to retain the graces and skills of childhood.

Walking in the inner world

Recognition of the inner world of the child client may imply entering that world with the child. This may be both invigorating and dangerous for both child and counsellor. In his *Introduction* to John Allan's book on Jungian-based work with severely disturbed children, James Hillman (1988) describes the dangerous worlds of children's fantasy, including witches and wizards, violence and death, from which the counsellor's training is largely alienating. He advises that 'To engage in the child's fantasy requires one to be engaged by one's own. To enjoy one's own dreams and be comfortable in one's own inscapes should be the first requirement for working with children' (p. xvi).

Luci (5+) describes a dream of the '"dead land"...Outside there are no flowers, no grass, only rocks'. Far from trying to distract or console her, Allan 'enters that place with her' (p. xvii).

Here are dangers for the counsellor who is not well grounded and one of the many dangers of empathy is over-involvement. I have mentioned the problems of empathic contact with my friend. We easily seduce one another into 'the dead land'.

Two of Catherine Storr's books for children explore this. In *Thursday* Bee succeeds in staying clear of the dead land where Thursday, in whatever dimension, languishes. Her emotional union with him does not drag her into his depression (Storr, 1974).

In *Marianne Dreams* (1964) Storr explores a dead land remarkably like that of Luci's dream. Marianne, confined to bed for many weeks, draws a desolate house and landscape in which are imprisoned Mark, a real boy who suffers from some life-threatening illness. Marianne draws, then dreams herself and Mark in the pictures.

Her daytime emotions about the real boy cause her to develop the drawing: her dreams present her with the dangers and problems effected by those emotions. In a tantrum of jealousy she turns the house into a prison and makes 'the fence round the sad little garden thicker and higher...Outside it were the great stones and boulders she had drawn before...' She draws 'more stones, a ring of them round outside the fence' (p. 55).

Eventually Marianne helps to rescue Mark but not before she has allowed this extraordinarily powerful empathic contact to cause him great harm.

The importance of balance and the twin traps of failing to maintain this at all times are clearly expressed by Brian Thorne: 'The task of empathic understanding can only be accomplished by a person who is secure enough in his own identity to be able to move into another's world without the fear of being overwhelmed by it' (Thorne, 1984, p. 119). A child lost in the labyrinth cannot be helped by a counsellor who not only loses the thread but also fears the monster at the centre.

Once the counsellor has entered the other's world 'he has to move around with extreme delicacy and with an utter absence of judgement'. He recognizes 'the danger the therapist could express understanding at too deep a level and frighten the client away from therapy altogether' described by Rogers as 'blitz therapy' (p. 119). Enter the labyrinth with the child, offer your hand, protect the way out but do not start laying about with your sword, murdering the minotaur yourself or explaining that it is really only a cardboard model.

The task is to be with the child who travels towards, meets and greets the monster, decides what to do next, and does it.

A cool head

Another pair of problems is identified by Geoffrey Sworder (1977) in *Counselling at Work*. He warns against reaching 'a stage where empathy is so strong that the counsellor inclines to take his clients' problems upon himself, and to feel somehow responsible'. Over-identification 'is likely to be unhelpful to his work, or even disabling, and he must try to stand back sufficiently to be objective'. (He has already warned about the high risk of suicide and divorce in counselling and psychiatry). Standing back, however, must be rightly balanced for taken too far, the counsellor 'will be seen as a remote, cold manipulator, lacking empathy , "playing God", and meeting his personal needs for power' (p. 82).

One temptation to play God may be in assuming that because the counsellor believes the contact with the child to be empathic, interpretation of the child's feelings is accurate. In intensive work with four young children who observed the murder of their mother by their father, a child psychiatrist and a social worker recognized 'that it is not always easy to understand what is being communicated, there may be several meanings to each communication and one can never be certain of having comprehended them' (Isaacs and Hickman, 1987, p. 35).

As the experience of empathy is crucially 'as if', so the interpretation of communication received, however empathically, must be regarded as 'perhaps'.

The reception of messages by either counsellor or client may lead to misunderstandings with grave results. Rowe indicates the danger of lacking 'both a strong sense of your own self and concepts in which to organize what you discover, which are concepts shared with other people'.

Sensing that a newly met person is

> under a guise of friendliness, really very angry I can organize this subtle information into, say, a question like, 'I wonder what he's angry about?' and, if I feel confident in myself, decide that his anger has nothing to do with me, or if it has, that he's a fool to get angry with so wonderful a person as me.

Lacking these concepts and without self-confidence, 'what I perceive is anger, danger and confusion' (Rowe, 1987, p. 362).

The killing waltz

Anger, danger and confusion are not only real but really felt by the client in relation to the counsellor, or vice versa. In a story set in a dancing class, Bowen (1983) captures the hideous relationship between Joyce James, a dancing-mistress and her victim/pupil, Margery Mannering. Hatred of the girl is the only passion in the teacher's life and the child knows this whenever they meet. Margery thinks, '"She'd like to kill me"' and the teacher thinks, '"I would like to kill her – just once". Her face had a hard wistfulness' (p. 255).

Teacher and girl exchange very few words but the hatred and fear are palpable. The climax of the story is a gruesome waltz. 'They did not speak; they heard one another's breathing; the girl's light, the child's loud and painful.' Margery's eyes are, 'stretched with physical fear like a rabbit's'. But the mothers (not one of whom belongs to Margery), sitting around the walls, say of the teacher, 'She really is patient and good...Look at the pains she takes with that poor little stupid...'. Pains, certainly, but given not taken. 'Don't hate her so's the others can notice', counsels Joyce's friend. But the others don't notice. They see only what they wish (pp. 258–9, 260).

Isaac Asimov (1990) in a novel set far from dancing classes, indeed, from twentieth-century Earth, captures the very present, down to earth feelings of a child. Marlene (15) is revealing to her mother an unusual and threatening gift:

> You're thinking that I know what you're thinking, but you're wrong. I
> don't read minds. I just tell from words and sounds and expressions
> and movements. People just can't keep what they think hidden.
> ...When I was a kid, everyone lied to me. They told me how sweet I
> was. Or they told you that when I was listening. They always had that
> look plastered all over them that said, 'I don't really think that at all.'
> And they didn't even know it was there. I couldn't believe at first they
> didn't know. But then I said to myself, 'I guess it's more comfortable
> for them to make believe they're telling the truth' (p. 65).

Empathy is a two-edged caduceus. What may be used to help and heal
may also maim and destroy.

But here is a last, healing word, a compassionate and hopeful
definition by Dorothy Rowe: 'Empathy is a precious human skill which
not only prevents us from being cruel but joins us to others. When we
experience empathy we are able, if only momentarily, to leave the
loneliness of being and enter another person's world' (p. 74).

Summary

Empathy is a word much used in the literature and discussion of
counselling. Interpretations and misunderstandings of the concept are
legion; it must, for example, be distinguished from **sympathy** and
thought reading. Definitions from **psychologists** and **counsellors** have
been introduced briefly. Empathy operates in two directions; the
counsellor **communicates** as well as **receives unconscious messages.**

Children are capable of empathy which may be **innate,** probably
from the first year of life. **Jungian** counsellors describe the dangers of
opening oneself to the nightmare world of severely disturbed children.
Counsellors must be **secure in their own identities** to avoid being
overwhelmed. Children receive negative as well as positive messages
and empathic responses may be **wounding,** even **destructive.** Great
care must be taken.

Empathy is a complex, difficult concept, a two-way channel of
communication of both good and ill, destruction and healing.

Link

Marlene may not be able to read minds but she can recognize the real
feelings of other people, through acute and minute observation. Most
people who realize this find her intolerable: most communication
relies it seems on dissembling. One of the greatest skills is to know
when and where to stop, to respect the privacy of the other person,

whoever s/he may be and whatever the context of contact. This is as important in working with children as with adults. Some aspects of this little discussed or respected topic are presented in Chapter 4, 'Tips, Dumps and Privacy'.

References

Allan, J. (1988). *Inscapes of the Child's World: Jungian Counseling in Schools and Clinics*. Spring Publications, Dallas, Texas.
Asimov, A. (1990). *Nemesis*. Bantam, London.
Bowen, E. (Wilson, A. (ed.)) (1983). *The Collected Stories of Elizabeth Bowen*. Penguin, Harmondsworth, The dancing-mistress, pp. 53–62.
Chaplin, J. (1988a). *Feminist Counselling in Action*. Sage, London.
Coles, R. (1986). *The Moral Life of Children*. Atlantic Monthly Press. Atlanta. Quoted in M. L. Hoffman, pp. 56–7.
Durant, D. N. (1978). *Arbella Stuart: a Rival to the Queen*. Weidenfeld and Nicholson, London.
Dryden, W. (ed.) (1984). *Individual Therapy in Britain*. Harper and Row, London.
Egan, G. (1990). *The Skilled Helper: a Systematic Approach to Effective Helping*. Brooks/Cole, Pacific Grove, California.
Eisenberg, N. and Strayer, J. (1987). *Empathy and its Development*. Cambridge University Press, Cambridge.
Gardam, J. (1987). The weeping child. In Lee.
Glasser, W. (1975). *Reality Therapy: a New Approach to Psychiatry*. Harper and Row, New York.
Hillman, J. (1988). Foreword. In Allan, pp. xiii–xx.
Hoffman, M. L. (1987). The contribution of empathy to justice and moral judgement. In Eisenberg and Strayer, pp. 47–80.
Isaacs, S. and Hickman, S. (1987). Communication with children after a murder. *Adoption and Fostering*, 11, (4), 32–5.
Jacobs, M. (1988). *Psychodynamic Counselling in Action*. Sage, London.
Jones, A. (1984). *Counselling Adolescents: School and After*. Kogan Page, London.
Lee, H. (ed.) (1987). *The Secret Self(2): Short Stories by Women*. Dent, London.
Lowe, P. (1988). *Special Needs in Ordinary Schools: Responding to Adolescent Needs; a Pastoral Care Approach*. Cassell, London.
McDowell, N. (1976). God and Heaven. In Mirror Group Newspapers, p. 36.
Mallon, B. (1987). *An Introduction to Counselling Skills for Special Educational Needs: Participants' Manual*. Manchester University Press.
Mearns, D. and Thorne, B. (1988). *Person-centred Counselling in Action*. Sage, London.
Mirror Group Newspapers (1976). *Children as Writers, 3*. Heinemann, London.
Murgatroyd, S. (1985). *Counselling and Helping*. British Psychological Society/Methuen, London.
Norman, B. (1991). Barry Norman on ... *Radio Times*, 25.4.91.
Renault, M. (1970). *Fire from Heaven*. Longman, London.

Rogers, C. R. (1961). *On Becoming a Person: a Therapist's View of Psychotherapy*. Constable, London.

Rowe, D. (1987). *Beyond Fear*. Collins, London.

Shapiro, L. E. (1984). *The New Short-term Therapies for Children: a Guide for the Helping Professions and Parents*. Prentice-Hall, New Jersey.

Storr, C. (1964). *Marianne Dreams*. Penguin, Harmondsworth.

Storr, C. (1974). *Thursday*. Penguin, Harmondsworth.

Strayer, J. and Eisenberg, N. (1987). Empathy viewed in context. In Eisenberg and Strayer, pp. 389–98.

Sworder, G. (1977). Problems for the counsellor in his task. In Watts, pp. 79–83.

Thompson, C. L. and Rudolph, L. B. (1988). *Counseling Children*. Brooks/Cole, Pacific Grove, California.

Thorne, B. (1984). Person-centred therapy. In Dryden, pp. 102–28.

Watts, A. G. (ed.) (1977). *Counselling at Work: Papers prepared by a Working Party of the Standing Conference for the Advancement of Counselling*. National Council for Social Service, London.

Wispé, L. (1987). History of the concept of empathy. In Eisenberg and Strayer, pp. 17–37.

4   Tips, dumps and privacy

Pressing the bruise

'Does that hurt?' I pressed the neck behind my stepdaughter's ears.
'Yes'. 'Does it hurt now?' 'YES!' Inexperienced in caring for sick
children and obsessed with discovering the facts, I pressed and
pressed, seeking, I suppose, confirmation.

Did I think the first 'Yes' had been a mistake, or a lie, or a genuine
response to a once-only pain? Fortunately she managed to convince
me that her neck did hurt and that the diagnostic phase was, please,
complete. We could proceed to the simple and effective treatment of
warmth and hot drinks.

My step-daughter's neck is long free of my ministrations but the
psychic glands of other children have been prodded by my over-
anxious fingers. For her, the prodding produced only a momentary
pain and could be halted by a yelp. The effects of pressing on an
emotional swelling or bruise may be less obvious and more painful.
The would-be helping adult may even be at risk of abusing the already
wounded child...

It seems to be very difficult to trust children to experience and live
and grow with their own feelings in silence. And in private
(Crompton, 1991, p. 31).

I wrote the article, of which the above is the beginning, towards the
end of 1990, as an early draft of my ideas on privacy and intrusion and I
was delighted that the editor of *Adoption and Fostering* considered it
to be of interest. Success in placing the paper led me to follow my initial
ideas into a number of places, many of them tips, dumps and
wildernesses.

A room of one's own

Privacy may not be considered a prime need of children, who live in
every respect publicly. The extreme example is the royal baby,
appearing before the public as an enlarging prenatal lump, posing for
photographs on the hospital steps, observed, recorded, commented on
through nursing and nursery, school and social life.

Even babies of commoners are routinely scanned in utero. Some
adult is always keeping watch, assessing, making demands. If things go
wrong, the usual tally of general practitioner, health visitor, playleader

and teacher may be augmented by paediatrician, nurse, psychologist, psychiatrist, education welfare officer, social worker and/or any number of therapists.

Space is shared at all times unless the dwelling is large enough or family small enough to provide an individual bedroom. Children living in their own homes may take their privacy, or lack of it, for granted. For many children, space and privacy are scarce goods.

Some girls in care were encouraged to comment on their living conditions. Sandra (15) wrote 'I feel and a few other lasses that we all should have a bedroom of our own, for more privacy. We feel if we had separate bedrooms we would not disturb anyone' (Benton Grange School, 1979, p. 18).

Sharon (12) considered that 'You should have your own bedroom because you might want a bit of privacy' and Joanne (12) wanted to take visitors into 'a room by myself and talk to them' (pp. 18,17).

Brenda Hawes (1979) who had spent her childhood in care, 'resented being stared at by all those helpful people from Councillors to Women's Institutes who came to look. It was like living in a goldfish bowl'. She believes that 'all children in care have the right to refuse being put on display for visitors' (p. 64).

A moving account of feeling on show is given by Catherine Houghton (15) in *On the Day when Mother Died (1976)*. 'There's nothing so horrible as seeing everybody waiting for you to cry, and whispering to each other when you don't. You hold your breath, pull faces and even pretend you've got a cold coming so that people don't see you'. She goes out and sees 'a group of nosy, chattering women...in a tight circle gossiping. I...knew by the looks on their greasy faces that they were talking about me' (pp. 104–105).

A crucial aid to privacy is the possession of a door to close, to say, physically or symbolically, do not disturb. 'I have a house with two doors, at the front and back. Both doors have locks. The many windows have locks too, and curtains, so that no one can either come or see in without my permission. If my telephone rings I may ignore it, or switch to "answer" so that, even if I hear, I need not respond. How many doors may a child lock?' (Crompton, 1991 p. 32).

Elizabeth Goudge (1936) presents a child discovering the bliss of privacy. 'At the orphanage she had slept in a dormitory with other little girls and worked and played and eaten in a seething horde, never knowing a moment's privacy day or night, and that had seemed so natural to her that loneliness, when it came, was terrifying' (p. 43).

Henrietta had been placed in a fictional nineteenth-century orphanage but children in school, hospital, community home or day care may still feel themselves to be absorbed in a seething horde. Henrietta is suddenly adopted and the exchange of dormitory for bedroom is a shock. But soon 'she knew that the most precious possession she had was her room and the privacy it gave her. She was immensely proud of it...In it she dreamed dreams and saw visions' (p. 43).

> A room of one's own in which to dream dreams. What child does not need that room, even if your physical walls may not enclose a private space?
> A private place in the mind. A private box. A drawer which noone else may open.
> The privacy must be decently guarded too. What value is being put on a life story book if only a Tesco bag is supplied to transport it between foster homes? What care of the child's treasured possessions, hauled round in an open cardboard box? (Crompton, 1991, p. 17).

If no larger private space can be provided, a special box may serve at least to symbolize privacy. Goudge (1950) describes 'a small wooden box with sea shells stuck upon the lid'. This contains the only relics of the dead mother of Stella, a foster child – 'a handkerchief, a coral, a locket – with some writing in Greek'. When she is given the box, Stella goes away to her own room, and sits on her bed. She may open the box which contains the key to her history and the only contact with her mother in private (p. 90).

But this is a child of some control for 'without giving herself time to think or feel, leaving all that for bedtime, she ran downstairs again to help...make the bread'. So private is she that 'Never, never, if she could help it, should Mother Sprigg know of the something in her that cried out in longing for her real Mother as it never cried out for Mother Sprigg'. Her foster mother is taken in and wonders if the child feels anything at all (p. 90). The child's privacy has been protected but at the cost of understanding.

It is important that Stella is allowed to open her box in private, to receive her messages without interference. Brenda Hawes asks that 'all children in care should have the right to open their own personal mail'. She remembered 'receiving letters addressed to me and feeling that all and sundry had read them before they reached me. Even birthday and Christmas cards were opened before I received them' (Hawes, 1979, p. 63).

Aline (15) wrote that 'We should be able to have our phone calls in private' (Benton Grange School, p. 18). In private in residential care would mean not being overheard by care staff, as well as peers.

A strange new element

Caring adults may be intrusive, even imprisoning, and there is little privacy in prison. Even the highest motives may have negative effects. The mother of Billy, in a novel by Rose Macaulay (1965) is an enlightened energetic woman but Billy complains, 'Mother'll never let me do what I want. 'Tisn't good enough for her, I wish people wouldn't *want* things for one: wish they'd let one alone. Being let alone...that's the thing' (p. 288).

Billy's problems are eventually easily solved, largely by time. For Paul (6) the intrusion is far deeper, the binding stronger. He is a hostage of his parents who, lacking the intervention of a Soloman, seem determined to rip him apart. The external action concerns swimming lessons. 'He looked like a prisoner offered a chance of escape, but the plastic water-wings, like some absurd pillory, kept him fixed.' He wants to escape from the terrors of the sea, which he hates, and the pressure from his father (Swift, 1978, p. 338).

At the moment of crisis he is caught, wanting to go with his mother but realizing that

> he was afraid of his father and his gripping hands. And he was afraid
> of his mother, too. How she would wrap him, if he came out, in the big
> yellow towel like egg yolk, how she would want him to get close to her
> smooth, sticky body, like a mouth that would swallow him. He
> thought: the yellow towel humiliated him, his father's hands
> humiliated him, the water-wings humiliated him: you put them on and
> became a puppet. So much of life is humiliation. It was how you won
> love (pp. 339–40).

What traps to have sprung so soon on the child. If the water does not drown him, the asphyxiating parents will. If he swims, his father will leave his mother; if he does not swim, his father will be angry: either way, Paul will suffer.

With only a few lines of the story left, what counsel for the oppressed child? 'There was no way out; there were all these things to be afraid of and no weapons.' But Paul's spirit and need for escape are strong. He realizes that 'perhaps he was not afraid of his mother nor his father, nor of water, but of something else'. Paul swims, freed at a stroke from his fear, maintained until then by 'unconsciouly pretending'. He swims, breaking the bond with his mother and 'half in panic, half in pride, away from his father, away from the shore, away, in this strange new element that seemed all his own' (pp. 340–41).

To discover one's own element, to become free from intrusion – a basic human need. The element, the place is both physical and intangible. It is also, sometimes, so secret that noone, not even the child, is aware of its existence. Swift's story shows Paul discovering not only the physical element, water, but also the emotional element of independence, the spiritual element of faith and the cognitive element of mastery. He uncovers secrets about himself of which his parents have no suspicion.

Sleeping beauties

Dennis O'Connor (1982) (educational psychologist and lecturer) tells a Sleeping Beauty story about Sandra (15) who, at the beginning of the tale, 'is overweight and has an unkempt appearance. Her performance at school is poor and she tends to make trouble for some of the class teachers whose assessments of her abilities are extremely low.' Following serious assault on a woman teacher, Sandra appeared in court, and when 'a social worker visited the home he was given a very hostile reception' and all offers of help were refused. She was placed on probation. Soon, Sandra attempted suicide, almost successfully, and 'On her return to school she presented as sullen, withdrawn and unmanageable' (pp. 32–3).

An educational psychologist reported:

> My early attempts at establishing rapport with Sandra had been met with a complete lack of response but as I proceeded with the sub-tests and began to feed back to her some approval for her performance she looked directly at me for the first time and began to volunteer small items of information about herself and her feelings quite apart from the responses required by the test, e.g. *she read a lot in private secrecy* due to the attitude of her family (p. 33) (my italics).

Moreover 'she loved Thackeray's novels and some of Shakespeare's tragedies'. Tests showing that Sandra had a superior intelligence did not surprise her, she was 'simply overjoyed that she could share her brilliance in a constructive way with someone who appeared to understand' (p. 33).

Her need for private secrecy had led Sandra nearly to death, the greatest private secrecy: the grave may be a fine and private place but none, I think, do there read Thackeray and Shakespeare. So secret had Sandra been that she had hidden an immense intelligence within a cerement of flesh and foolishness. Only her nearly successful attempt to hide herself completely brought her the miraculous opportunity to live abundantly.

Hiding even, or particularly, from oneself, is a common form of privacy seeking. As a child-care officer I spent much time with 'Karen', the young single mother of two sons who hid her face under a thick mask of make-up, covered as completely as possible by her hanging black fringe. The secret thus hidden was perhaps a key to her chaotic personality. Karen hid not only behind cosmetics and hair but also within an invisible cloak which involved in her own chaos anyone who tried to come near. A Sleeping Beauty who had not, by the time I ceased contact, begun to awaken.

Like Karen and Sandra, Penny needed to maintain secrecy even from herself, hiding physically so that she 'used to cover the mirror in my bedroom because I did not want to see myself' (Golding, 1990, p. 19). Her social worker told Penny's story in a reconstruction from 'her own words and the facts of the case, as if Penny were telling the story' (p. 18).

Sexually abused by her stepfather from the age of 7, Penny was forced to maintain this terrible secret until at 13 she disclosed it to the police. She had tried to obtain help at 7 but had not been believed. Her invaded privacy caused her integrity to be questioned, a further abuse. She withdrew into enforced sleep. Described by her school teacher as 'miserable and bedraggled, very backward indeed, a child with no love in her' (p. 18).

Like Sharon, Penny sought the ultimate privacy, death, taking the same brand of anti-depressant tablets with which her mother had also attempted suicide: 'I want to die' (p. 19).

For Penny, as for Sharon, there would be an awakening. Help came from her social worker, a group for sexually abused girls at the hospital and good fostering. At 14 'The nightmares have stopped and I sleep properly. I'm able to eat too and have put on some weight. I had my hair cut and Anne said to me: "Penny, you've got lovely blue eyes. I could never see them before"'. Penny had, unlike Karen, emerged from behind the concealing curtain. Eventually she would be able to enjoy her hair as 'shiny these days' and to 'like looking at myself in the mirror' (p. 19).

A Sleeping Beauty has awakened from nightmare into healthy sleep. A Lady of Shalott can use her mirror not to avoid nightmare but to reflect health (a use to which Tennyson's poor lady never put her glass).

Extraordinary privacy and pathological fear of intrusion are portrayed in Tennyson's Lady of Shalott, a maiden imprisoned in a tower as surely as Sharon in her fat, Penny in her silence and Karen behind her cloak of chaos. The Lady lives through her mirror, weaving into her tapestry the reflection of life. Confrontation with reality, seen directly through the window instead of mediated through the mirror, causes the curse to come upon her and, it seems, her death (Tennyson, 1832).

What is the curse? How does she die? Why is the withdrawal from her retreat fatal? I owe to my husband the idea that the curse might be interpreted, as the schoolgirl euphemism would have it, as menstruation, and that the Lady dies, not literally, but from unawakened (and terrified) pubescence into sexually aware womanhood; metamorphosis rather than death.

The sighting of Lancelot, a mature but unattainable male, shocks the Lady into making not only three paces through the room but also an impulsive step into taking initiative and risk. Not long before she has been unsettled by the reflection of 'two young lovers, lately wed'. Dissatisfaction with her lot has set in:

'I am half sick of shadows', said
The Lady of Shalott.

What killed the Lady? Fear of life? Or did she leave her outgrown maidenhood to set up a flourishing weaving business – in Lincolnshire, no doubt, where Tennyson first saw the

Long fields of barley and of rye
That clothe the wold and meet the sky.

What floated down to Camelot? A corpse? Or the cast off skin of a new woman?

And why this digression into poetry? Myth is deeply important as both reflection and map, and ignored at peril. Through asking questions about the Lady, for example, it is possible to look with fresh perspective at apparently intransigent problems of living individuals.

The Lady's privacy is not inviolable. She can be reached and apparently destroyed by intrusive thoughts about young lovers and feelings about Lancelot. Sharon and Penny could be unbound by care and respect; intrusion had only tightened the bonds.

Some unbinding takes a long time, until it becomes safe to leave the private place. 'Gary', in a residential special school provoked, and gave signs of enjoying, punishment; he would incite other boys to hit him and show pleasure until he was punched. He would then sit in a corner with his thumb in his mouth, crying, until running away to climb a tree and remain high and private but not alone.

Residential social worker 'Lee' would follow at a safe distance, sit at the bottom of the tree and wait without speaking.

Eventually Gary would descend and allow Lee to put an arm round his shoulder. In due course he tolerated other, female, staff touching him too. Like Robina Prestage (1972) beneath Kim's tree Lee understood the importance of building, slowly, trust. No good could derive from running after Gary or screaming and shouting and Lee considered the question of why Gary climbed the tree too delicate to ask. Lee, the only keyholder to Gary's private place, had to ensure that he remained calm and unchanging. Had he ever lost his temper or snapped, he would have become like too many other adults in the boy's experience. He knew that the tree times were crucial because there, then, something was happening.

For Gary and Lee the time testing was long and ended with a dramatic ordeal. Gary suddenly threw at Lee all the abuse he had received from his father. The final form of the enchanted victim is often the worst but the would-be rescuer must hold on, however horrifying the transformation. Lee recognized that the worker who achieves the child's trust may receive the full force of undammed feeling, now safe to be expressed.

For some children the hiding may be almost complete, the hedge of thorns all but impregnable. Margaret Hunter (1987) (psychotherapist) worked with Julia (7) whose foster parents 'found her stilted, aloof, unable to show emotion of any kind except for theatrical outbursts in which she noisily sought attention'. At school she was 'disruptive and inattentive', making little progress. To her foster mother she showed no 'spontaneous affection, no warmth..., no coming for comfort or love'. The foster mother 'grieved. "You can't feel anything from her"' (p. 26).

Julia, who is regarded as 'frozen', can eventually be helped to discover love, to become real, like Kay in *The Snow Queen* whose frozen heart melts when his snow blocks spell the word *eternity* (Andersen). Communication with Julia is in fact achieved through the *Snow White* story with its appropriately named 'frozen' heroine.

Catherine Dunbar, another Sleeping Beauty, could not be unfrozen, even by love. 'She died at peace with God, with herself, with us, and with a heart full of love.' But she died at her own wish, ending seven years of anorexia nervosa, when she wrote in her diary 'I can't open the door to life' (Dunbar, 1987, pp. 118, 70).

Her mother records that, within a few days of her death, 'Catherine was so loving, so giving, but knowing she wanted to die was something we could not come to terms with...it was like living a nightmare, a nightmare I desperately hoped to wake up from and discover that none of it was real' (pp. 114–15).

The totality of Catherine's withdrawal into the long-term, complete denial of life led to the ultimate privacy, death. On the way from health at 15 to death at 22 she gave up, among so many gifts, her womanhood – for cessation of menstruation is a consequence of starvation. Catherine's voyage to Camelot was truly that of death.

Dens, dumps and limbo

Some of the most vivid and intense life of children takes place in their own chosen private places, very often tips and dumps and patches of wasteland unclaimed by adults.

At 13 or so, my friends (Chris, Sue, Anita) and I walking home from school, the long way round, slipped between old metal railings into a narrow copse bordering a field. What we did I don't remember. I suppose we continued that perpetual conversation which had occupied us on the mile so far walked. I do remember the feelings of excitement, a little guilt and fear (suppose we were *caught*!) and pride of possession, for this group self-selected by the direction of our homeward walk, had a secret place of which even other friends must not know.

On my first visit to 'Mark' he showed me the den, built with help from his foster parents in an overgrown part of the garden. My childhood home had a large garden, much of it a lovely tangle under old fruit trees. Here I lived richly in my cave within the russet branches, the secret walk behind ragged box hedges and nested in the scented deep grass. The life of imagination could grow, the griefs of my teen-years be nursed. Within the untenanted orchard I could be myself. And the beauty of Gerard Manley Hopkins' *Spring*, read under the great old pear tree, has never left me.

Mossy Trotter's wilderness is invaded by an adult:

> 'It's a *paradise* for children', Miss Vera Silkin said, standing under the lilac tree by the gate, and looking across the common. Mossy knew what the word 'paradise' meant. It was a place like heaven. And he wondered how Miss Silkin could know that it was heaven.
>
> Standing where she was she could not possibly see the beautiful rubbish dump among the bracken. This had been his private paradise from the moment he discovered it. It was a shallow pit filled with broken treasures from which, sometimes, other treasures could be made. People had thrown away old bedsteads and rusty bits of bicycles, tin cans, battered coal-buckets for making space helmets from. If he could only find two odd wheels, he could build himself a whole bicycle, he thought. And every afternoon when he came home from school, he went to the rubbish dump to see if there were any luck (Taylor, 1967, p. 9).

The need for a personal, secret paradise goes deep. Adults may *know* the place but they do not *see* it. Bowen (1983) shows great understanding in *The Jungle*. A lonely girl, Rachel (14) discovers a place of her own, out of bounds of her boarding school, 'an absolutely neglected and wild place; nobody seemed to own it, nobody came there but tramps'. Rachel makes a terrible mistake: she takes a false friend to her jungle and when she returns on her own, the friend is there before her, in possession. Paradise lost (p. 231).

The limbo place reflects and receives the limbo state of being: being 14, being between friends. Janet West (1990) describes a number of young children suspended between addresses; they could hardly be called homes when, for example, Peter (8) had already had 23 addresses. The author recognized 'the "in limbo" phenomenon' in course of play therapy. Her vignettes do not reveal whether these children had, in their multiple places of sojourn, any private jungles but I imagine that the playroom became the next best thing (pp. 11–15).

Peter 'had a vivid, rich fantasy world. In the playroom he and I travelled many oceans, traversed the stars, and he was a cornucopia of a provider'. Physically forced to travel from house to house, Peter, given control for a while, chose space inhabited by no-one who could fail or demand of him. Unlike Rachel, he was fortunate in having a friend who would be likely to understand (p. 13).

Another child in limbo is Roger (9), sad subject of Bowen's story, *The Visitor* (1983). Awaiting the death of his mother, the imminence of which no one will acknowledge, it is appropriate that his inner state is reflected in his environment – a spare-room in someone else's house:

> He had never before slept in anybody's spare-room; theirs at home
> had been wonderful to him: a port, an archway, an impersonal room
> with no smell, nothing of its own but furniture (p. 124).

Janet West's Peter has spent his whole life in spare rooms and we may wonder whether Roger will again in his childhood feel, anywhere, at home or be like Geraldine (also about 9), whose mother having died, has been abandoned by her father with her grandmother. Her charming room is minutely described:

> But here (you might notice) vacant little Geraldine seemed to exist
> with difficulty. Every time her reflection flitted out of the looking-glass
> the whole of Geraldine seemed to become mislaid.

(One thinks of Penny who would not look in her mirror).

> A huge rubber ball balanced on top of the bureau, Geraldine's
> stockings straggled over a chair; every day she trod biscuit-crumbs into
> the carpet. The air smelt faintly of peppermint, from her tooth-
> powder. Otherwise this was a guest-room: ready, but someone never
> arrived (p. 431).

Geraldine has no place of her own at all. In her limbo she experiences intense and violent hatred for everyone. The prettiness of the room in which she enacts life is in ghastly contrast to the wasteland of her emotions.

Wastelands, wildernesses, endless moors and walled bomb sites, these appear throughout our lives and our literature. The need of the child is never outgrown. Elijah and Jesus withdrew for periods of retreat into desert places. Jane Eyre, running from the attempted bigamous marriage and Gothic horror of Thornfield Hall, endures a purifying ordeal on the high moors:

> To the hill, then, I turned. I reached it. It remained now only to find a
> hollow where I could lie down, and feel at least hidden, if not secure.
> But all the surface of the waste looked level. It showed no variation
> but of tint: green, where rush and moss overgrew the marshes; black,
> where the dry soil bore only death (Brontë, 1966/1847, p. 356).

Maggie Tulliver at 17 finds in the Red Deeps a place of privacy and freedom, a stone-quarry, 'so long exhausted that both mounds and hollows were now clothed with brambles and trees, and here and there by a stretch of grass which a few sheep kept close-nibbled' (Eliot, 1979/1860, p. 304).

In summer this is a place of great beauty but its importance to the embattled Maggie is invisibility from her home, and neutrality. The

Red Deeps is not owned. Presumably someone does possess title to the land but essentially it is not used or useful, except to the few nibbling sheep. Here is a land in limbo, unclaimed but not, like a desert or mountain, dangerous.

The central action of *Thursday* (Storr, 1974) takes place in a bomb site 'peaceful and deserted' where 'the sound of the city's traffic was distanced...a hum which you could ignore, could forget'. It is crossed by pathways, 'some of them marked out by the original ground plan of the houses which had stood there', one corner 'overgrown with brambles, and another...occupied by a mound, now grassed over'. The dead houses are already being resurrected in 'the year's new growth, the heartless, persistent miracle of the seeding, the leafing and flowering of the season's weeds' (pp. 63–4).

The place is perfect. The child has no responsibility for its maintenance and can do no harm. The strange, temporary life of the site provides reflection of and setting for the changing, between-worlds life of the child. Bee enters her bomb site through a gap in a hoarding. Maggie reaches the Red Deeps 'by a narrow path through a group of Scotch firs' (p. 305).

The way into the special place may be hidden and narrow or dangerous. Barney enters his dump dramatically when, wishing that 'he was at the bottom of the pit...the ground gave way'. He 'felt his head going down and his feet going up. There was a rattle of falling earth beneath him...Then he seemed to turn a complete somersault in the air, bumped into a ledge of chalk half-way down, crashed through some creepers and ivy and branches and landed on a bank of moss' (King, 1963, pp. 8–9).

Just so did Alice more slowly descend the rabbit hole into Wonderland (Carroll, 1982/1865). Alice, who 'was not a bit hurt', continued to follow the White Rabbit into adventure. Barney, who has 'decided he wasn't dead', encounters the Stoneage man Stig (whose name in Swedish means *path*). Alice will eventually wake up. But has Barney been dreaming?

In the wilderness

Sometimes the unclaimed land is the setting for ordeal. The Arthur Ransome books are particularly famous as the (awfully competent) children survive in the wilderness. Joan Robinson's *Charley* (1971), convinced through a misunderstanding that she is unwanted, camps alone in a wood, eventually stealing milk and eating dog biscuits. No Stig or White Rabbit. The wonderland becomes a place of menace and rescue by humans is desperately needed. Charley discovers not only a remarkable talent for painting but also the ability to be loved as she begins to consider the reality of other people.

Within her wilderness, physical and emotional, Charley grieves for her, as she believes, unlovedness. Tips and dumps are dramatically reflective settings for the recognition of loss. Catherine Houghton wrote 'I didn't go out into the country where "misty-eyed weepers", always seem to cry in the "solitude of a leafy glade". I went to the county tip. It suited my mood. It was dead, Mum was dead' (Houghton, 1976, p. 104).

One of the saddest experiences of my social working life was discovering with Mark that a tip was, literally, dead. He had talked with such vigour about the rich life enjoyed with his brother, foraging in the dump local to their home (before traumatic reception into care). What toys had been uncovered, what adventures dared.

Our first stop on a precious day touring the important places of his early childhood (he was still only 10), was to be the dump. But we found only a large rough field between the river and the railway. We searched, transported into a crazy world. A man approached us, diverting his tractor. Kindly he offered a range of alternatives but none was *the* tip. Slowly we faced the truth. The dump was dead, buried under tarmac, imprisoned by 20-foot high wire. Full grown, expensive cars were penned over the place where damaged Dinkies might have been treasure trove.

The purpose of our journey was to help Mark bring together the threads of his life and many moves, but this was a too cruel blow. 'Why?' he asked me as we walked sadly past the horrible enclosures, 'Why do things have to change?'

Perhaps it is always a mistake to seek again our magic lands. But, once known, our tips remain in memory and cruel remembrance of physical disappearance is often soon eased away as the true experience retains life. Although I have seen more than once the modernized Welsh mountain cottage where I spent happy months at 3 years and weeks at 12, I cannot retain any image of the present 'real' place. Alive is the old house through the eyes of the little girl.

Sometimes the unclaimed land represents not only privacy and freedom from the pressure to be anyone but oneself but also a place as unloved and unwanted as the child herself, to which new life may be brought. Rumer Godden (1989a) tells of Loveday, a little London girl who makes, against tremendous opposition, a garden in a bomb site. As every year I greet the spring in my own country garden I recall her struggle to obtain 'good garden earth'.

And who could improve on the evocation of loneliness, the children saved by the sad secret wilderness which they themselves save in *The Secret Garden*. What magic greater than to be with orphaned plain Mary 'standing *inside* the secret garden', having at last found the key. Treading gently into the garden, 'stepping as softly as if she were afraid of awakening someone', she is a sleeping beauty who will awake as she awakens this haunted, haunting place. 'Is it all a quite dead garden? I wish it wasn't' (Hodgson–Burnett, 1951/1911, pp. 69,70).

Like Paul discovering his new elements, the sea and lack of fear, Mary finds earth and something to care about. For both children the way to life is through mastery, discovered in privacy, free from intruding adults. They have escaped from limbo.

Tips, dumps and other private unclaimed places are the child's own choice as 'space in which to explore those feelings and sensations which have no words, which are undifferentiated, because they are too painful, too confused, or are memories from pre-verbal years. Children have very little time in which they are allowed just to *be,* without questions, criticism, help or expectations' (Gillespie, 1986, p. 19).

Where would you like to sit?

Space, physical and temporal, is essential for counselling children. The space and convenience of the meeting place may be of much less importance than privacy and atmosphere. Lawrence Shapiro (1984) (psychologist) recalled that 'With limitations of time and space, I had to completely reconceptualize my ideas about therapy. Since I worked in empty broom-closets and in the back of gymnasiums instead of well-equipped play-therapy rooms with two-way mirrors, I usually carried all my materials in a large box'. (p. v).

Donald W. Morrison (1977), writing on school counselling, advises that 'A request for privacy should be honoured and every attempt should be made to find a suitable place for non-interrupted consultation. To allow other activities to interrupt an individual consultation...is to communicate to the child that his problem is unimportant'. He depicts an environment where not even a broom cupboard is easily available and suggests resort to the telephone.

Yet somewhere can always be found. During my work with children in 1989–90, I carried materials in a large shopping bag. Since it was not possible to work with Mark in his foster home and there was no office within miles, I met him once a week from school and asked, 'Where shall we go today?' The answer was always the same, despite the possibility of an interesting castle and an inviting river: 'To the café.'

In view of staff and customers we considered the painful places of his life. The waitress, who soon got to know us, thought we were doing extra homework and admitted us to the quieter, residents only end of the café. Unconsciously she helped my work of trying to develop Mark's confidence by engaging him in debate over the day's drinks, including remembering what he had chosen last time.

I always asked, 'Where would you like to sit?' Children have few real choices and in relationships with professional adults, practically none. Choices can be problematic. I remember the anxiety on the first day back at school – Which class room? Would I sit next to my best friend? In the back corner by the window?

I still find it hard to enter a strange room and be invited by the owner, social or professional, to sit where I like. I want to prowl (in private), try the tempting settee (but too low?) the elegant windsor (a commanding position) and the sensible armchair near the table (for papers and coffee cup). I also want to know where my host is going to sit. Goldilocks may have carried this to extremes, but her instinct is familiar.

We do, I am convinced, have individual special places on the earth and others within those places. One of the difficulties of moving house is the loss of the possibly unconsciously loved special place. Children who move often may not have time to identify a place and soon lose those they do find. Children in hospital will be given places – beds – but do they find homes? a corner of the playroom, for example?

Bowen (1983) expresses this elegantly. Gavin (8) has come to stay with a friend of his mother. 'She vaguely glanced round her drawing-room, as though seeing it from his angle, and, therefore, herself seeing it for the first time'. She asks Gavin 'her first intimate question – "Where do you think you would like to sit?"' (p. 690).

The woman will soon humiliate the child through appalling manipulation and thoughtlessness. The question may be intimate but she is not really interested in either Gavin or his answer. His privacy will be assaulted, his feelings exposed.

As with Mark in the café the private place need not always be free of other people, for privacy is a quality. Mark and I were protected, aided by the courteous waitress. It is not only that noone took any notice of us but also we were able, for a short time at least, to feel alone in a place of our own. I think we both left something of ourselves there.

When Mark moved to another foster home we had to find a new place. At about this time, Mark also lost his dump. Only writing this chapter led me to understand the activity of our first meeting after his move. We drove off to look for the sea. Miles and miles in sweltering sun, getting lost in twisting lanes and misled by redundant sea walls. We never found the sea. I think we had really been seeking a new private place and the following week we found it, a river bank where we could *be* together. As with the café, Mark would choose to go there, learned the landmarks en route, and had much control of how we spent the time – walking, finding dead crabs, watching cargo ships, drawing, writing stories.

Confidentiality

An important aspect of privacy, more complex than it may at first seem, is confidentiality. The child should be able to feel confident that what is communicated within counselling sessions is not communicated outside. Morrison comments:

The student needs to know that the teacher is able and willing to keep confidential the statements made during personal problem-solving conferences. The teacher simply must remember that a violation of the confidential nature of an individual consultation is irresponsible and will surely destroy the potential benefit of the teacher's intervention (Morrison, 1977, pp. 119–20).

Unconsciously the counsellor may inform colleagues, or other clients in the waiting area that the session has been, for example, tough. The walk (brisk, drooping, relieved) to the door; the tone of 'Goodbye'; the facial expression as the child recedes; the collapse with coffee; the celebration of a breakthrough.

Deliberately the counsellor must share much of the experience with a designated consultant or perhaps colleague group and in many agencies, to write case notes.

Reluctantly the counsellor may have to pass on, preferably with the child's permission, information, for example, to police about alleged sexual abuse. Ford and Merriman (1990) note that 'it is usually acknowledged that there are some exceptions' to absolute confidentiality 'where some considerations have even more importance than the individual's right to privacy...where there is severe threat to the life or safety of someone who, because of his age or mental state, cannot look after himself' including 'Young children and elderly confused people' (pp. 88–9).

Shapiro suggests that

Children are used to being talked about by people who care for them; it happens all the time with their parents, and they can accept this as a part of life. They do not necessarily distrust the therapist who also talks to their parents, as long as the therapist's intentions are made clear from the beginning of the treatment (Shapiro, 1984, p. 10).

The greatest fear may be of communication between counsellor and parents, for example, 'that the therapist will report to his parents that he has been stealing again' or 'how angry she is with her father, causing him to leave the home'. Maybe 'the therapist will tell her parents about her sexual feelings towards her teacher. Every stage of childhood has its secrets, and every child must be assured that the therapist respects him or her' (p. 9). Even where, for the safety of the child, confidentiality must be broken, the child must be treated with respect. Humiliation and betrayal, in the name of rescue, are so close.

'Bella' was admitted to hospital because of stomach pains but discharged home when no medical cause was found. Investigation by 'Jan' a social worker who had met her on the ward led to disclosure that Bella had been sexually abused by her uncle. Jan had visited her at school. 'Bella could, in the right circumstances, and with a caring and familiar worker, tell her story. Once.' But the story would have to be told again, to the police. At a meeting in another place, Bella refused to talk or be videotaped.

> Her privacy, invaded first sexually by her uncle, then clinically in hospital, had now to be sacrificed to official strangers.
> Only to the social worker had she *chosen* to reveal herself and the social worker had been prevented from respecting Bella's confidence.
> Bella's secrets, inside and out, would have to be made known to many adults before her privacy could be restored. Like her hymen, it could never again be intact (Crompton, 1991, p. 31).

Confidentiality may be breached by devices intended to protect.

It may also be broken at the wish of the child, either informally (discussing sessions with friends/parents) or formally (inviting a third party to attend sessions). Presumably a counsellor would have a say in this and I have found no account of a child introducing another person within the health and social services.

However, solicitor Mike Morris (1986) wrote that a girl (16) whom 'he had represented many times, mainly for theft offences from shops, telephoned me and said her friend aged 14 had received a solicitor's letter and was very upset. Could I help? I was fascinated'. Both girls came in and 'As the three of us talked, or more precisely as the two of them talked in my presence, far more emerged about the 14-year-old girl and her current difficulties...simply because of the presence of the older girl. We had a marvellous talk.' He found that clients' friends could in other cases be drawn in 'to tremendous effect', and that confidence had 'not been breached, the friends rising to their new role as legal assistant/confidante' (p. 55).

A useful set of guidelines is provided by Munro, Manthei and Small (1989) who recognize that clients feel safe to speak freely within the counselling relationship if they can trust counsellors to keep their secrets but that a variety of circumstances may lead to breach of confidentiality.

1. The client should know where she stands in relation to confidentiality. For example, if case discussion is routine within an agency, the client should be told this.
2. where referral to another agency or consultation with another family member seems appropriate, the client's prior permission should be sought.
3. When a client specifically requests confidentiality regarding a particular disclosure, this must be respected.
4. Where confidentiality has to be broken because of the law or because of danger to the client's life, she should be informed as soon as possible.
5. Records of interviews should be minimal, noting only what is essential within the particular agency setting. Records should be locked up, shared only with authorised recipients who would also be

bound by confidentiality and destroyed when the counselling relationship is terminated.

6. An atmosphere of confidentiality is even more important than any verbal assurances of it. If, for example, during the interview note-taking is considered essential, the counsellor could offer to let the client see what is being written or even write it herself. Confidentiality then takes on a new meaning for her.

7. Confidentiality, when part of a professional code of ethics, should be upheld (pp. 9–10).

Guidance is also given in the British Association of Counselling *Code of Ethics,* Appendix 1, (1984).

The intrusive counsellor

An unintended breach of confidentiality may be intrusion into a child's life by the physical presence of and meeting with the counsellor. Shapiro refers to 'the client's right to privacy about his/her treatment, and the intrusion or disruption that the treatment causes in the life of your client'. He regards the 'issue of intrusion' as 'a more common problem in the child's school than in his home. Children are very sensitive to their status with their peers, and having a "therapist" is rarely considered something to brag about.' However much children may 'seem to enjoy therapy' and be 'deeply attached to their therapists', they may be 'embarrassed to be in therapy', not wishing the therapist to visit school or 'be seen by their friends'. He warns of the danger of a child becoming 'so self-conscious that the therapy will be undermined' (Shapiro, pp. 9–10).

I did worry about meeting Mark after school, waiting with the mothers, but he greeted me cheerfully with no sign of embarrassment. I also worried when, collecting conkers in the churchyard, I saw other boys approaching. I wondered what Mark would feel about his odd companion and prepared to fade behind a tree. Mark, however, greeted his friends naturally and the boys invited me to admire their chestnut collections.

More serious may be well-intentioned intrusion by caring adults. Carl Rogers (1961) recognized intrusion through over-earnestness:

I discovered a published account of an interview with a parent, approximately verbatim in which the caseworker was shrewd, insightful, clever, and led the interview quite quickly to the heart of the difficulty. I was happy to use it as an illustration of good interviewing technique.
Several years later...I was appalled. Now it seemed to me to be a clever, legalistic type of questioning by the interviewer which convicted this parent of her unconscious motives, and wrung from her an admission of her guilt. I now know from my experience that such an

interview would not be of any lasting help to the parent or the child. It made me realize that I was moving away from any approach which was coercive or pushing in clinical relationships, not from philosophical reasons, but because such approaches were never more than superficially effective (pp. 10–11).

In the position of client, and particularly of child client, it is very difficult if not impossible to restrain the counsellor and to avoid intrusion. The counsellor wields great power: interpreting, probing, giving choice of continuing or stopping contact may apparently offer power to the client but does it always do so? Everyone has experienced being client/patient in childhood and, for example, counsellors accredited by the British Association of Counselling have received and receive counselling themselves. Even so, perhaps counsellors are not always aware of their impact on clients or sensitive to the difficulties which a child may experience in managing such an unusual and often bewildering relationship.

Some time ago I found myself unexpectedly in the role of child client when, despite a formidable range of defences, I felt disturbed to the extent of, much later, writing about the experience (Crompton, 1991). I had not felt able to discuss the event and my feelings with the other person involved but my writing led her, with much courage, to contact me. What made her letter particularly moving was that she had herself experienced something very similar, being placed in an unexpected and uncomfortable 'client' position and learning, as I had, from the 'inside'. She had been shocked and distressed by the revelations of my reponses to our interaction.

This led me to regret that I had lacked the maturity, courtesy and common sense to approach her directly at the time: but I have learnt further that the child in me who felt so exposed at the time had been unable to make a direct response. The chronological children with whom we work are unlikely to have the repertoire of communication means available to me (writing articles, letters) or the opportunity to continue interaction with the counsellor after conclusion of official contact, so that frustrations and anxieties raised during and by the contact may never be expressed to and with the right person.

For me the initial painful experience and my endeavours to manage it have led to more than one good outcome and I have been able to learn about myself and to alter my behaviour, becoming more direct. But for the child client, the ill-effects of unrevealed and unresolved difficulties with the intrusive counsellor may emerge at other times, other places.

Every 72 seconds

The most common form of intrusion by caring adults is questioning. In the opinion of a sensitive doctor, 'the one idea of adults, when conversing with children, seemed to be to ask them question. Extremely vulgar and ill bred...It was not his way to win confidence by questioning but only by the unspoken invitation of his vast compassion' (Goudge, 1950, pp. 170, 73).

Rumer Godden (1989b) learnt about the danger and discomfort of questioning from her daughters and mother in law. In her diary for May 1953 she noted 'I have to learn that, when the girls come in, I must not ask questions. I remember...Florence and her questions as soon as I came in at the door. For some reason it was like sticking pins into me and all the experiences melted away' (p. 160). All those pricking questions to which the bewildered answer can be only 'I don't know'.

Novelist Jane Gardam (1983) describes spirited rejection of intrusive questioning by Phoebe (6 – also known as Beams). Child psychologist Mrs Winterschladen was 'wild and fat and her dress was lacking a button. She held a cup of tea in her hand and had an excitable moving eye' (p. 82).

Her room was 'the untidiest room I have ever seen in my life...It wasn't busy, or warm or comforting...It was a frantic place in which was no peace. She sat down and tried to look motherly and comfortable and you've never seen such a tight dress'. Since Beams thinks that Mrs Winterschladen is an optician, the consultation heads rapidly into confusion. 'I made conversation as best I could, suggesting that perhaps we might tidy up a bit before she started on my eyes. "Eyes?", she said..."Eyes? No darling, first we're going to play some games"' (p. 83).

The bewildered Beams is assaulted with dance, song and eventually art:

> Then she tried to make me draw a lot of shapes (which I couldn't) and do a lot of sums (which I couldn't) and then she showed me a lot of pictures where I had to point out things I couldn't see and she made a great fuss about it all being great fun really and then wrote very earnestly in the book for hours and hours (pp. 83 – p. 4).

All this leads to the great question which, we must suppose, the psychologist regards as penetrating to the heart of the child's alleged problem: '"Tell me, Phoebe darling, does Mummy love Daddy do you think?" I remember so well the sort of hopeful look in her eyes that I can't believe it was six whole years ago. "Is Mummy *happy* with Daddy do you think?"' (p. 84).

Beams is helped at last by a doctor who asks no questions and meets the real girl.

Hargie, et al. (1981) comment on 'the appeal of questions in the media' and summarize two pieces of research in the classroom. In one 'on average, the teacher asked a question once every 72 seconds'. In the other, where the children were aged five – seven, '36% of the teachers remarks were questions' (p. 66).

Statistics without context are meaningless but these do themselves raise questions. What questions were those teachers asking every 72 seconds? How much time did that give for answers? What was made of the answers?

On Hugo's first day at school (in Maria Gripe's story, 1974) the teacher explains that 'in school children have to sit still and be quiet. The teacher does the talking, and the children just answer when the teacher asks them a question. Hugo listens attentively to this, but looks frankly astonished. "Now that's odd", he says. "What's so odd about it?" the teacher asks.'

Note that she can't resist asking a question, and one which might be received as a put-down. But Hugo takes it seriously. 'There's no sense in our answering, when we don't know anything. We're the ones who ought to ask the questions' (p. 59).

How much opportunity have children involved in some form of counselling to ask the questions? In the view of Josie, who had been in care, social workers: 'don't gain your trust and respect because they are too inquisitive. They shouldn't ask questions – they should wait until you're ready to tell them' (Crompton, 1982, p. 6).

Josie wrote of her experience especially for my book but not at my direct request. The person who could command enough trust and respect in a number of young people for them to write about their feelings was herself 16 and still in care. Under her chosen pseudonym *Dorna* she wrote that social workers

> make you feel a total idiot. I mean they'll say to you 'well how is such and such?' You know they already know so you say 'What you asking me for, you already know'. They usually reply 'But I want to hear off you'. Now what is the sense of that? The only thing they want is to be able to say to their bosses 'Fred told me all about the incident in his own words'. All of a sudden they think they've got you where they want you. People only tell them what they don't mind anyone else knowing. The kids only tell them as much as they want them to know, nothing else (pp. 9–10).

Not all children and young people are as able as Dorna to respond so briskly to apparently intrusive questioning. She and her colleagues had been alienated and hurt by the insensitivity of those who should have been most sensitive.

Lifting the burden

The last aspect of privacy to be discussed in this chapter is *reverse intrusion*. Adults often withhold information from children, usually on the grounds that the children would be upset. I refer again to Bowen's story of Roger whose agony, waiting for news that his mother has died, was increased a millionfold by the failure of well disposed adults to acknowledge the truth with him (Bowen, 1983).

Concluding their account of work with four children following the murder of their mother by their father, Isaacs and Hickman (1987) comment, 'It might be questioned whether it would not be better to let the children forget their terrifying experiences, to spare them further suffering'. However follow-up studies indicate 'that permitting anxieties to be buried results in the anxieties persisting and contributing to chronic personality changes' (p. 35).

Withholding predictably painful information and avoiding appalling subjects may lead to far more damaging intrusion when, inevitably, the truth is discovered. Who is really being protected?

Georgina (8) was searching through her adoptive mother's underclothes drawer when she 'found a secret that did not belong to her adoptive mother'. This was indeed 'her own secret, the answer to herself, and why her mother never came to take her away. She found a pile of yellowing newspaper cuttings, with photographs and graphic descriptions'. Georgina's mother had been 'the last woman to be hanged in Britain...when Georgina was three and a half'. The little girl 'recognized her dimly, a hazy picture, carefully cherished and embellished, for all those years. But it was her. This Ruth Ellis was her Ruth Ellis, her lost, and longed-for mother' (Toynbee, 1985, pp. 99–100).

The line between protection, secrecy and lying may be very faint. Adults who maintain their own comfort, privacy may take an unwarranted risk on the part of the children. Georgina 'told no one for years that she had found out about it. She was too afraid of the trouble she would get into for having looked into that underclothes drawer to dare reveal her knowledge. The sexual taboo of looking into the drawer combined with the knowledge of her mother's crime, and the world's crime against her mother' (p. 101).

The child's intrusion into an adult's privacy prevented the child gaining that help needed because of that adult's mistaken fear of invading the child's privacy. In such mazes tragedy flourishes.

Joan Wheeler (1990) writes of discovering her birth family when at 18 she received a life-changing telephone call: 'Even though you don't know me...it is important that you listen to every word I say. Don't scream, don't ask questions, just listen. Everything will make sense in time...I am your sister' (p. 22).

This revelation intruded into the girl's life: 'I was in shock' and led to much unhappiness within the adoptive home. Secrets held for 18 years turned into time bombs. People who had withheld information to protect privacy were deeply wounded. Fortunately the eventual outcome was happy and Joan Wheeler concludes:

> The secrecy, deceit, and pain could have been avoided by the use of a more open system – a system which is slowly gaining acceptance today

by promoting honesty, integrity and healing through ongoing communication and education. No one said it better than my adoptive father when he learned I had been found by my birthfamily. 'A tremendous burden is lifted. I'm glad the secret is out' (p. 27).

For Penny, too, healthy life could begin only when the secret was out. But fear of adults and their protection of their own privacy, led to disbelief and further intrusion when at 7 she first tried to reveal her stepfather's sexual assault.

'I told the doctor. Mum said that I was telling lies because I was jealous of Mandy, my baby sister...the doctor agreed with Mum and talked about sending me to child guidance. I never tried to tell anyone again. I was too scared and thought no one would believe me.' Much later her mother would reveal that 'she'd suspected Jim was having sex with me but had pretended not to know' (Golding, 1990, p. 18).

Here is a dilemma: how to distinguish between intrusion and avoidance; how to respect privacy and provide protection. There are no simple answers but two base-guidelines: know thyself and listen to the children.

> The quiet victories come so quiet. Essential, but overlooked (Asimov, 1990, p. 415).

Summary

There are may ways of **intruding on privacy** – physical, emotional and spacial. **To be left alone** is as important as to be in receipt of attention. The (ongoing) **discovery of oneself** has to be achieved in private. The maintenance of privacy may be an unhealthy **secrecy**, as when children hide anxieties and problems, abilities and emotions. Children choose **personal private places** – often **tips, dumps and wildernesses**. Sometimes these reflect a **limbo** state of being, sometimes they represent a **lost time** of greater happiness. Sometimes child and wilderness together achieve **new life**. Everyone needs to discover the **right place**.

Privacy is an important aspect of **confidentiality** and of **interpretation** and **assessment** and may be intruded on by **questioning**. **Reverse intrusion** is the failure of respect represented by witholding information. To distinguish between **intrusion** and **avoidance, respect for privacy** and **provision of protection** can be achieved only if counsellors **know themselves** and **listen to the children.**

Link

At the end of Chapter 1 I asked 'How can any communication take place without silence?' It is impossible really to listen if one's head and environment are full of noise and the most important communication often occurs within the spaces between words. Textbooks are notably silent on this essential topic. Following and developing the theme of **privacy**, Chapter 5 offers 'A Few Feet of Silence'.

References and Further Reading

Andersen, H. (n/d). *Fairy Tales*. Ward Lock, London.

Asimov, I. (1990). *Nemesis*. Bantam, London.

Benton Grange School. (1979). What I feel I am due. In Harris and Hyland, pp. 16–18.

Bowen, E. (Wilson, A. (ed.)) (1983), In *The Collected Stories of Elizabeth Bowen*. Penguin, Harmondsworth, The return, pp. 28–34; The visitor, 124–35; The jungle, pp. 231–41; The little girls' room, pp. 425–34; Ivy gripped the steps, pp. 686–711.

British Association of Counselling (1984). *Code of Ethics and Practice for Counsellors*. BAC, Rugby. See also Dryden, et al., pp. 425–36.

Brontë, C. (1966/1847). *Jane Eyre*. Penguin, Harmondsworth.

Burton, H. (1968). *In Spite of All Terror*. Oxford University Press, London.

Carroll, L. (1982/1865). *Alice's Adventures in Wonderland*. Chancellor Press, London.

Carter, A. (1981). *The Magic Toyshop*. Virago, London.

Comyns, B. (1989). *The House of Dolls*. Methuen, London.

Crompton, M. (1982). *Adolescents and Social Workers*. Gower/Community Care, Aldershot.

Crompton, M. (1991). Invasion by Russian dolls: on privacy and intrusion. *Adoption and Fostering*, 15, (1), 31–3.

Dunbar, M. (1987). *Catherine: a Tragic Life*. Penguin, Harmondsworth.

Eliot, G. (1979/1860). *The Mill on the Floss*. Penguin, Harmondsworth.

Ford, J. K. and Merriman, P. (1990). *The Gentle Art of Listening: Counselling Skills for Volunteers*. Bedford Square Press, London.

Gardam, J. (1983). *The Summer After the Funeral*. Penguin, Harmondsworth.

Gillespie, A. (1986). 'Art therapy' at the Familymakers Project. *Adoption and Fostering*, 10, (1), 19–23.

Godden, R. (1989a). *An Episode of Sparrows*. Penguin, Harmondsworth.

Godden, R. (1989b). *A House with Four Rooms: Autobiography Vol. 2*. Macmillan, London.

Golding, V. (1990). Speaking out leads to survival. *Social Work Today*, 21, (38), 18–19.

Goudge, E. (1936). *A City of Bells*. Duckworth, London.

Goudge, E. (1950). *Gentian Hill*. Hodder and Stoughton, Dunton Green.

Gripe, M. (Austin, P. B. (trans.)) (1974). *Hugo and Josephine*. Pan, London.

Hargie, D., Saunders, C. and Dickson D. (1981). *Social Skills in Interpersonal Communication*. Croom Helm, London.

Harris, D. and Hyland, J. (eds) (1979). *Rights in Residence: a Review of the Residential Care Association*. RCA Publications, London.

Harwood, R. and King, F. (eds) (1978). *New Stories '3: an Arts Council Anthology*. Hutchinson, London.

Hawes, B. (1979). Rights in retrospect. In Harris and Hyland (eds) pp. 63–64

Hodgson-Burnett, F. (1951/1911). *The Secret Garden*. Penguin, Harmondsworth.

Holgate, E. (ed.) (1972). *Communicating with Children*. Longman, London.

Houghton, C. J. (1976). On the day when mother died. In Mirror Group Newspapers, pp. 104–106.

Hunter, M. (1987). Julia: a 'frozen' child. *Adoption and Fostering*, 11, (3), 26–30.

Isaacs, S. and Hickman, S. (1987). Communicating with children after a murder. *Adoption and Fostering*, 11, (4), pp. 132–5.

King, C. (1963). *Stig of the Dump*. Penguin, Harmondsworth.

Macaulay, R. (1965). *Told by an Idiot*. Collins, London.

Macaulay, R. (1983). *The World My Wilderness*. Virago, London.

McMaster, J. (ed) (1982). *Methods in Social and Educational Caring*. Gower, Aldershot.

Mirror Group Newspapers (1976). *Children as Writers, 3*. Heinemann, London.

Morris, M. (1986). Communicating with adolescents. *Adoption and Fostering*, 10, (4), 54–5, 71.

Morrison, D. W. (1977). *Personal Problem Solving in the Classroom: the Reality Technique*. Wiley, New York.

Munro, A., Manthei, B. and Small, J. (1989). *Counselling: the Skills of Problem-solving*. Routledge, London.

O'Connor, D. (1982). Assessment in practice. In McMaster, pp. 28–42.

Porter, G. S. (1905). *Freckles*. Murray, London.

Porter, G. S. (1959/12). *A Girl of the Limberlost*, Brockhampton Press, Leicester.

Prestage, R. O. (1972). Life for Kim. In Holgate (ed.), pp. 98–107.

Robinson, J. G. (1971). *Charley*. Collins, London.

Rogers, C. R. (1961). *On Becoming a Person: a Therapist's View of Psychotherapy*. Constable, London.

Shapiro, L. (1984). *The New Short-term Therapies for Children: a Guide for the Helping Professions and Parents*. Prentice-Hall, New Jersey.

Storr, C. (1974). *Thursday*. Penguin, Harmondsworth.

Swift, G. (1978). Learning to swim. In Harwood and King (eds), pp. 323–41.

Taylor, E. (1967). *Mossy Trotter*. Chatto and Windus, London.

Tennyson, A. (1832). *The Lady of Shalott*.

Toynbee, P. (1985). *Lost Children: the Story of Adopted Children Searching for their Mothers*. Hutchinson, London.

West, J. (1990). Children in 'limbo'. *Adoption and Fostering*, 14, (2), 11–14.

Wheeler, J., born Sippel, D. (1990). The secret is out. *Adoption and Fostering*, 14, (3), 22–7.

5 A few feet of silence

Living silence

> Silence is an important word in my vocabulary. Working with music, I
> have used it more than men in other professions. I know how one can
> speculate with silence, measure it, set it apart. But then, sitting on that
> rock, I was living silence; a silence that came from so far off,
> compounded of so many silences, that a word dropped into it would
> have taken on the clangour of creation. Had I said anything, had I
> talked to myself, as I often do, I should have frightened myself
> (Carpentier. 1968, p. 99).

Silence: gift or deprivation, desirable or dreaded. As Quaker and
writer, I recognize the silence celebrated, lived by Alejo Carpentier's
composer. I need long periods on my own, no one speaking to me or
expecting me to speak, no one interfering with the sounds in my head
which may become words on a page.

I need too the silence shared with other people, often more rich and
communicating than conversation. On 17 January 1991, the first day of
the Gulf War, only a silent Meeting brought relief from the nightmare:
words heightened anxiety, silence healed. All day I heard screaming in
my head until, in a safely shared silence, I could listen to and still them.

It is often the experience of Quakers that several people sitting in
silence together find themselves thinking about the same matter (and
not the obvious 'news' of the day). A quality of communication is
achieved through and within living silence.

Internal silence is best achieved within external silence but external
silence by no means guarantees internal peace. One internally silent
Quaker Meeting was held in the foyer outside a university chapel. An
ecumenical service had taken the place of our regular, advertised
Meeting. We could choose to join in fully, to sit in silence, or to hold
our Meeting elsewhere. We chose the last when we saw that the words
of the hymns were not in accordance with our beliefs. We felt that our
'exiled' silence was honesty because we could neither collude (join in)
or consent (sit in silence).

Such a decision might be very difficult for a child with an an adult
who did not feel able to use silence creatively or positively. We, as
adults who were making a free choice with the support of one another,
could sit in a public place, in silence, and be undisturbed by the noises
around us – hymn singing from the chapel, people passing, doors

slamming. A child making some equivalent choice might have been called delinquent, withdrawing, truculent, withholding.

Providing and protecting an environment of silence may be one of the greatest contributions of a counsellor. Children have so very little opportunity for silence, particularly shared with an adult.

After a terribly stressful experience for 'Mark' (10) during which, as a social worker, I had been present, we went for lunch to a quiet café. On the way we talked a little and Mark ordered his meal cheerily, giving no sign by word or action that he had just received a devastating blow.

Once seated, we became silent; no chat, no stories and certainly no questioning about feelings. Though the mask might not be given up altogether he could for a time relax, ponder, rest before re-entering everyday life.

Psychologist 'Joel' recognized 'the need for the adult to sit comfortably, making no demands, centred; then the children don't feel they have to *do* anything. If children feel any kind of pressure they don't feel free to offer what they can', a freedom which can be helped by silence.

The importance of the silence may be to enable clear thought and attention to inner voices (parents, grandparents, teachers, friends or chosen mentors whose philosophy and language we admire), or to recognize and pull together our scattered selves. Such peacefulness may be difficult to achieve, with results both enlightening and daunting.

Letting go

Bowen (1983) describes a young woman, Lou, lying alongside a severely physically handicapped girl, Josephine, in a summer garden:

> At first she was so nervous, she thought the lawn vibrated under her spine. Then slowly she relaxed. There is a moment when silence, no longer resisted, rushes into the mind. She let go, inch by inch, of life, that since she was a child she had been clutching so desperately – her obsessions about this and that...How anxiously she had run from place to place, wanting to keep everything inside her own power.

She realizes that

> Josephine stores herself up, and so what she wants happens, because she knows what she wants. I only think I want things;...I feel life myself now. No wonder I've been tired, only half getting what I don't really want. Now I want nothing; I just want a white circle (p. 519).

Josephine has told Lou that she need not talk to her; her silent immobility itself provides the environment for Lou to risk stillness and the discomfort of insight. The girl, still chronologically a child, aids the woman, still clutching so desperately at life since childhood and so, emotionally, still in a child state.

Joel helped another clutching, tense child. 'Amy' (16) suffered from alopaecia, panic attacks, sickness and headaches. She was bright and expected to pass examination but often refused to go to school. A few years ago she had endured both bereavement and sexual assault.

On one occasion she arrived for a session and asked to be excused because she had a headache. Joel encouraged her to try at least to become free of that pain. At Joel's direction, Amy lay on the floor and relaxed, from her toes. She reported feeling very dizzy, her head spinning and very agitated. Joel told her to slow down, asking what she would need to do so. 'A brake pad.' 'So bring one in.' 'It's all black.' This changed to white when the 'brake pad' slowed the spinning and then went through a range of colours. Amy felt that she was floating, thinner, had long luxuriant hair and was dressed in white. She felt good.

But then she felt dark and cold: Joel said, 'Bring in the sun.' For half an hour this pattern continued, good images becoming disastrous and Amy bringing in what was needed to repair and restore, for example, different colours.

Eventually her hands raised spontaneously to the very place where her hair was being lost. Like Lou clutching at life, perhaps, Joel suggested that Amy had been pulling at and out her hair. Whatever the reason for and meaning of that action, Amy was helped and restored by her counsellor's recognition of her need for peacefulness, lack of pressure, inner silence. During this encounter words were used and exchanged but in service of the necessary quality of silence. Joel did not, for example, encourage or pressurize Amy to interpret her lifting hands.

'Rob', a reclusive boy, was seen by many people as depressed even mad. During sessions in a hospital child and family unit, psychiatric nurse 'Kay' gave him permission to be silent. Knowing that he was good at art she would say, 'You can draw if you like: would you like to be quiet?' and gave a length of time for the shared silence. Rob would become very calm. Kay too enjoyed the quiet, becoming absorbed and demonstrating that she was valuing him and what he chose to do.

In due course he began to initiate conversation, eye contact and smiles, whereas Kay's first endeavours to engage him verbally had been resisted.

Till the cows come home

Child psychiatrist Geoffrey sat for 45 silent minutes with one boy but for Robina Prestage (1972) the silence lasted for 15 hours. Kim (9) 'silently assented' to see the social worker at the child guidance clinic after school:

> Thus for fourteen long weeks he arrived promptly, acknowledged my greeting with a non-committal nod and proceeded to climb the two pear trees with the ease and agility of a monkey – a mute monkey! Not one word did he address to me during these 14 tree sessions although I came to realize that he was communicating with me in other ways...he would...answer politely any question I might put to him, but I soon realized that this was valueless and confined myself to comments when I felt them applicable...I had nothing to go on except my intuition of this silent child.

Unlike Kay, Robina Prestage did not enjoy these involuntarily shared silences and confessed to feeling 'depressed, bored and angry'. She was rewarded however when 'At the end of the fifteenth session he uttered his first voluntary remark. "See you next week"' (pp. 100–101).

It may sometimes be very difficult to recognize tiny positive elements in or sequel to a child's silence. Elaine Dorfman (1951) considers that 'If the therapist is truly convinced that the hour belongs to the child, he will not feel the necessity of urging the child to play or to talk' (p. 244). Perhaps the child will show no response at all within the sessions, not even 'See you next week'.

Dorfman finds that work must often 'be adjudged successful, on the bass of reports of altered behaviour' from elsewhere. Of several examples, one is a boy (13) who was 'referred for his explosive outbursts of aggression, and for his long-standing "torturing"...of a girl in his class'. Verbal contact with the therapist was very slight and he spends most of his hour 'seated at the window, his back to the therapist, counting the numbers of the various brands of automobiles which pass' (pp. 244, 245).

Eventually 'he throws his tally-sheet on the therapist's table and stalks out'. After 10 sessions, 'the therapist tells him that she saves the hour for him, but that he need not come any more if he does not wish to. His reply is, "Whaddya mean, not come any more? I'll come till the cows come home!"' He is doing well at school: 'His teacher has "become fond of him because he is so helpful and cooperative" saying "Why, I don't know what I'd do without him!"' (p. 245).

The way he was

The environment of accepting silence enabled these children to work, silently and internally and, without discussing whatever problems were perceived by themselves and/or the concerned adults, to change. Such an environment may also attract direct verbal release. Goudge (1950) described the comforting room and presence of the doctor to whom 'Patients and pupils, and many who came to consult...about problems other than physical or intellectual...poured their troubles into the comforting depth of his comprehending silence' while he 'learned more from the shadows round the eyes and the play of expression about the mouth than he did from the flow of confused words, tumbling about his ears' (p. 71).

One of the most interesting examples of a child relishing and responding to another person whose communication is entirely without words is Barney who, when staying with his elderly grand-parents, meets in a dump a Stone Age man whom he calls 'Stig'. Stig is a magic combination of imaginary friend and real person (although many imaginary friends are more real than flesh and blood humans) (King, C., 1963).

Stig speaks no English, verbalizing incomprehensively 'in his strange grunting language' (p. 13) but his influence is immense. With and through him, Barney develops confidence and skills in ways which no deliberate, verbally communicating adult could have achieved. Barney chooses Stig as a friend: communication is fun and non-threatening and Barney can feel both control and achievement. I await the Stig School of Counselling.

Writing this chapter reminds me constantly of the over-emphasis on exchange of words, at least in Western culture – the anxious desire to have feelings and experiences owned by being described. With Mark I had to learn and respect that 'I don't know' implied both that he did not know and that the topic should be closed. All too often I tried to collect in words responses which were perfectly clearly expressed in other ways. The need for words is often the demand of an adult to square things up and off, to control.

Virginia Axline (1971) recorded the confession by Dibs' mother that she constantly tormented him with demands to 'pass this test and that test – always, always he had to prove that he had capacity. *He had no peace*'. Do adults regard 'peace' as an essential of childhood? (p. 147) (my italics).

Dibs had peace in two places. As for Kim with Robina Prestage, we may suppose that he found peace with his counsellor. But there was one other, his grandmother. 'They had a good relationship with each other. He relaxed with her. He did not talk much to her. But she accepted him the way he was and she always believed in him' (p. 147).

We don't talk much about it

For Dibs and his grandmother not talking much betokened peace. For many children the not-talking derives from fear, not knowing what to say. In his endpiece to a children's book about death Hugh Jolly (1982) writes 'Because we are all frightened by death, we don't talk much about it.' But he warns against such harmful breaches of silence as 'Grandpa has become a star' (p. 25).

The inability of adults to face painful facts and find clear honest words, maintaining self-protecting silence may force children into another kind of silence for if the subject is too terrible, or too (apparently) negligible for the (apparently) strong, all-knowing adult to confront, why should the child expect attention? I have written before about the cowardice and cruelty of withholding truth (although not in those terms) (Crompton. 1990).

A particularly moving insight may be found in *The Visitor* (Bowen, 1983). Roger (9) is staying with kind neighbours while his loved mother is dying. He knows this but no one will acknowledge the fact, let alone enable him to reveal his feelings. Denial forces him into fantasy and terror.

During breakfast his unspoken thoughts run constantly on death. There is 'a monstrous tea-cosy' printed with parrots 'so brilliant one could almost hear them screech. Could a world hold death that held that cosy?' The Miss Emerys are very kind, solicitous, anxious:

> were they perhaps wondering if he *knew*, how much he knew, and whether they ought to tell him?...Roger could hear them saying, 'Little motherless boy, poor little motherless boy!' and they would snatch him and gather him in, and each successively would press his head deep into her bosom, so deep that perhaps it would never come out again (pp. 127–8).

Roger's response is terror and flight: 'he must escape, he must escape, he must escape...Yesterday had been one long intrigue for solitude...telling a fib and slipping away from his father' (p. 128).

The inappropriate silence of the adults leads him to imagine ways of forstalling the news which he dreads, until he is forced to recognize that he is afraid. 'He was a little boy, he was afraid of the pain of death..."I *must* know, I can't let them tell me. Oh, help me, let them not have to come and tell me! It would be as though they saw me see her being killed. Let it not have to be!"' (p. 133).

But Roger's father comes to him in the garden. Terror increases and covering his ears he screams 'I *know*, I *know*!...Go away, I can't bear it. I know. I tell you'. He screams on, resisting his father's efforts to calm him until, 'When his own voice dropped he heard how silent it was. So silent that he thought his father was dead too...' (p. 134).

Here is the silence of exhaustion, of non-communication, a kind of death, of betrayal. The story ends with a terrible withdrawal as the defeated, bewildered father leaves and the boy retreats into a fantasy of heaven (pp. 134–5).

This story offers as could no textbook a brilliant image of silence misused. One more reference illustrates how adults talking for the sake of it may lead children to long for their silence. Roger fears his father reaching out to 'grab him with "Come on, old man, let's talk. Let's talk for a bit". And they had nothing to say, nothing. And at any moment this man who had no decency might begin talking about *her*' (p. 128).

Fading around the edges

The adult's desire to be seen to be communicating and to elicit response, by failing to allow the child peace at the right time, may lead to long-lasting withdrawal.

In a story by Janice Casey (1978) Jane is being left at boarding school by her mother and aunt. 'Obediently she kissed her mother on the cheek and felt her clutch. "Good-bye", she said. But she had already said good-bye in bed the night before.' She has used up that piece of emotion and needs now 'to go down the path and leave them. She did not want to go on saying good-bye until she felt regret…"Can I go now? she said"'. Later her teacher is amazed at her apparent lack of emotion; her feelings have been dammed up, silenced (p. 37).

I am reminded of Eileen Holgate's comment: 'Adults somehow have a capacity to silence children' (Holgate, 1972, back cover). The children may continue to use words to us but only to cover muteness. The withdrawal and silence of Dibs is described in detail by Axline, the expression of his feelings of hostility and revenge towards father, mother and sister.

Ninny, the invisible child of Tove Jansson's story (1973) is mute too. The 'social worker' Moomin, Too-ticky explains why to the Moomin foster family:

> You all know, don't you, that if people are frightened very often, they sometimes become invisible. Well. This Ninny was frightened the wrong way by a lady who had taken care of her without really liking her. I've met this lady, and she was horrid. Not the angry sort, you know, which would have been understandable. No she was the icily ironical kind…She was ironic all day long every day, and finally the kid started to turn pale and fade around the edges, and less and less was seen of her. Last Friday one couldn't catch sight of her at all. The lady gave her away to me and said she really couldn't take care of relatives she couldn't even see'…'Does she talk?'…
> 'No. But the lady has hung a small silver bell around her neck so that one can hear where she is' (pp. 105–107).

Many children lack even a small silver bell; and who can understand that chime, even when heard? The bell had been attached to mute invisible Ninny by the ironic abusing lady for her own convenience, not to aid the Moomin child's communication. Silence was to be broken only involuntarily as a warning of her unwanted presence.

Ninny's withdrawal was stimulated by deliberate cruelty, the wish of her care-taker to destroy the child's sense of self. Such assault, such response, must be familiar to all who counsel children and young people.

Emotional assault, often unintended but arguably more common than physical cruelty, forces uncounted numbers of Ninnys to fade, to withdraw their true selves. The silent self hides behind ever beaming competence or tries and fails endlessly to gain approval.

Jocelyn Chaplin (1988a) explores how children cover over, 'forget' their failed attempts to achieve true selfhood. Her composite adult client 'Louise' discovered that 'her present feelings of rage at never being taken seriously were connected to a mother who always laughed at her'. As with Ninny, the ironic lady had stimulated withdrawal. Chaplin writes of women who may have decided to 'give up trying, or complaining, at an early age' and later that 'Things that happened to us as children can still go on affecting us, especially if we have deliberately forgotten them, because they hurt too much' (pp. 60,61,64).

Here is silence become terrible, the destroyer of truth, the environment of deformity. Most terrifying are unseen unknown enemies, the thief in the night, the knife in the dark. In silence, perhaps alone at night, fantasies may become strangling fears. Small anxieties about health, unshared, may assume the proportions of unappealable death sentences.

'Carl' approached a student counselling service after a chest x-ray had proved, terrifyingly, positive. He had no one with whom to share his fears, including the suspicion that the assault of illness might prove that he was a bad person. He could tell neither parent because throughout his childhood only good, happy things might be shared with his mother. Only reports of success were acceptable: difficulties at school, broken friendships, health worries had to be born in silence. In addition, the mother blocked communication between Carl and his father.

Student counsellor 'Mary's' warm acceptance enabled Carl to face the mounting terror within his isolated silence and to at least attempt to break the long silence with both parents. Perhaps, I thought when I was told about Carl, the release from silent terror would in itself be a powerful aid to healing the physical illness, both body and spirit strengthened.

On the very day that I met Mary I read Chaplin's (1988a) account of Julia who, at the beginning of counselling 'insisted...that her child-hood had been happy all the time'. But in the third session she began to cry. 'She told me that she was always expected to be cheerful and to think how lucky she was. But actually she had been miserable sometimes. Her parents had often missed her school shows and that had hurt a lot. Once she had run away and they hadn't even noticed' (pp. 64–5).

This recalls a Woody Allen story: he is kidnapped; his parents leap into action – they rent out his room. Like Ninny, Julia is invisible; her parents neither notice the absence of her physical presence nor recognize the silence of the real girl.

Because, I suggest, most of us are more or less hiding and silencing our own cries it is often difficult to recognize, let alone to reach behind the masks and gags of other people. Everyone has some disability or may at any time be suffering from some lowering of spirits or assault on health. My own demon is migraine and at times I fear suddenly to be struck effectively blind with associated impairment of speech and thinking. A doctor's letter in a magazine shocked me when, asking for sufferers to volunteer for a research project, reference was made to non-sufferers as 'normal'. When I suffer from a migraine I am disabled but not less normal than usual, not ab-normal. I do not, thanks to a sympathetic husband, suffer silently (migraine or any other physical, emotional, spiritual or social distress). But many people do endure pain and anxiety alone, screaming inwardly with smiling faces.

The haunted tree

Bowen (1983) describes the effects of shock on Myra, introduced, although 19 and married, as a 'mannerless, sexless child', a 'cold little shadow across a hearth'. Here is a woman *manquée*; something has arrested her development (p. 463).

One night Lancelot, a house guest, discovers Myra in the library. He hears through the keyhole only a silence in which he receives such horrifying images that he thinks he is going mad; no knight in shining armour he. Another guest, Mrs Bettersley, bravely enters the library but, surviving for a minute the total 'silence and stillness', she is beaten back by the same images, projected from the immobile girl (p. 466).

Without benefit of any counselling handbook, Mrs Bettersley wins through the ghostly silence of Myra's locked memory. A sad sleeping beauty whose evil fairy gave her not peaceful slumber but nightmared sleepwalking, Myra speaks at last, appropriately in bed as though she were sleeping, but with her body rigid: gripping with both hands Mrs Bettersley's arm' (p. 468).

At boarding school when she was 12, a friend who considered that she had been betrayed by Myra, hanged herself in the apple tree, favourite haunt of the girls. That night, Myra had gone into the garden and seen Doria hanging but told no one. While she was very ill, the tree was cut down and adults denied that it had ever existed. No wonder that Myra is haunted and suffers recurrent nightmares; although many people know, 'no one will speak of it' (p. 470).

So many silences: Myra's silence towards her erstwhile friend Doria (except to laugh at her); her failure to seek help for the girl; the lie of the nurse – a very potent kind of silence; the inability of anyone to speak of the nightmares experienced by and with Myra. All conspiring to increase the nightmare itself, the guilt and secret widening, taking ever deeper hold and threatening to destroy not only Myra herself but also those near her. The 12 year old has become frozen as the sexless child and shadow, physically, emotionally and spiritually.

The courageous counsellor who frees the girl to become a woman, first by breaking through that silence as surely as ever a prince cut down a thorn hedge, is not unscathed. But on that, other than to say that 'The victory aged her', Bowen is silent (p. 470).

Silence may be maintained collusively by adults who either invest in the unawakening of the child (chronological or child-in-adult) or fear to face the truth behind the hedge; thorn hedges look very pretty when covered in blossom.

In this Bowen story, I find it interesting that the usual fairy tale order is reversed. The imprisoned princess is saved by neither marriage nor the 'knight', Lancelot, but by the 'mother' whose methods include total care, taking Myra away on her own and whose access to the bedroom is completely non-sexual. To achieve this, Mrs Bettersley has to overcome her own fears, of the haunting itself and of failing. Although feeling cruel as she does so, she overcomes Myra's resistance to talking, her wish to maintain the silence (p. 467).

Difficult to bear

Mrs Bettersley's fear of this silence is well founded but for many counsellors the silence of a child may seem threatening because of the need to be seen (heard) to be achieving, doing something. How often we fail to contact a friend after bereavement because 'I didn't know what to say', a cowardly silence preventing a simple, loving message. How often in this noise-filled society do we fear that lack of verbal response equals failure?

Dorfman is brisk: 'A therapist who feels rejected when the child fails to pour out his troubles will only add to the child's anxiety by his display of his own. If the therapist cannot feel comfortable, it might be better for him to avoid offering therapy to children over 10 or 11 years of age' (p. 247). I suggest that such a therapist is either in the wrong job altogether or deserves careful and loving counselling and support from colleagues.

Referring to 'The American cultural emphasis on self-expression, on speaking one's mind, having one's say', which has relevance for practitioners in European-based cultures too, Alfred Kadushin (1972) writes of the difficulties of silence which might 'seem an unacceptable form of behavior'. Of his several comments, one echoes Dorfman:

> the social worker...feels a professional anxiety at the thought that
> continued silence signals a failing interview. It is no surprise, then,

that inexperienced interviewers tend to feel uncomfortable with silences and tend to terminate them prematurely. It takes some measure of confidence and security for the interviewer to permit a productive silence to continue. It also requires that the interviewer accept the fact that a silence is not necessarily an attack against him (p. 193).

Silence on the part of either child or counsellor can be used as, and/ or an indication of, anger, hostility, punishment, boredom, confusion, control, sulking. Kadushin noted only that silence is *not necessarily* an attack and there is no reason why a child should not reject a counsellor or anyone else using any means, including silence. In any such situation it is for the counsellor to be alert and sensitive, receiving and using the possibly hurtful messages. Trying to force an angry or sulking child to speak can have no good effect.

Kadushin also notes that 'In general social interaction, we feel compelled to talk even if we have nothing to say' (p. 193).

Talking for the sake of it not only wastes the opportunity for productive silence but may also produce false messages, even lying. A mother recalls her family's involvement with 'the family guidance place...The next time they asked Michael about his tantrums, and why he didn't want to go to school. But we saw that he began inventing things just to cover the silence...In fact we all began inventing to fill in the gaps' (Nicolson, 1989, p. 19).

Telephone counsellors need particular skills in using silence. The telephone

> is a great encourager of lies. You may hold the receiver in one hand and a book or pen in the other while assuring your interlocutor that she has your full attention. You may yawn or grimace to yourself while promising that you are enormously looking forward to meeting her soon. You may say you are in London when you are really in Leeds.

The silent part of message giving, non-verbal cues, cannot be transmitted or received and total silence may occur involuntarily due to mechanical error, or voluntarily because the other person has gone. 'All too often that desperate plea "Are you still there?" is met with the silence which shows that indeed you have gone' (Crompton, 1980, p. 89).

I wrote that in 1980 before ChildLine was established and telephone counsellors for children were trained 'how to speak into silence and to try to engage the child in conversation' (Eaton, 1990, p. 21). Speaking into the invisible silence may be unnerving, trying to hold children who may be distressed and afraid – afraid of the situations they want to report, of being caught with the telephone, of the telephone itself, of you and what you may say or, worse, do. And yet, may not a child be glad of an accepting silence, the anonymous stranger waiting, calmly, unseen and unhurrying, for the eventual word?

A few feet of silence

Whatever the difficulties and potential negative aspects of silence in counselling children I must emphasize the benefits. Children experience few opportunities for silent contact with adults or even silent time alone.

They are subject to the constant noise of talk and teaching, television and stereo headsets, noise in the family, the playground, the classroom, the supermarket, the place of work. The Tower of Babel may have been a ruined Assyrian-Ziggurat but it rises again in every city, blares from every loudspeaker, whispers in every ear. We are noise-dependent, drugged.

External noise is reflected in and reflects the internal noise which inhibits true growth and development, leaving no space for inwardness. The desperate need of a young woman mirrors that of many children:

> if she had only a few feet of silence of her own, to exclude the world from, to build up in something of herself (Bowen, 1983, p. 32).

One of the greatest gifts a counsellor can offer is a few feet of silence. So simple. So difficult. So rare.

Summary

Silence is essential both individually and in company but is very difficult to achieve. A great gift from counsellor to child may be **aid to**, **sharing in**, and **protection of silence** and **peace**. But silence may also be inimical to health, for example, if information is used as a **weapon** or **betokens fear** and **paralysis**. It is important for the counsellor to be comfortable with and recognize the implications of silence. Then the counsellor can offer the gift of 'A Few Feet of Silence'.

Link

Silence, individual and shared, is essential for real **listening** and **communication** and helps attention to the deepest places of the person. Through ideas and experience of a number of writers, children and adult, academics and practitioners. Chapter 6 explores ideas about the spiritual life of children and its importance in counselling, beginning with the image of the person as 'A House with Four Rooms'.

References

Althea, (1982). *When Uncle Bob Died*. Collins, London.

Axline, V. (1971). *Dibs: in Search of Self*. Penguin, Harmondsworth.

Bowen, E. (Wilson, A. (ed.)) (1983). The return, 28–34; The visitor, 124–35; The apple tree, 461–70; Look at all the roses, pp. 512–20. *The Collected Stories of Elizabeth Bowen*. Penguin, Harmondsworth.

Carpentier, A. (de Onis, H. (trans)) (1968). *The Lost Steps*. Penguin, Harmondsworth.

Casey, J. (1978). *Tamed Strawberries*. In Harwood and King (eds), pp. 37–50.

Chaplin, J. (1988a). *Feminist Counselling in Action*. Sage, London.

Crompton, M. (1980). *Respecting Children*. Edward Arnold, London.

Crompton, M. (1990). *Attending to Children*. Edward Arnold, London.

Dorfman, E. (1951). Play therapy. In C. R. Rogers. pp. 235–77.

Eaton, L. (1990). At the end of the line. *Social Work Today*, 21, (48), 40–41.

Goudge, E. (1950). *Gentian Hill*. Hodder and Stoughton, Dunton Green.

Harwood, R. and King, F. (eds) (1978). *New Stories. 3: an Arts Council Anthology*. Hutchinson, London.

Holgate, E. (ed.) (1972). *Communicating with Children*. Longman, London.

Jansson, T. (Warburton, T. (trans.)) (1973). *Tales from Moomin Valley*. Penguin, Harmondsworth.

Jolly, H. (1982). In Althea, p. 25.

Kadushin, A. (1972). *The Social Work Interview*. Columbia University Press, New York.

King, C. (1963). *Stig of the Dump*. Penguin, Harmondsworth.

Nicolson, O. (1989). More than a playground problem. *Social Work Today*, 7.12.89, 18–19.

Prestage, R. (1972). *Life for Kim*. In Holgate (ed.), pp. 98–107.

Rogers. C. R. (1951). *Client-centered Therapy: its Current Practice. Implications and Theory*. Constable, London.

6   A house with four rooms

A house with four rooms

> There is an Indian proverb or axiom that says that everyone is a house
> with four rooms, a physical, a mental, an emotional and a spiritual.
> Most of us tend to live in one room most of the time but, unless we go
> into every room every day, even if only to keep it aired, we are not a
> complete person (Godden, 1989, p. 13).

To my mind this house is a square so that every room touches every
other room. No room is larger than any other, none has a better view
or richer furnishing.

Throughout this book I visit all four rooms, showing child and
counsellor as complete persons. I have chosen to devote a whole
chapter to the spiritual room because not only does it interest me but
also I think that this aspect of adults and children together is not greatly
explored in the literature of counselling, care and welfare.

I sought material from religious traditions other than Christianity
but I can write only as who I am – white, middle-class, middle-aged,
female, brought up and educated within western European Christianity. As I must write from my own inwardness I hope that readers
will mediate ideas and illustrations through their own experience.

My own belief as a Quaker is in 'that of God in every one', that the
spirit of and in every person is the Spirit of God. I am required to
adhere to no creed or dogma and follow no ritual or liturgy.

I propose to associate the words *religion/religious* with systems of
belief, organization, practice, group, community. *Spirit/spiritual* is the
crude metaphor for that which is transcendent, which creates, loves,
survives, worships. It is as possible for the spirit to thrive without
religion as it is to be religious without nurturing the spirit or engaging
in worship. In this chapter I intend to discuss children in terms of both
religious and spiritual needs and hope that distinctions and syntheses
will be clear. I do not expect that my use of language will always be
precise.

A useful working definition of *spiritual* is provided by John Bradford
(1978) (Chaplain Missioner for the Children's Society) in the discussion paper *The Spiritual Rights of the Child*, 'a *growing* attunement to
and rapport with the transcendent values and ultimate realities of life',
elaborated thus:

The term 'transcendent' includes reference to something 'Other' which may, paradoxically, be both 'within' and 'Beyond'.

The use of the concept 'spiritual' should not be taken as meaning non-material, since this would be to suggest a dualism in which things material are considered antipathetical to the spiritual. A better view, it is suggested, sees the spiritual embracing and permeating the material.

It is important also not to glibly equate 'spiritual' with 'religious' – in the sense of being in some way connected or associated with a world faith *organisation*. The writings of Camus, Sartre and Solzhenitsyn highlight well the spiritual dimension which this Statement has in mind. The phrase 'pertaining to the soul' gives a useful focus (p. 7).

Not something we talk about

The spiritual room is, it seems to me, least visited. Sex, money, death, even disability, have shed many of their long worn taboos but who would confess to a stranger that she was troubled in spirit?

During a brief period as social worker with a family placement unit I spent hours discussing with applicants to foster or adopt their experiences of and attitudes towards sex, employment, family life, finance, childlessness, bereavement. Few of 'my' applicants professed any religious belief. 'Enid', for example, attended a non-conformist chapel. Although I felt that hers was by no means a Sunday-best religion, we did not discuss her beliefs or their effect on her day-to-day living or view of child care.

Where applicants expressed no interest in religion (as attachment to a church, mosque, synagogue, temple) and/or belief in a spiritual dimension to life, there was no discussion. It did not occur to me to enquire whether a baby would, whatever the beliefs of the adopting parents, be offered opportunities to attend, for example, a local Sunday school.

Had applicants expressed firm views, perhaps being members of a religious community, no doubt we should have discussed at length. *Lack* of apparent interest attracted, from me at least, no probing.

Yet the sexual, employment and family history and present lives of applicants had to be pursued and reported. Failure of a sexual relationship or unresolved feuds with parents might have been regarded as contra-indicators for eligibility to bring up children born to other people. However deeply I might have enquired into bed and purse, I felt constrained in the face of non-belief in or indifference to the spirit. I felt that to question about non-belief would be an intrusion. The very existence of my own beliefs inhibited me from discussion with people who professed no beliefs. Yet an interviewer whose sex life was full and satisfying, or happily or sadly non-existent, would have been expected to discuss in depth and write about the topic of sexuality.

Whether or not some religious belief is held is not in itself relevant. But the reasons for this and attitudes towards, for example, members of other groups or non-believers, must be of considerable significance in meeting, assessing, placing and counselling children and those who care for them.

Charlotte Allen (1991) (a mature student nurse) finds 'spirituality as a topic for discussion has the status of footnote. Any attempt to expand on its meaning or significance is met with blank stares, dazed expressions. Tutors who allude to God are received with muffled hoots and "Bible basher" taunts' (p. 52).

She believes that 'Recognising the real importance of religion for others is important' (p. 52). But that real importance may not be benign. Tim Tate (1991) warns that

> whilst our secular society may choose to ignore or even ridicule all forms of religious worship, what matters is not what we believe, but what the followers of any particular sect or cult accept as reality. Faith in a personal God or a personal Devil may make little sense to some people, but to the devout Christian or satanist, it is central (p. 58).

The *Children Act, 1989* (Department of Health) requires placing agents to take into account religious beliefs and preferences of children and young people in care. I am not clear whether, and if so how, spiritual needs and welfare of children are to be attended to and assured.

Practically, how much importance is attached to the experience and interest of a child for whom finding a welcoming bed at all is difficult enough? 'Sara' was received into care as a non-conformist but nominally converted to the established church on a review form. Successive foster placements included two families, each deeply involved with denominations whose beliefs and practices, while Christian in foundation, were in detail very different one from the other.

In both placements Sara was lovingly included into the worship and wider life of the churches, becoming a member of these communities as well as of the foster families. Faced with a very difficult decision regarding the placement, one family prayed together and involved its church community, endeavouring to learn the right course of action. Eventual adoptive placement was with a family whose life did not include regular attendance at any place of worship. Part of Sara's life which had been important and positive for several years was, almost certainly, suddenly curtailed.

In 1991 some children removed from home following allegations of abuse, were involved with their families in a well-established dissenting religious organization. They were denied access to representatives of their organizations while in care, thus being deprived of an important aspect of their usual way of life.

The spiritual care of children away from home must include both continued attendance at appropriate place of worship and encouragement of the life of the spirit. Erna I. Goulding (1984) writes as Associate Vice President for Patient Care at the Children's Hospital of Philadelphia:

> Recently I renewed acquaintance with a nursing colleague. When I told her I had been asked to write the foreword to a book on the spiritual needs of children, she responded, 'Great! We have been assessing every other need of children; it's about time we paid attention to that one'.
>
> I would not call my friend religious, but she does recognize a neglected dimension of care. This concern is felt by nurses, physicians, chaplains, social workers and others who work in hospitals with children and parents (p. 6).

She comments that

> The concept of whole-person health care is a relatively recent development. For years the medical professions assumed that hospitals run by religious groups would give some attention to spiritual needs. In secular hospitals...the patient's religion was a private matter and could be dealt with by calling in the patient's own priest, pastor or rabbi.
>
> In children's hospitals, spiritual needs were usually left to parents. For years, fears of death and dying were hushed up as inappropriate for conversation, or like sex, they were met with 'Ask your mother or father when they come in' (p. 7) (re-pararaphed).

Although individuals arranged Sunday-school classes, chaplains and other hospital staff found difficulty in dealing with 'the complex situations and crises presented by children and families who populate children's hospitals' (pp. 7,8).

The book to which Goulding writes the *Foreword, Spiritual Needs of Children* (Shelley, et al., 1984/82) reflects the 'hard work and wise counsel' of a 'task force...of professionals representing several areas of child care including social work, nursing, medicine, education and chaplaincy, as well as parents' (p. 8).

Goulding identifies some situations where adults are confronted with the spiritual needs of children:

- the staff nurse on the evening shift who is embarrassed when a little girl asks if she will listen to her prayers;
- the nursing student who is told by a school-age boy that he does not think he will mind dying since his mother said he would see God;
- the parent whose child asks again and again, 'Why am I sick? Does God hate me?'
- the Sunday-school teacher who tries to comfort the crying boy who does not want to go to heaven if he has to leave his dog behind.

. . .

- the hospital chaplain who has counseled adult patients who fear anaesthesia and possible death but has not talked to children in the same situation.
- the intensive care unit nurse who longs for the right words to comfort a suffering child – she knows that not all suffering is physical and relieved by medication (p. 7).

In the *Foreword* to the English edition of this North American book. Janet Goodall (consultant paediatrician) writes, 'We were all children once, but most professionals – and even many parents – have retained very little idea as to how children think. By being insensitive to this enormously important area we can inflict on young children much unnecessary bewilderment and hurt' (Goodall, 1984, p. 10).

She notes that

> For many, the idea that a young child may have serious questions with a spiritual content can itself be a difficult concept to grasp. Physical symptoms can arise from both spiritual and emotional upsets and it is helpful to be reminded and informed about ways of exploring these areas sensitively. Whereas older children may be glad of a more dispassionate counsellor, pre-school children will be more likely to ask questions of their parents, who may well need help themselves before being able to tune in and respond adequately (pp. 10–11).

Ages, stages and language

Goodall advises that 'There is no easy way to instant rapport with a sick child, but by knowing something about the stages of conceptual development and by listening to individual children, we can begin to gauge more effectively the right wavelength for successful communication'. She finds it 'extraordinary that the areas of conceptual and spiritual understanding have been so neglected' in paediatric training (p. 10). There has, I suggest, been similar neglect in the training of counsellors, social workers, doctors, foster parents and others concerned with the care of children.

Shelley offers 'Summaries of how various aspects of spiritual development fit into the theories of Erikson and Piaget' which 'are usually taught in schools of nursing'. She notes that 'Each provides a different emphasis and complements the other. Neither is the final authority. The study of spiritual development is a wide-open field with a great need for solid research from a nursing perspective' (p. 23).

I am not competent to discuss such theories and space in the present book does not permit reproduction of the entire tables. The following extracts offer a flavour:

Table 1: Piaget's Stages of Cognitive Development As Related to Spiritual Development
Sensorimotor Stage (under age 2) – Understanding of God is vague, associated with parents. Prayer may provide comfort and deepen bond between parents, child and God. Responds to environment of love and warmth. No sense of conscience. Wise use of diversion better than punishment for wrongdoing (p. 24).
Table 2: Outline of Spiritual Development As Related to Erikson's Eight Ages of Man: (1963) Lois J. Hopkins, M.S.N.
Prenatal Period – Developing child's environment is influenced by love, joy, good health. Preparation of parents for task of child-rearing includes their own spiritual well-being, as well as plans for child's religious upbringing.
Birth to Age One – Stage of basic trust vs. basic mistrust. Child needs a dependable environment, security in care, and love from a mother figure. Ability to trust, which develops during this stage, is essential for a growing faith in God.
...
Age 12–18 – Stage of identity vs. role confusion. Adolescent rebellion against parents may include rejection of the religious beliefs of their upbringing. Becomes more interested in a personal relationship with God, but may be opposed to institutional religion. Often begins asking deep religious questions, but hesitates to discuss them with peers for fear of ridicule (p. 25).

The interpretations of the basic theories are made within a Christian framework.

Arthur (1985) discusses Erikson's model as applied to religious education, including lengthy consideration of 'the critical tension faced by the adolescent as being that strung out between a sense of identity and the threat of its obverse, role confusion'. He quotes Jersild (1963) who 'is careful to stress that there is much of the adolescent left in all of us whatever chronological age we may happen to have reached' and who defines 'final maturity in terms of developing a sense of compassion' (pp. 50.51).

Greer (1980), reviewing a range of studies, records that David Elkind (1971) 'has demonstrated a similar developmental sequence in Jewish, Protestant, and Catholic children's understanding of their religious identity'. He notes that, 'it is now commonly taken for granted by educators that children's religious thinking follows the developmental pattern from intuitive, to concrete operational to formal operational thought' (see Piaget: Goldman, 1964 (Greer, 1980, p. 24).

He concludes that

Studies of religious development must take particular account of the fact that religious insight and understanding cannot be analysed neatly into the cognitive and the affective domains. The growth and interaction of religious thinking and feeling must be a priority in future research into religious development in childhood and adolescence (p. 28).

Fowler (1981) discusses the development of faith in six stages with a prologue, under these headings:

Infancy and undifferentiated faith
Stage 1. Intuitive-projective faith
Stage 2. Mythic-literal faith
Stage 3. Synthetic-conventional faith
Stage 4. Individual-reflective faith
Stage 5. Conjunctive faith
Stage 6. Universalizing faith (pp. 119–213).

Berryman's (1985) paper *Children's Spirituality and Religious Language* does not take an ages and stages approach but is included in this section because it reviews 'seven major lines of inquiry into religious experience and its religious language' comprising the 'traditions' of Freud, William James, cognitive-developmental, taxonomic, multi-dimensional, social psychology, and Montessori (Berryman, 1985).

Berryman describes his paper as 'an inquiry into the relationship children have with God' which 'will be called "spiritual". The child's spirituality is assumed to be a comprehensive relationship with God that involves the whole person in an ultimate way just as one's dying and death does' (p. 120).

Space permits attention to only one of the traditions discussed in this paper. Berryman explains that the focus of William James

> was not on the origin of religious experience but on its inability to be reduced to any other human experience. 'It is as if there were in the human consciousness a sense of reality, a feeling of objective presence, a perception of what we may call "something there"' (James, 1902). It is the feelings, acts, and experiences of individuals in solitude who 'apprehend' themselves to stand in relation to whatever they consider divine (Berryman, 1985, p. 121).

Berryman finds that

> The Jamesian Tradition's focus on the more positive aspects of the religious experience and the significance of religion during transition periods in the life cycle are of great importance in this area of study. The great transition period that lasts approximately from 5–7 years is one deserving as much attention. If we had a better-informed approach to that period, the religious crisis of many adolescents might not be so destructive. In the United States the loss of ultimate meaning for adolescents has become a major concern, because of the increasing rate of suicide among the nation's teenagers (pp. 124–5).

While this is in the language of and directed towards educators, I find in it much of relevance to counsellors in all fields. The use of language, the attitude of the adult, the relationship with the child, all are of universal significance:

> To teach the art of using religious language requires a mature artist because one must steer carefully between two ancient and deceptive rocks that guard the narrow passage into the open sea that lies beyond ordinary experience. The sharp rocks of blasphemy (thinking that one is God and can know what every individual child needs and how religious language ought to be used) are on one side. On the other side are the dangerous rocks of idolatry (teaching religious language as an end in itself as if it were to be worshipped instead of God).

We need to 'become more aware of what it is not only to be a child but also what it is like to be like a child' (p. 127).

Charlotte Allen finds that a problem for nurses is lack of 'a *language* of spirituality with which we all feel comfortable', while recognizing that 'Even with a common language, it may still be an intensely private matter for us or our clients. Developing spiritual self-awareness does not give us permission to launch into the fray, using every encounter as a spiritual truth session' (p. 53).

Questions of belief

Language and the attribution of meaning were fundamental to the study of Kibble, Parker and Price (1981) into religious beliefs amongst adolescents, a survey conducted in two secondary schools. Pupils aged 13–16 were

> asked to indicate their agreement with one of the following statements:
> (a) You are certain that there is a God.
> (b) You believe that there is a God but you are not completely certain.
> (c) You are not sure whether there is a God or not.
> (d) You do not believe that there is a God at all.

The resulting numerical analysis of responses is given and reasons for choices recorded, for example, 'I believe there is a God because more and more is being spent on surveys to find out about God and Jesus' (p. 31) (Kibble, et al., 1981, p. 31).

The final comment recorded was made by a third-year boy 'obviously struggling to work out what is real and what is not' in response to a question about belief in 'a powerful, supernatural force greater than man': 'There are so many strange things that happen and it makes my mind think. So I would say yes..., just to be safe. If you were to look at it logically it would seem there wasn't. But it makes you wonder' (pp. 34,35). The first Spiritual Right defined by John

Bradford (1989) is 'The opportunity to have moments...of *wonder*' (p. 42).

Questions were designed to inform the adults about the attitudes of young people of a certain age. It is not clear what action resulted from the study, for example, in the role and attitudes of counsellors within the schools. For many of the pupils, the questions must have stimulated trains of thought and further questions; you cannot ask people about their beliefs without recognizing that you are possibly encroaching on delicate ground. Indeed the paper is entitled *The Age of Uncertainty*. I wonder if those who took part in the survey were enabled to ask questions of their own at the time and/or afterwards.

Kate Cairns (1990) writes after 14 years experience of residential care that

> All the children I have lived and worked with have been deeply concerned with moral and religious questions. 'What sort of person am I?' 'How am I to live my life?' These have not been idle musings, but the fundamental uncertainites which have established the basis and shape of a child's approach to living.
>
> I have become convinced that the search for meaning and direction is of critical concern for children. This is more so when their image of themselves is cloudy or flawed, as is often true for children in care. Such questions may not be answered but must be addressed (p. 27).

Children talking

The section on models and theories began with the advice of Janet Goodall that the attainment of 'rapport with a sick child' could be helped 'by knowing something about the stages of conceptual development and by listening to individual children' (p. 10). I consider the second part of that advice as more important.

Preparation for this chapter led me to many examples of children and young people talking and writing about their beliefs and religious/ spiritual experiences, from the responses to Kibble's survey to autobiographies, novels and autobiographical novels (for example, *Oranges are not the Only Fruit*, Winterson (1985)).

Nearly all the literature to which I have access is drawn from the Western Christian tradition. An exception is the account by an adult Quaker of his Jewish boyhood.

Harvey Gillman (1988) was brought up in Manchester in the 1940s– 50s to think of himself 'as Jewish both religiously and ethnically' (p. 41).

> Being Jewish was a matter of belonging to the group that was called Yidden and which others called Jews. Even when I became very

'frumm', that is religious. I still knew that some people were none the less Jewish even though they never went to the synagogue and perhaps only had the haziest notion of Judaism. In my strict Hebrew school that I attended every evening after junior school from the age of eight or nine we were taught that non-religious Jews were bad Jews, yet they were still Jews to whom we owed solidarity. Suffering was the common lot and suffering led us to stick together (p. 42).

He speculates that

If I was asked as a child what I believed constituted the Jewish religion I should have answered perhaps: praying three times a day, observing the Sabbath, eating only Kosher food, obeying my father and mother (though in this commandment I was always somewhat remiss), studying the first five books of the Old Testament, and fasting on the right occasions. This is still what constitutes Judaism for many Jews. All these activities are communal ones; they spring from personal commitment and are at the same time the basis of community (p. 42).

Harvey Gillman

rejected the Jewish religion as a teenager. The learning I had received seemed stale to me. Instead of leading to wisdom and understanding it had become a negative code. Instead of leading to a feeling of unity with the whole world it was leading to a separatism that I felt stifling. The more I read the more I rejected. At the same time I longed for more real communion with the world around. It would be a communion based on the real me, as I understood it then (p. 44).

His rebellion, fuelled by the writings of Dostoievsky and James Baldwin,

led neither to communion nor to the grand deed. It left me more alone than ever. I was no longer at home in the Jewish community, nor did I feel at home among my gentile friends. Indeed I had few friends. Books were my most faithful companions. My adolescence then was a long exercise in loneliness (p. 45).

At 18 he attended a Quaker Meeting but 'was soon in the desert again, obsessed with, therefore violently against, the idea of God'; the journey towards eventual membership of the Religious Society of Friends would be long (p. 45).

These extracts offer rare insight into the experience of a child/young person growing up in and rejecting the way of life of one religious community and seeking, not without suffering, the true home for his individual and continuing spiritual development.

Like Harvey Gillman, Yvonne Stevenson (1976) was brought up within a family whose religious beliefs and practices were inextricably intertwined in everyday life. Unlike him, her adult experience led her completely and irrevocably away from any form of religious tradition.

Born and brought up in an Anglican vicarage, the young Yvonne had a very lively sense of Jesus who, with herself and *Black Beauty* 'formed a trio of friends'. Once, sent home alone from a beach outing in disgrace,

> My heart jumped in panic at having to make such a big journey alone, but I hid this under a pirouette of complete contempt. Without another glance behind, Jesus and I made off at a dignified pace. Once out of sight I became completely happy. The high-banked lanes were covered in flowers, and I could peer among their leaves until my eye caught a tiny thing moving, a spider or an ant perhaps, and I could watch its busy ways, unmolested and unhurried.
>
> After dawdling for some time I suddenly decided to do the opposite and race. Black Beauty immediately appeared at my service, and I mounted him and made off. Jesus tearing along at my side. We formed a splendid trio, all galloping along magnificently. In fact, there were times when we all three became prancing, foaming horses; or I would mount the cab seat, flourish the whip over the other two horses and we would become a rollicking and swaying carriage and pair. Shrieks of warning came from my mouth as people turned round to stare and make way. The galloping lasted all the way home, driving out my fear (p. 17–18).

At 16 her 'religious preoccupations assumed their height' and she

> thought more and more about the actual physical sufferings of Christ on the Cross. Would the flesh of His hands and feet have been torn by the weight of his body? If so, might not the nails have worked their way through the knuckles of His hands? Did the knuckles touch sufficiently to prevent this? I often felt my hands, pressing in between the bones to decide whether they could take the weight of my suspended body (p. 42–3).

In order to test whether she could suffer for God as had such saints as Joan and Sebastian, she decided that *'I would drive a nail through my hand'* (p. 43). She found the necessary equipment and putting the nail in position

> raised the hammer. At that very instant the gong went for tea. It was a message from God, telling me to stop – just as He had told Abraham to stop before he slew Isaac. I put the nail and the hammer down and sat trembling. Surely that gong had been timed by God. God did not wish me to cause Mother and Father unhappiness by having me ill with poisoning and a stiff right hand for ever afterwards. I suddenly felt my mother's love all about me, as if she were bending down with her arms around me saying, 'No, child, that isn't the way at all' (p. 44).

Yvonne spends a few more uncomfortable minutes, shivering and receiving a stern talking to from 'the Voice of God', leading her to acknowledge that she has been 'fancying and imagining and ruminating along false lines. With a great sigh I got up, utterly disgusted with myself, and began to walk, rather unsteadily, downstairs' (p. 44).

Clive Penman (1986) writes from long experience of teaching in a Quaker boarding school: 'I have come to the conclusion that a "religious" child is a disturbed oddity' (p. 76). Yvonne Stevenson's behaviour might indeed appear disturbed, her interpretation of the Christian message extraordinary. Yet her account shows how she used the experience to grow, to apply reason to emotion and make an important step in her development.

Eating in outward calm, she decides that

> I would have to think much more seriously about what I really wanted to do when I grew up, and stop thinking about Joan of Arc and the saints and martyrs. They had suffered to bring civilisation to the level it had now attained. What was I going to do about it – about helping forward civilisation?...I felt years older, just as I had...after Mother had told me about adultery (p. 45).

In late adolescence she discovered the uncomfortable difference between preaching and practice when holidays from boarding school 'seethed with wrangles, arguments and scenes and I was the centre of them'. These occurred 'almost invariably at Sunday dinner, for the simple reason that I had just heard an excellent sermon by Father which would set me thinking about Christian principles' by emphasizing 'the humble origin of Christ' and the Apostles who were 'for the most part...working men' (pp. 54, 55).

At home, however, 'all values were reversed. Here were working-class maids waiting on us, handing us the vegetables correctly, from the left side, potatoes first, vegetables second, all as it should be...Did Christ, at the Last Supper, ask John to jump up and wait on Him? Then why should we?' The result of Yvonne drawing such inconsistency to her father's attention was for him 'to explode with exasperation' and for her 'to get a reputation – in his eyes – for extreme stubbornness' (p. 55).

Eventually, at university Yvonne suffered a devastating spiritual crisis from which she left all forms of organized religion. 'Did I or did I not believe in God? I could no longer even say my prayers' (p. 139).

Towards the end of her autobiography she writes 'It will be an immense step forward, if, on the global scale, we human beings can begin to discover even a little faith in our own human nature.' She considers that 'religion *divides* the good from the bad, which form God, Satan, and so on. Religion therefore makes a mockery of "faith in human nature". It has *no* faith in human nature. Religion lowers our capacity to tolerate ambivalence, to accept disease as well as health, death as well as life' (p. 189).

Yvonne Stevenson concludes her *Preface* (written 30 years after the rest of the book, when she felt ready to publication) with a comment on the unconscious violence of my sweet-natured headmistress who preached to us Sunday after Sunday on the need...to dedicate ourselves to the service of God, to become part of the Body of Christ, and so on. The violence started in my nursery, really; the only pictures on the walls were of Jesus, either surrounded by children of all nationalities, or carrying a little blonde-haired English girl. Later on, at the age of nine or ten, I...was presented with...*The Lives of the Saints.* All the illustrations were of white-faced holy people with hands pressed together. This relentless conditioning continued to my college days: whereupon London University flung its arms wide and said: 'Here you are! Now you can believe *anything!*' No wonder I needed a transcendental experience to release me from my mental straightjacket (p. x).

For Sarah Ferguson (1987) too, religious experience in her adolescent years proved intense and eventually unmanageable, perhaps because she received no support, no counselling at that time. Yvonne Stevenson at least could record the advice of a school chaplain: 'If at the end of a year or two of college life you suddenly find your beliefs become no longer tenable, *hang on to the ethic* – the ethics of Christianity...Hold yourself suspended in doubt for a year or two, and let your own conclusions grow in their own time'. The girls realized that 'it didn't need words to tell us that he himself had been through what he had described' (p. 71).

(Since Yvonne Stevenson (a pseudonym) died in 1987 it has not been possible to thank her for permission to quote from her wonderful book. I am indebted to Nicolas Walter of the Rationalist Press Association for this information.)

Sarah Ferguson's account of her spiritual life is made in a long address to her dead psychoanalist:

I had been so fervent a believer when I was a child and adolescent, seeing angels through the plain lattice windows of the village church of my aunt, and at home, going willingly to matins and evensong with my grandmother, where I had visions of Christ passing down the nave. Altars covered with their embroidered cloths concealed the most precious treasure of the universe. I was always the only communicant at the early service on New Year's Day, and I accepted transubstantiation without question. The presence of Christ constantly by my side was what kept me alive. I punished and mortified my spirit so harshly that I was not strong enough to keep up with my intensely secret life of worship.

When I was 18 I broke and I decided that what I had prized so highly was only emotional, and that intellectually I could accept nothing. One evening I became hysterical with weeping. My father came to see me and said I could only cry if I had a reason. I closed up entirely then. I had lost my faith. Even the visions which appeared before me shortly before his death – I dismissed.

As an adult she feels her

> emotions to be nearer the usually invisible truth than my feeble
> intellect and reasoning. I am not so ardent or faithful as I was before,
> and I am more full of sin, but Christ once again is everywhere. Rarely
> supporting and comforting me but His presence is a reality which I
> know I have to go far to reach (Ferguson, 1987, p. 79).

Sarah Ferguson described her spiritual crisis long after the event.
Particularly poignant is the comment that her father inhibited her
expression of doubt and grief. Writing to a counsellor who can never
read her words, she recalls a time when, had a counsellor been present
and able to listen, much suffering might have been spared, then, and in
time to come.

The experience of religious practice and language is often very
bewildering for children (and adults). In my early teens I used to blush
when recital of the Creed required me to use the forbidden word
womb. Forbidden because at school the scripture mistress always cut
those verses in the Bible which included embarrassing words. We
would be bidden to read, for example, Genesis chapter 25 omitting
verses 23 and 24. Quite how we were to avoid the appalling verses was
never explained. The contaminating description was:

> 23…Two nations are in your womb, and two peoples, born of you,
>   shall be divided…
> 24When her days to be delivered were fulfilled, behold, there were
>   twins in her womb (Genesis, 25).

At church parade, in front of the Boy Scouts, it was appalling to be
required to say so awful a word and, worse, associated with a verb
whose meaning was unknown to me and deeply embarrassing: 'He did
not abhor the Virgin's womb.' The use of a dictionary might have made
all plain but to associate prayer book and dictionary did not occur to
me. Whatever *abhoring* was, perhaps I thought it too dreadful to
discover.

The narrator of Jeanette Winterson's (1985) book had also to work
out not only her own salvation but also the meanings of unmentionable
words. Jeanette and her mother read the Book of Deuteronomy
together:

> Whenever we read about a bastard, or someone with crushed testicles,
> my mother turned over the page and said, 'Leave that to the Lord',
> but when she'd gone, I'd sneak a look. I was glad I didn't have
> testicles. They sounded like intestines only on the outside, and the
> men in the Bible were always having them cut off and not being able to
> go to church. Horrid (p. 42).

Anxious to save her school friends from damnation, Jeanette finds herself involved in a bewildering interview with her headteacher who complains that she seems

> 'rather pre-occupied,...with God...Your sampler, for instance, had a very disturbing motif'. [THE SUMMER IS ENDED AND WE ARE NOT YET SAVED.]
> 'It was for my friend....and she gave me three mice in the fiery furnace' (p. 41).

Jeanette is questioned further:

> 'And why,...do you terrorise, yes, terrorise the other children?'

Two mothers have complained that their children have nightmares:

> 'I have nightmares too.'
> 'That's not the point. You have been talking about Hell to young minds.'
>   It was true. I couldn't deny it. I had told all the others about the horrors of the demon and the fate of the damned. I had illustrated it by almost strangling Susan Hunt, but that was an accident, and I gave her all my cough sweets afterwards.
> 'I'm very sorry,...I thought it was interesting' (pp. 42–3).

The girl is depressed:

> What was all the fuss about? Better to hear about Hell now than burn in it later...Mrs Vole wrote to my mother, explaining my religious leanings, and asking my mother if she would moderate me. My mother hooted and took me to the cinema as a treat. They were showing *The Ten Commandments* (p. 43).

Eventually Jeanette and the church part company. But on a visit home she reflects: 'I still don't think of God as my betrayer. I miss God who was my friend' as she tries 'to find the balance between earth and sky' (p. 170).

God was lost by Ruth Fawell (1987) when at 12 her mother died and she

> broke away from the Church of England in which I had been brought up together with my sisters. With the literal mind of a child I felt that I had been betrayed by the promise of the church service – 'where two or three are gathered together in thy name thou will grant their requests'. I and others had requested pleadingly and passionately that my mother should live, but she had died and our happy family world which had been so dependent on her serene and loving personality had fallen apart.
>   By the time I was at university I was a very questioning and vocal agnostic who refused to turn to the east in chapel prayers and who had

to be asked to leave a Christian apologetics group because I would not cease to query the existence of God. My searches led me to other churches and groups, but it was only after the tragic death of my agnostic father, a noble, gifted and disinterested public servant, that I felt an insistent need to discover purpose in the universe.

During my adolescent years I had been painfully aware of the abyss of meaninglessness that lay beneath my father's useful and active life because of the loss from which he had been unable to be healed and that had caused the bottom to fall out of his life (pp. 110–11) (re-paragraphed).

She would become a Quaker and a social worker.

For Ruth Fawell, two experiences of bereavement resulted in spiritual crisis and decision, first to renounce an idea of idea God, next to seek purpose in the universe. Her response as a 12 year old to the death of her mother in 1910, recalled in old age, is echoed by Catherine Houghton aged 15 in 1976:

Aunt Alice would always fold her hands piously and murmer, 'even death is not unkind, when living love is left behind'.

Death was unkind though. It had torn me from my mother. It had separated us with a rift that not even all my determination could cross, unless – unless nothing. Human flesh is cheap, the world is over-populated, but I'm not going. My mind just ached – yes, my mind. I felt fatigued. Something unconscious plucked at my twisted thoughts, slowly and painfully separating them into clearer strands. A half-remembered, childishly lisped hymn sprang to my lips, 'Yes, Jesus loves me'.

I felt abused. 'All right', I shouted, 'If He loves me, why has He taken Mum away?'

I stopped, feeling extremely pleased with myself. I had confused my Creator, I had proved him wrong. Triumphantly I thought, 'Let Him get Himself out of this one' (Houghton, 1976, p. 104).

Desperately needing to cry, she finds a private place, the gas works, not ideal but she is able to cry and to feel 'better cleansed – they use that word in the Bible. I seemed to have a, "thing", on God that day which was ridiculous as I hadn't set foot in a church since I was four. It made me feel queer though, walking past a church' (p. 105).

Catherine regards God as 'only for the, "Holy Joes", not for the likes of me. I swore, I drank, and once I had smoked, but Mum had found me and made me smoke the whole packet and then read my Bible for an hour, after which I was dutifully sick and blamed it all on "readin" that rubbish' (p. 105).

But in the privacy of the gas works she becomes

aware of a growing juxtaposition between myself and another energy. I had a companion, Mum would see me alright. Mum would watch me. She was somewhere I'd never see but she could see me. We made an uncanny link; an electric energy contact came with the realisation that everything wasn't finished. Even though my little world was temporarily shattered I knew the glass was not broken, only cracked and would repair slowly...I felt hurt, but calm,...(p. 105).

Catherine's spiritual experience evaporates when during the funeral she sits 'alone in church; the reassurance I had felt the day before deserted me. Where was my Mum? In a large wooden box with imitation brass handles which would rip off if you pulled them' (p. 106). Neither mere presence in a house of religion nor experience can mean anything without a context. Ruth Fawell rejected the church and the God which she felt betrayed her. I do not imagine that Catherine Houghton returned to the church in which she found none of that comfort, the stirring of her spirit that had reached her in the gas works.

Children dying

The young people quoted in this above group of extracts are united by deep religious/spiritual experiences which led to change, either away from any religious observance at all or into some new organization. They were chosen to illustrate the importance of the dimension of life both at times of crisis and in focusing the whole texture and context of being.

I found numerous examples of a child deriving great help from an individual image of God. For many people, God-language is difficult, even disengaging; comments by a Baptist hospital chaplain in *Is God a Teddy Bear? Images of God* (Rodgers, 1984) are helpful:

At times I feel like a person with a net, trying to catch a butterfly. Just as I feel close to understanding a person's relationship with God, the person changes direction. My own image of God constantly changes too as I discover more about God's many-faceted nature. Parents and children who are sick perceive God differently according to their spiritual needs of the moment. Sometimes those perceptions are accurate understandings of the character of God, and sometimes they are attempts to make God in their own images (pp. 91–2).

He recalls some counselling which failed: 'Job, in his anguish, tried several images of God to understand his tragedy. His comforters added their own images and relationships to Job's, yet left him without comfort' (p. 92).

He describes the experience of John (8) suffering from leukaemia:

His mother was a deeply committed Christian. His father was also a believer, but his faith was more philosophical than experiential. Several times John's illness went into remission. These were good times which his parents never interpreted as miracles. His mother constantly reminded John and herself of God's presence. She read the Bible and prayed with John daily.

Finally, the leukemia became severe. John would get scared and lash out, but his mother assured him that God understood, cared and was with him – sort of like the bedraggled teddy bear at his side. He could vicariously take jabs with the syringe and the bops on the head when John was angry, and still be there to comfort him.

Finally, bleeding mouth ulcers and infection began. John's last admission to the hospital was painful, frightening and long. His mother continued to assure him of God's love, which seemed to comfort him. One day John's mother told me that John was disappointed because he had missed Holy Communion while in the hospital. I offered to bring him the bread and wine if he could tolerate it. John smiled. I returned and conducted a Communion service in his room. Despite the sore ulcers in his mouth he managed to swallow the bread and sip the wine with a straw from a little Communion glass. I reaffirmed God's presence in our closing prayer. John died several days later. That Last Supper was deeply meaningful – to John, to his mother and to me (p. 98).

Rodgers suggests that 'In many ways, God came to John as a teddy bear, willing to take all of his bumps and bruises and anger, and still offer him comfort and forgiveness' and that 'Sometimes when God comes to those who are suffering, he comforts them, like a teddy bear. Our job, as comforters, is to help them recognize that comfort' (pp. 98, 99).

Such language and imagery may not appeal to all readers. The central message I take to be that, for a child who had been brought up within a particular religious tradition (in this case free church Christianity) and who felt at ease with the language and images of that tradition, the continuation and adaptation of practice and belief within the contexts of hospital, illness and dying was of the greatest importance.

What could be of greater significance, comfort and beauty than that last communion service shared in the dying child's own room? What kinder counselling than that given by the chaplain to both boy and mother? During the last few days of his life, the boy was enriched by respect for his wishes and beliefs, the recognition of his individuality and importance.

Perhaps it is inevitable that accounts of illness and death seem more likely than other life crises to include reference to the spirit. Suzanne Schuurman (1987) a member of the Baha'i faith, records the death of her son Tristan:

His eyes opened wide and he looked out into the room. My arms were cradling his head, so I did not catch their look. Enunciating clearly, he said with a sense of grateful relief, 'I'm so glad that I'm a Baha'i...because...'. The last word faded away. There was a slight spasm and he went limp. I cradled his head for some time, still listening to his shallow breathing....

She writes to her mother:

> On the bed Tristan lies dying. His breathing draws on the wellsprings of life. So painfully, with so much travail is that breath inhaled, convulsing the whole chest, and, after an agonizing pause that lasts and lasts, exhaled with a rattle through the pale dry lips half-glued with mucous. How beautiful his face is, calm and withdrawn. The fine lines of his nose and cheekbones and the pale moonlight colour of his hair move me.
>
> He is at home and we orbit around him, around his center of stillness, but as he withdraws farther and farther into that unconscious world where the spirit waits in the antechamber of the other worlds, we draw closer together, pulled in by the gravity of his being and of his passing from being (pp. 218–19).

Tristan dies after 17 years of struggle with impaired health. A fever in infancy led to assessment that 'he would be nothing but a vegetable'. But, as Roger White quotes from a letter in his *Foreword*,

> Tristan walked and talked, laughed and loved, and believed in Baha'u'llah with a devotion that inspired all who knew him. We remember him at Conventions, going from table to table, visiting with friends, uplifting them with his radiant spirit...Beyond the veil of physical afflictions lived a soul brilliant with the gifts of God; we have been blessed to know him (p. v).

(After reading almost the final draft, Robert Holman reminded me that life and death decisions are made by girls who are faced with the possibility of abortion, with important spiritual implications for mother and unborn child and for those helping her, including counsellors. I have neither space nor time to develop this but add this sentence, at the last minute, for others' consideration.)

Solitude and community

Spiritual experience is by no means, of course, confined to illness and dying. Elise Boulding (1989) refers to several children whose lives were healthy and happy. Here is Benjamin Bangs who between 11 and 12 sometime in the late seventeenth century

> was much given to diverting myself in running, wrestling and foot-ball playing, which was much practiced in the part of the country where I lived, and my company was very much desired by such...Being one day by myself, not far from the place of our habitation, I met with such a visitation, as I had been altogether ignorant of before, in which a sweet calmness spread over my mind; and it rose in my heart, that if I could but keep to this, what might I grow up to in time? It much affected me, and rested with me for some time (p. 25).

Göte Klingberg of Sweden (1959) described a boy who, one October evening, 'was left at home alone to look after a sleeping little brother. He tried to bolster his courage by thinking about God. Suddenly, he felt that God was *there*, around him, in him, as he sat by his brother's bed' (in Boulding, 1989 p. 22). Klingberg also narrates how a girl (12)

> described a long walk home from a friend's house in the late afternoon. It was growing dark, and the path lay through a gloomy wood. 'I imagined that God walked by my side and that I said: Dear God, take care of me on the way. And I imagined that God answered: "See I am with you". Then I felt very calm as I went along' (p. 22).

Elise Boulding herself remembers

> a small girl all alone in a rowboat in the middle of a quiet mountain lake at high noon. Scarcely big enough to handle the oars, she sits alone feeling the warmth of the sun, the cool blueness of the water lapping softly at the boat, and the immensity of the fir-covered hills all around. She is bursting with warmth and bigness and silence. This is home. It is belonging. It is joy (p. 27).

We may all remember those times of peace and exhilaration, of something greater than the sum of our parts but the spiritual experience and interest of children and young people is not confined to solitary lakes or mountain tops.

Boulding describes two high-school boys in a (Quaker) discussion group on

> 'Nurturing the Spiritual Life of our Children'. It had been agreed in advance that the participation of young people in any discussion group would be encouraged, and these two young men took the program committee at its word.
>
> There was a distinct uneasiness in the group as they sat down with us. What were they doing there, in a discussion on spiritual life and particularly the spiritual life of children? It turned out that they were very concerned about spiritual life, their own and that of adults.
>
> They had thought a lot about it. They had more to say than a number of adults present. And they had advice for adults on how to relate to the spiritual life of children: 'Listen to them. Find out what is going on.'
>
> We adults fumbled for a way to relate to these boys who were being so frank and open with us. Respect for children was talked about. The boys brought up equality. What does equality for children mean, the adults wondered. No problem for the boys. Equality meant being recognized as equally human, equally aware, equally searching. Not equally knowledgeable – not in everything, anyway.
>
> But it turned out there were some things these boys knew that we didn't know. It often doesn't occur to us how interested children are in the things we do. (p. 41) (re-paragraphed).

Catrin Prys-Williams (16) wrote to her mother about the religious life of and in an English Quaker boarding school. 'She enthused on the pleasures of positive participation. Her peers at her former school, a large comprehensive, had regarded anything but outright apathy at morning assembly as very bad form' (Prys-Williams, 1986, p. 68).

Catrin appreciated not only Meeting for Worship but also

> the Meeting as a community: 'I went with M. to a mini-discussion after morning Meeting on Sunday. There was good ground coffee and the discussion about Meeting for Worship, was quite interesting...It was nice to be back in a sort of Meeting atmosphere where adults accept you on equal terms and yet feel a bit protective towards you and there was that nice sort of coffee-time chat feeling you get [at home] before the hunted looks start to chase across the faces as people remember their burning roasts (p. 69).

Catrin also

> commented from time to time on the quality of the compulsory Sunday Meeting for Worship, expressing great pleasure in a good one and exasperation with ministry too blatantly for the good of the dear children. Ministry from pupils was very rare. She was most appreciative of ministry given at some personal cost and warmed when she felt everyone in the Meeting on an equal footing as humble learners. But even an undistinguished Meeting for Worship seemed to provide a welcome opportunity for calm and reflection in the midst of a frequently noisy community life (p. 69).

As young adults, although still at school, the two North American boys and the Welsh girl found no discrepancy between the practice of religion and everyday life. They visited their four rooms every day. Any assessment or counselling service offered for whatever reason (for example, career choice, illness, separation, bereavement) would have been deeply deficient if this integral part of their lives should have been ignored.

Of innocence and experience

In discussion of goals and values of bringing up children, Michael Rutter (1983) (professor of child psychiatry) writes that

> Some may be concerned that I have introduced the term spiritual so late in my discussion of goals. However...I do not make a distinction between the sacred and the secular. All the qualities to which I have referred derive out of a set of spiritual values, and themselves have a spiritual component (p. 41–2).

The four rooms are visited daily, naturally and spontaneously; health, wholeness are achieved when the individual exercises in and enjoys every room with undeliberate vigour.

Nicola McDowell (10) (1976) finds no barriers between everyday life on earth and in heaven:

> My sister Fiona thinks that God is a clown. But I think God is a ghost with no feet and floats about on air. He wears a white gown and a blue belt and black hair with a halo over his head, but he has not got a beard he is not old he is young looking. I think Heaven is a place where you go when you die and you get a place to yourself and in it there is a machine where you can look down on earth and see how your family is getting on.
>
> I always think about God in bed I always find it is the best place to think about him. One night I thought about when I die it will be like going to sleep and when I wake up I shall find myself outside the gates of Heaven.
>
> I always think that when I go to Heaven I shall meet my Nana and we shall shake hands and go off talking about things. I always talk to my Nana whose [sic] dead and I always think she's listening. I tell her what happened today and may tell her jokes. I always think they can hear what you think. I get the feeling that some body is listening or watching me but I never know how (p. 36).

This lovely piece of writing is, for me, the most moving of all my references. By now (1991) Nicola must be 25 and both she and Fiona have surely changed their images of God. Does she still talk to her Nana and tell her jokes? Her vision of communication, death and Heaven may no longer be so clear and pragmatic but perhaps her sense of the intangible, the other than physical, has developed.

Whatever the eventual experience of Nicola, I hope it was not as devastating as that of Markus Natten (12) (1979) whose poem *Childhood* may be seen as a vision of departure from Eden:

> When did my childhood go?
> Was it the day I ceased to be 11,
> Was it the time I realised that Hell and Heaven,
> Could not be found in Geography,
> And therefore could not be,
> Was that the day!
>
> When did my childhood go?
> Was it the time I realised that adults were not all
> they seemed to be,
> They talked of love and preached of love,
> But did not act so lovingly,
> Was that the day!

When did my childhood go?
Was it when I found my mind was really mine,
To use whichever way I choose,
Producing thoughts that were not those of other people,
But my own, and mine alone,
Was that the day!

Where did my childhood go?
It went to some forgotten place,
That's hidden in an infant's face,
That's all I know (p. 6).

Here is a child whose need of love and counselling screams from the page as surely as Nicola's post-mortal chatter smiles. What happened to make him realized 'that adults were not all they seemed to be?' How devastating those words 'They talked of love and preached of love. But did not act so lovingly'. Who were they? What did they do? What has become of the wounded boy? Hell may not be found in geography but Markus seems to have found it in and around himself. 'Hell is other people' wrote Sartre (1944); 11 seems very young for such a discovery.

William Blake depicts the blighting of young life in *The Schoolboy*:

O! father and mother, if buds are nipp'd
And blossoms blown away,
And if the tender buds are stripp'd
Of their joy in the springing day,
By sorrow and care's dismay,

How shall the summer arise in joy,
Or the summer fruits appear?
Or how shall we gather what griefs destroy,
Or bless the mellowing year,
When the blasts of winter appear? (Blake, 1927/1757–1827, p. 67).

As with all the other children in this chapter, if a counsellor meeting Markus Natten had ignored his spiritual needs, how could the boy have been helped towards health?

Markus Natten's poem is not wholly about loss and betrayal. His third verse reflects independence and self-responsibility but in the context of the whole poem, it is a lonely bravery. I am sure that anyone involved in counselling has met that sense of lost childhood, whether in someone still chronologically a child (Markus was only 12 when the poem was published) or physically adult. What did the loss of Hell and Heaven mean to him? What did those non-geographic concepts symbolize?

Abuse of the spirit

A child who suffers abuse, in whatever form, is surely in Hell. The disturbing cases of ritual abuse focus particularly on abuse inflicted on body, mind and emotions by adults involving varieties of ceremony. I shall not discuss this but I am clear that whatever really *happens* there is evil in the intentional attitudes and behaviour of some, perhaps many, people towards children. If children are involved in religious practices known as 'satanic' they are put at the very least at risk of spiritual confusion, at worst of perversion. (For a detailed discussion see Tate, 1991.)

For many people holding strong belief in the traditions and practice of one Christian denomination, the tradition and practice of another denomination may be regarded as un-holy. A loved and loving relation of my own was for some years seen as unkind by his devoted sister because, since she did not belong to his strict evangelical group, he feared that she could not be eligible to accompany him to heaven; his unkindness derived from his urgent need to convert and save her.

Not only through devotion to not-god may children suffer spiritual abuse. In the name of religion, children can be taught to hate as well as love, to seek revenge as well as reconciliation. As excursion back to the life of Edmund Gosse in the mid-nineteenth century evokes vividly the response of an 8 year old boy to an assault on his spirit, well meant but leading to disillusionment when 'my Father and I, though the fact was long successfully concealed from him and even from myself, walked in opposite hemispheres of the soul, with "the thick o' the world between us"' (Gosse, 1949/1907, p. 207).

But at 8:

> It was my Father's plan from the first to keep me entirely ignorant of the poetry of the High Church, which deeply offended his Calvinism; he thought that religious truth could be sucked in, like mother's milk, from hymns which were godly and sound, and yet correctly versified; and I was...carefully trained in this direction from an early date. But my spirit had rebelled against some of these hymns...A secret hostility to this particular form of effusion was already, at the age of seven, beginning to define itself in my brain, side by side with an unctuous infantile conformity (p. 63).

Studying together the Epistle to the Hebrews,

> My Father's religious teaching to me was almost exclusively doctrinal. He did not observe the value of negative education, that is to say, of leaving Nature alone to fill up the gaps which it is her design to deal with at a later and riper date. He did not, even, satisfy himself with those moral injunctions which should form the basis of infantile discipline. He was in a tremendous hurry to push on my spiritual growth, and he fed me with theological meat which it was impossible for me to digest.

Some glimmer of a suspicion that he was sailing on the wrong tack must, I should suppose, have broken in upon him when we had reached the eighth and ninth chapters of Hebrews, where, addressing readers who had been brought up under the Jewish dispensation and had the formalities of the Law of Moses in their very blood, the apostle battles with their dangerous conservatism. It is a very noble piece of spiritual casuistry, but it is signally unfitted for the comprehension of a child.

Suddenly by my flushing up with anger and saying, 'O how I do hate that Law', my father perceived, and paused in amazement to perceive, that I took the Law to be a person of malignant temper from whose cruel bondage, and from whose intolerable tyranny and unfairness, some excellent person was crying out to be delivered. I wished to hit the Law with my fist, for being so mean and unreasonable (pp. 64–5) (re-paragraphed).

There was occasional relaxation from this Epistle and 'not always was my flesh being made to creep by having it insisted that "almost all things are by the Law purged with blood, and without blood is no remission of sin". In our lighter moods, we turned to the "Book of Revelation", and chased the phantom of Popery through its fuliginous pages' (p. 65).

The elegance and distance in time of Gosse's autobiography may defuse the intolerance of his father's beliefs. But the editor of the Penguin edition comments, 'That Edmund Gosse remained sane is extraordinary' in the light of what 'The elder Gosse...did to the mind of a brilliant and sensitive son' (back cover).

Gosse could triumph 'over the stifling dogmas of his childhood', overcoming abuse. But what of the child victims of religious intolerance today? Fionnuala Bogues (16) was attending the Dominican Convent school in Belfast when she wrote this poem (1979):

The Lost Years
They talk, the older folks.
And paint a rosy past.
Oh! I am tired of hearing
How things were in Belfast.

They talk and tell me stories
Of the good times they once had
And the more they talk about it all
The more it makes me sad.

For I cannot remember
A childhood free from strife,
To me the bombs and bullets
Are just a way of life.

So I have just one question
To ask our violent men.
What about my wasted childhood.
Can you bring that back again?
(Bogues, 1979, pp. 84–5).

By what right do we abuse children in the name of *any* god?

If Edmund Gosse was spiritually abused by too much enforced time in an oppressively furnished fourth room, many more children are abused by neglect, the key to that room being denied by the uninterested adult. In this is my main concern. I have tried in this chapter to show some of the ways in which children demonstrate interest in and experience of the life of the spirit. I know that readers may interpret away any of these illustrations and there is no science, no research, no statistics, no organized data to prove the existence of the spirit.

If the adult – parent, residential carer, counsellor, nurse, field-worker – regards life as containing only three or even two rooms, the fourth room of the child may be unvisited until it too appears to disappear. In my own experience, the room of the spirit cannot be closed down, sold off or demolished: but it needs to be regarded as integral to the whole house, and aired.

I am writing not about the virtue of attending church or synagogue, mosque or temple but about the need of the healthy child to be nourished in spirit as well as body. Caring adults should recognize emotional deprivation but do they perceive the effects of spiritual neglect?

The spiritual rights of the child

In 1978 the Church of England Children's Society published a paper on the spiritual rights of the child 'as a contribution for discussion during the International Year of the Child, 1979' (Bradford, 1978, p. 1).

The five rights identified elaborate Principle 2 of the United Nations Declaration of the Rights of the Child, 1959:

> The child shall enjoy special protection, and shall be given
> opportunities and facilities, by law and by other means, to enable him
> to develop physically, mentally, morally, *spiritually* and socially in a
> healthy and normal manner and in conditions of freedom and dignity.
> In the enactment of laws for this purpose the best interests of the child
> shall be the paramount consideration (p. 3).

The rights of spiritual initiation, expression, choice, support and protection are summarized thus:

> 1. A child or young person has a right to the best of the spiritual
>   heritage of the culture into which he or she is born.

2....to express his or her spiritual belief in private and/or public without discrimination.

3....to deepen, doubt or alter the spiritual commitment into which he or she is being nurtured or educated.

4....to schooling, family life and other institutional support which shall be complementary to his or her spiritual development.

5. A child, especially in his or her early life, has the right to such protection from spiritual damage and handicap as is reasonable and appropriate (pp. 12–13).

All five rights are elaborated in the discussion paper but I wish here to concentrate on the last one. On this John Bradford includes four points of which the first is particularly relevant to the present chapter:

It is possible for a child or young person to suffer spiritual damage for example by cruelty or violence, from the atmosphere of extreme ugliness or squalor and acute deprivation, or through the influence of the impact of damaging ideas (not excluding the possibility of these being through the mass media) which decry the principle of humanity and respect for the inherent dignity of the human person. Such experiences may result in what might be called 'spiritual handicap' (p. 11).

(A condensed version of this paper is included in Harris and Hyland, 1979, pp. 32–9).

In a later paper, Bradford discusses four cardinal spiritual rights, *wonder, joy, inner serenity* and *relatedness with others,* noting that many children live in conditions which are inimical to enjoyment of these rights (Bradford, 1989, p. 42).

The faith of the counsellors

I did not expect to find much material for the present chapter; my problem in the end has been selection. Friends and associates from various parts of my life have shown great interest in the subject and have provided me with ideas and literature. Moreover a number of the counsellors to whose accounts I have referred elsewhere, comment on the life of the spirit.

For the counsellor this may be an area of doubt and difficulty. Extracts in this section are chosen to illustrate the experience and viewpoints of adult counsellors whose particular beliefs may be very different one from another but who share the conviction that the spirit, however defined, must be involved in any human interaction. (The title of this section was used by Paul Halmos for an influential book in 1965.) David G. Benner (1991) (a professor of psychology in Canada) expresses this in terms of psychotherapy which he regards as 'in essence a psychospiritual process...Therapy, which may appear to ignore the spiritual aspects of functioning, does not in fact do so. Rather it always shapes and supports some type of spirituality' (p. 11). I find no distinction here between 'psychotherapy' and my liberal use of 'counselling'.

Benner continues that

> People do not have to be talking about God to be expressing spiritual problems. Struggles associated with the search for meaning to life, or with the quest for identity, wholeness or even fulfilment – all contain spiritual elements. But so do problems that seem on the surface to be even more purely psychological, such as depression, marital conflicts, and anxiety. Once we begin to understand the diverse ways in which people mask their experiences of and responses to the spiritual quest, we can become more discerning of the presence of the spiritual in the problems presented in psychotherapy (p. 11).

He warns against using the therapeutic relationship 'primarily for spiritual direction' (p. 13) and offers guidance:

> One way in which we can give permission for raising spiritual matters is to enquire about the person's religious history. It is amazing how often therapists who routinely enquire about developmental, medical, interpersonal, academic and vocational aspects of history never once ask about religious upbringing and current functioning. Clearly, religion has replaced sex as the taboo of our age.
>
> We can open the door to spiritual considerations in therapy in an even more direct way by telling those with whom we work, in an early session, that we view the spiritual as inseparable from the psychological. My experience with such a statement has been that people respond to it readily by raising matters which they judge to be spiritual in nature. Sometimes these may be explicitly religious, at other times more broadly existential, and sometimes esoterically mystical. Always, however, it has served to enrich and broaden the therapy (p. 12).

He emphasizes that 'The focus should always be on the person's experience' (p. 12) which can be recognized by

> listening to the story behind the story. Therapists easily listen only to symptoms and complaints while missing the meanings of these symptoms to the sufferers. Sometimes the spiritual quest is the main theme of the story presented to us in therapy, as for example by the person who presents with existential questions about the meaning and purpose of life.
>
> Usually, however, the psychological themes are dominant and the spiritual must be discerned as the underlying story. This underlying story is the vital one and if we do not understand it we fail to understand the meaning of the other person's experience. If we learn to listen with an ear attuned to spirituality we are able to discern the underlying story and we have a context for making sense of the

person's life. We can then help him know his own story and this may be one of the most important benefits of a course of psychotherapy (Benner, 1991, p. 11) (re-paragraphed).

With regard to pastoral counselling, Foskett and Jacobs (1989) identify three stories 'the client's, the counsellor's, and the religious story' all of which 'Have to find their place and interaction with each other for the ultimate benefit of client, counsellor, and the religious vision' (p. 262).

They add:

> Given the essential body-mind-spirit unity which underlies theological ideas about the nature of persons, current thinking about spirituality, and the concerns of holistic healing, there are grounds for a greater *rapprochement* between these different activities.
>
> There is evidence that those who guide the spiritual development of others are finding parallels between their own discipline and Jungian thought in particular. As pastoral counsellors begin to realise this interest, it is to be hoped that they will in turn explore the benefits of closer links with spirituality (p. 263) (re-paragraphed).

The reference to Jung leads easily to Allan's (1988) work on *Jungian Counseling in Schools and Clinics* and in particular Hillman's *Foreword* describing the Platonic and Romantic theory that the child's soul descends from an archetypal world, endowed with Wordsworthian clouds of glory. 'A being close to angels, it arrives knowing everything essential...its collective unconscious is replete with primordial awareness' (Hillman, 1988, p. xiii).

Hillman proposes that 'The soul's difficulties with its descent into the world show up in counseling as', for example, adjustment disorders or autism, anti-social behaviour and 'other ills catalogued in our textbooks of abnormal psychology'. The counsellor is 'a midwife to the psyche' (pp. xiii–xiv).

He offers an interesting perspective on the use of music, art and literature in counselling children, considering that beauty is an essential guide and that the arts should 'take primary place in the teaching and counseling of children'. He finds that 'psychology, education and social studies seem completely unconscious of its importance in moving the soul deeply, so that beauty has become the Great Repressed in the training of professional counselors'. The arts are also important in helping to connect the child's 'first world of imagination' and 'the actual world into which it descends'. (p. xiv)

At about this point in writing, 'Tim' (5) explored my garden. Still small enough to be dwarfed by the fennel lining tiny brick paths across the flower border, he led 'Eva' (2) past lavender and feverfew onto the clover-full lawn. 'It's like Narnia' he said, the magic land reached through the wardrobe (Lewis 1950). In the summer garden the worlds of imagination and actuality, of myth and the living moment were fused, as wonderful for me as for him. We had not met before and exchanged few words. But as I showed him the physical path, he offered me a new way into my own garden. His spirit was very much awake.

To Eva the fennel and flowers formed a high hedge separating her from her parents and safety. Perhaps for her the garden belonged not to Aslan the holy lion but to Jardis the wicked witch.

Tim attends Sunday school and was happily wearing a badge with a religious theme on his T-shirt. If he should need the services of a counsellor, would Narnia be the setting?

Hillman is concerned about the effects on adults of the ideas of developmental psychology which, he suggests, propose a distortion of life, in which 'a person is caused by history' so that 'childhood has been declared the source of all disaffected behavior' and is regarded as 'basically miserable'. He finds that much counselling focuses on unhappiness, seeking memories of abuse and shame instead of beauty and joy (pp. xv–xvi).

He sees young people seeking through 'sensuous transcendence in sounds, speeds and sex for an altered state of mind' to counteract life as 'soulless and joyless' and recollecting unconsciously 'something else, something more, which they would find again, sometimes by suicide' (p. xvi). To counter this depressing view of the deterioration of childhood, Hillman writes of 'a *vision* of children' (p. xvi). Without vision, of what use is action?

Vision is involved too in Chaplin's (1989) advice that

> Counsellors need to be able to tune in to the level on which they can 'see' the human soul in front of them. The soul is neither male nor female. It is simply their being, their essence, their point of connection with all the other energies that dance around the universe. To be able to connect with and love this aspect of the person, whatever is brought to the counselling sessions in terms of problems, is a vital part of the healing process (pp. 229–30).

Following no single religious model or myth, Chaplin (1988a) demonstrates the essential integration of ancient symbols and images 'in our own psychological cycles, to help us understand ourselves better and to grow and change' without the 'need to "worship" those ancient images.' She describes 'the snake and its symbol, the spiral' which 'seemed to represent the rhythms of the eternal life-force itself as it curls and spirals through the universe' appearing 'as the primordial form of nature herself as she emerges out of chaos'. The model 'has been used for thousands of years, even after the rise of patriarchal religions, as a symbol of the journey of the soul' and still representing 'the power of human nature to transform itself, to change and to grow between opposites'. Chaplin refers to 'the concept of interconnected opposites' including the Jungian model' (pp. 11, 12, 17).

The religious/philosophical base to which Petrůska Clarkson (1989) refers throughout her introduction to Gestalt counselling is Zen. Every chapter is headed with a short parable from the Zen tradition which requires the total involvement of the whole person in every moment (see, for example, Reps, 1971).

She emphasizes that

> A cornerstone of the Gestalt approach is its emphasis on the wholeness of the person in the counselling relationship, not just the intrapsychic or merely the interpersonal dimension. In the counselling process different aspects of a person may be emphasised at different times. These will probably include intrapsychic behavioural, physiological, affective, cognitive and spiritual aspects of the client's life.
>
> The counsellor, however, will always have as a guiding principle the integration of all the many facets of that unique individual. The acceptance and celebration of this multi-dimensional wholeness is also considered a possible goal for the client. This is not 'imposed upon' the client, but is based on a belief that human beings want to experience their wholeness, individual richness and integration of diversity (Clarkson, 1989, p. 17) (re-paragraphed).

Spiritual does not imply attachment to any one, (or any at all), religious group. For example, Gestalt child psychologist 'Joel' was interested in Taoism.

For social worker Reba Bhaduri (1990) the literature and traditions of India provide a base and perspective, gaining much insight from the *Bhagavad Gita*:

> Faith is the central theme in *Gita*. Ideologies of progress and a belief in the quality of life underpin social work as well. *Gita* takes faith a step further. Faith in inner spirit and the eternity of humankind helps the worker to draw strength to reach out into the lives of people who may have lost all sense of meaning (p. 16).

When Saleem (11) died in hospital and Siraj (6) 'manifested similar symptoms of liver disease', Reba Bhaduri 'felt overwhelmed by the daunting tasks of helping the family cope with Saleem's death, preparing them for the second son's illness and motivating them to accept help from the hospital for Siraj. I anticipated that the parents would be angry with hospital staff for not being able to save the elder son' (p. 16).

Visiting the family, she

> felt my training did not prepare me enough to face such eventualities of life. The parents wouldn't even hear of taking Siraj to the hospital where their son was 'killed'. The doctors were asking anxiously how much time I needed to persuade the parents. It was running out for Siraj. The sooner doctors could start the treatment, the better the chances for his survival (p. 16).

Now the law of *Karma* became 'most helpful', bringing 'a sense of containment rather than control' so that 'Workers need not be preoccupied by the anxiety of whether they are going to "solve the grief"' (p. 16). In her 1991 paper Bhaduri develops this: 'The desire to be seen as helpful is heavily related to egoism' (p. 15).

Reba Bhaduri regarded her duty as 'in being there containing the situation' although sometimes 'tempted to take over' and feeling 'anxious, thinking I should "do" something' (1990 p. 16).

The need for containment lasted for a long time but 'After months of my regular visits, the parents agreed to take Siraj to the hospital for a check-up. The transcultural approach kept me going. I could resist the doctor's pressure of hurrying the situation' (p. 16).

Juan Mascaro (1962) whose translation of the *Bhagavad Gita* I sought after reading this article, writes of *Karma*:

> All life is action, but every little finite action should be a surrender to the Infinite, even as breathing in seems to be the receiving of the gift of life, and the breathing out a surrender into the infinite Life. Every little work in life, however humble, can become an act of creation and therefore a means of salvation, because in all true creation we reconcile the finite with the Infinite, hence the joy of creation. When vision is pure and when creation is pure there is always joy (p. 32).

As with counselling and all work of helping, (all work) we are constantly under such pressure to *do*, to be cost *effective*, to hurry: yet the *being* is of most account.

One sentence of Reba Bhaduri in particular (referring to 'research of bereavement') has given me much to think about: 'social workers with an unwavering faith in a spiritual life seemed more at peace while working with clients experiencing life's tragic eventualities' (Bhaduri, 1991, p. 15). She does not say 'workers who attend church regularly' or 'observant Jews' or 'Muslims who have completed the Haj'. The important words are *faith, spiritual life* and *peace*.

It is not always easy for people in the role of counsellor to think in the language of religion or even to integrate private and counselling selves, perhaps keeping *spirit, faith*, and so on for family and church. Brian Thorne (a counsellor of the Rogers/Person-centered tradition of great experience) found himself suddenly able enter a new dimension of communication:

> It is clear to me now that the decision to trust the feeling of interrelatedness was the first step towards a willingness on my part to acknowledge my spiritual experience of reality and to capitalise on the many hours spent in prayer and worship. It was as if previously I had refused to draw on this whole area of awareness in the conduct of my therapeutic work. In my zeal not to proselytise it was as if I had deliberately deprived myself of some of my most precious resources in the task of relating to my clients. Once I had opened myself to myself,

however, I was capable of experiencing the communion of souls, or the membership one of another, which is a fundamental given of the spiritual life.

I still remain convinced, of course, that it is iniquitous to use a counselling relationship for evangelising. I am no more likely now to talk of God or religion in my counselling work than I was in earlier years.

The difference is that I now attempt to be fully present to my clients, and this means that I do not leave my eternal soul outside the door. Interestingly enough, it has also meant that I am far less disembodied in my behaviour than I used to be. My acknowledgement of my spiritual self has led to the discovery that I can indeed use my whole self, including my physicality, through touching. When I am bold enough to use my own uniqueness it seems that I am enabled to offer a tenderness which moves the soul while embracing (sometimes literally) the body.

I admit to considerable embarrassment as I write these words, and yet I have come to believe that the person-centred counsellor has a particular obligation to be honest about all his or her attributes and to be prepared to acknowledge their potential contribution to the counselling relationship.

For my own part I know that if I had continued to deny the therapeutic significance of some of the deepest parts of my own being I might never have tumbled to the fact that I have a capacity to express tenderness both physically and spiritually. Perhaps it is in the offering of this gift that I give the highest expression to my unique self, and that is why it always feels a risky undertaking where vulnerability and strength are present in equal measure. Nowadays, however, I know that I usually have no option but to take the risk (Mearns and Thorne, 1988, p. 37) (re-paragraphed).

At all points the counsellor must 'remain true to himself' and 'cannot divorce himself from his own social, moral, and spiritual values. He has a right to them. But he must know himself, recognise his values and be honest about them' (Munro, Manthei and Small, 1989, p. 6).

In 1964 Noel Timms (author and then-lecturer in social work and a Roman Catholic) proposed that

It is perhaps in religious belief and practice that a person's values are most clearly apparent and yet the relationship between religion and casework has received little attention in social work...A new appraisal of the subject seems opportune and the questions now requiring answers could perhaps be based on an assumption of the importance and significance of religious belief and feeling in human beings; this is not something to be hidden away or dissolved by analysis (Timms, 1964, p. 62: in Moran, 1968, p. 94).

Nearly 30 years later such an appraisal is still, it seems, awaited, although confessing to visiting the spiritual room may be beginning to provoke less embarrassment than in recent decades. While laudable to attend, for example, church, it has in many circles been in poor taste to discuss religion (except between consenting adults).

After completing the first draft of the present chapter, I was privileged to visit John Elvidge, retired from service in the field of residential child care including as a Home Office Inspector. Preparation for this visit had stimulated me to order my material and I thought I should be clear about what I hoped to learn. During a few minutes silence and privacy before I set out, I realized that I needed no questions, no direction, for the importance of the visit was in meeting the person. I should learn by listening, by being with him, not by mentally completing a questionnaire.

Soon after my arrival, unexpected visitors came in. But not visitors at all: 'This is our oldest son' said John. Both the young man and his wife had lived in the residential unit in the care of John and his wife Margaret. Becoming 18, leaving care, did not sever the links of love and true relationship: 'When we part, recognize that I still exist, I'm still available – I've got a telephone by my bed – remember you can come back at any time.' Children who need care and/or counselling have lost in greater or less measure, the security essential from birth and before. Counsellor and carer must demonstrate that 'there are safe people in the world'.

This safety is a product of the unconditional love and availability of the caring adult, of helping the hurt child to feel *good enough* and develop that inner security without which no amount of economic embrace can be of any value.

For John Elvidge, there is no distinction between faith and work and as part of his belief and experience, he transmits powerfully the total integration of spirit, mind and body, of vulnerable children in young adult bodies, of the need always to show love. God is a real, active presence. A child may talk to a counsellor about feelings and fears but 'tomorrow you may be very sorry you told me. It's all right, it's safe – there were three of us here and He's invisible.' The invisible spirit holds the child and counsellor in safety together.

I have written above about abuse of the spirit. John Elvidge adds a dimension, for if the child's image of God as Father is based on the experience of a vindictive, angry, punishing Earthly father, the image of God may reflect such attributes and the growing child be cowed or frightened away. Full and true development of the spirit, the whole person, is impossible if the image of God is warped.

This idea is developed in the *Taking Care* pack (compiled by an inter-church group with the National Children's Bureau; Armstrong, 1991):

Abuse, particularly sexual abuse, raises questions about the nature of the 'family', about what a 'father' is and what the parental role is. Religious language often depends on a positive view of the value and trust placed in fathers, parents and family. For an abused child (or an adult with childhood experience of abuse) there may be real difficulties in this type of theological language which may have an effect on the child's spiritual life. For the abused child confusion may arise between the language in which the spiritual life is presented and the experience such language aims to represent (p. 18).

Feelings aroused by abuse

may not be fully recognised but may lead to strong reactions against traditional language which represents God as Father or as protector, or indeed to the range of 'family language' used in religious thinking (p. 18).

Robert Holman adds the need for forgiveness, noticing 'that children who have been abused (as well as the abusers) want to receive a sense of forgiveness'.

Writing this chapter has been a journey of discovery and I am reluctant to put away the pile of material still beside me. But this *is* a chapter, not a book.

Central to the theory and practice of counselling children is helping freedom of access to all four rooms – spiritual, mental, emotional and physical, unbarring doors so often blocked by prejudice, nonsense, fear and apathy. Only the child can hold the key but the counsellor may help the unlocking.

The more we respond to the ALL the more personal we become (Teilhard de Chardin, in Moran, 1968, p. 17).

Summary

Using the image of the person as **a house with four rooms, physical, emotional, mental and spiritual**, this chapter has explored the spiritual room of childhood, a room which is often unvisited and ignored in training and practice of people caring for and/or counselling children. Insights from work with children in hospital lead to discussion of ideas about spiritual development, language and **questions of belief**. First person accounts of **religious experience in childhood** reveal much **depth** and **variety**, **joy** and **despair**. Attention to the fourth room may be of particular importance when a child is dying but the spirit is always in need of **recognition and nurture**, thriving in both **solitude** and **community**.

Although the spirit itself cannot be harmed, spiritual development can be impaired by **neglect and abuse**. Children have **spiritual rights** and **problems** and the **spiritual story** is a crucial element of counselling. The **spiritual/religious beliefs of counsellors** are integral to the whole person engaged in any **therapeutic relationship**. 'The more we respond to the ALL the more personal we become', living fully in our four rooms.

Link

Engagement in religious ceremony is a way of expressing aspects of spiritual belief. The four chapters which follow explore self-expression and communication through the arts (as recommended by Hillman, 1988), including **art** and **music**. Expression of spiritual belief and religious practice centre on narrative, on stories of the worshipped gods and of the individuals who worship them. Chapter 7 presents some ways of understanding and telling such stories through **myth** inviting the reader to 'Enter These Enchanted Tales'.

References and Further Reading

Allan, J. (1988). *Inscapes of the Child's World. Jungian Counseling in Schools and Clinics*. Spring Publications, Dallas, Texas.

Allen, C. (1991). The inner light. *The Nursing Standard*, 5, (20), 52–3.

Armstrong, H. (1991). *Taking Care: a Church Response to Children, Adults and Abuse*. National Children's Bureau, London.

Arthur, C. J. (1985). Religion, identity and maturity: some remarks on Erikson's 'Eight Ages of Man' and religious education. *British Journal of Religious Education*, 7, (2), 48–53.

Benner, D. G. (1991). *Counselling as a Spiritual Process: Lingdale Paper 17*. Clinical Theology Association, Oxford.

Berryman, J. W. (1985). Children's spirituality and religious language. *British Journal of Religious Education*, 7, (3), 120–7.

Bhaduri, R. (1990). Counselling with Karma. *Social Work Today*, 21, (33), 16.

Bhaduri, R. (1991). A sense of Karma. *Social Work Today*, 22, (33), 14–15.

Blake, W. (1927/1757–1827). The schoolboy. In *Selected Poems of William Blake*. Oxford University Press, London, pp. 66–7.

Bogues, F. (1979). The lost years. In ed. P. Muldoon below.

Boulding, E. (1989). *One Small Plot of Heaven: Reflections on Family Life by a Quaker Sociologist*. Pendle Hill Publications, Wallingford, Pennsylvania.

Bradford, J. (1978). *The Spiritual Rights of the Child: a Discussion Paper*. Church of England Children's Society, London. See also Harris and Hyland.

Bradford, J. (1989). Spiritual rights and religious rights in the 1989 convention. *Children Worldwide*. International Catholic Child Bureau, 16, (3), 41–3.

Cairns, K. (1990). Climate for learning. *Social Work Today*, 21, (38), 26–7.

Chaplin, J. (1988). *Feminist Counselling in Action*. Sage, London.

Chaplin, J. (1989). Counselling and gender. In Dryden, Charles-Edwards and Woolfe, pp. 223–36.

Chardin, Teilhard de. In Moran (1968).

Clarkson, P. (1989). *Gestalt Counselling in Action*. Sage, London.

Department of Health. (1989). *Children Act*, HMSO.

Dryden, W., Charles-Edwards, D. and Woolfe, R. (eds). (1989). *Handbook of Counselling in Britain*. Tavistock, London.

Elkind, D. (1971). The development of religious understanding in children and adolescents. In Strommen, pp. 677–8. Quoted in Greer.

Erikson, E. (1965). Eight ages of man. In *Childhood and Society*. Penguin, Harmondsworth, pp. 239–66.

Fawell, R. (1987). *Courage to Grow*. Quaker Home Service, London.

Ferguson, S. (1987). *A Guard Within*. Collins, London.

Foskett, J. and Jacobs, M. (1989). Pastoral counselling. In Dryden, Charles-Edwards and Woolfe (eds) (1989), pp. 252–65.

Fowler, J. W. (1981). *Stages of Faith: the psychology of human development and the quest for meaning*. Harper and Row, San Francisco, Calif.

Gillman, H. (1988). *A Minority of One: a Journey with Friends. Swarthmore Lecture*. Quaker Home Service, London.

Godden, R. (1989). *A House with Four Rooms: autobiography; Vol. 2*. Macmillan, London.

Goldman, R. (1964). *Religious Thinking from Childhood to Adolescence*. Routledge and Kegan Paul, London. Quoted in Greer (1980), p. 24.

Goodall, J. (1984). Foreword to English Edition. In Shelley, et al., pp. 10–11.

Gosse, E. (1949/1907). *Father and Son: a Study of Two Temperaments*. Penguin, Harmondsworth.

Goulding, E. I. (1984). Foreword. In Shelley, et al., pp. 6–9.

Greer, J. E. (1980). Stages in the development of religious thinking. *British Journal of Religious Education*, 3, (1), 24–8.

Halmos, P. (1965). *The Faith of the Counsellors*. Constable, London.

Hamilton, H. A. (1963). *The Religious Needs of Children in Care*. National Children's Home; London.

Harris, D. and Hyland, J. (eds) (1979). *Rights in Residence: a Review of the Residential Care Association*. RCA publications; London.

Hillman, J. (1988). Foreword. In Allan (1988), pp. xiii–xx.

Houghton, C. J. (1976). On the day when mother died. In Mirror Group Newspapers (1976), pp. 104–106.

Hull, J. M. (1991). *God-talk with Young Children: Notes for Parents and Teachers*. Birmingham Papers in Religious Education No. 2. The University of Birmingham and the Christian Education Movement 1990.

James, W. (1902). *The Varieties of Religious Experience*. Random House, New York. Quoted in Berryman, p. 58.

Jersild, A. T. (1963). *The Psychology of Adolescence*. New York. In Arthur, p. 5.

Kibble, D., Parker, S. and Price, C. (1981). The age of uncertainty: religious belief amongst adolescents. *British Journal of Religious Education*, 4, (1), 31–5.

Klingberg, G. (Boulding, E. (trans)) (1959). A study of religious experience in children from 9–13 years of age. *Religious Education*, 54, (May, 211–16. Quoted in Boulding (1989).

Klink, J. L. (Wilson, R. A. (trans.)) (1972). *Your Child and Religion*. SCM, London. (Wilson, R. A. (trans.)) *[Kind en Geloof.]* Uitgeverij Ambo n. v. Bilthoven. N. L.

Lewis, C. S. (1950). *The Lion, the Witch and the Wardrobe*. Geoffrey Bles, London.

McDowell, N. (1976). God and Heaven. In Mirror Group Newspapers p. 36.

Mascaro, J. (trans.). (1962). *The Bhagavad Gita*. Penguin, Harmondsworth.

Mearns, D. and Thorne, B. (1988). *Person-Centred Counselling in Action*. Sage, London.

Mirror Group Newspapers. (1976). *Children as Writers, 3*. Heinemann, London.

Moran, M. (1968). *Pastoral Counselling for the Deviant Girl*. Geoffrey Chapman, London.

Muldoon, P. (ed.) (1979). *The Scrake of Dawn: Poems by Young People from Northern Ireland*. Blackstaff Press/The Arts Council of Northern Ireland, Belfast.

Munro, A., Manthei, B, and Small, J. (1989). *Counselling: the Skills of Problem-Solving*. Routledge, London.

Natten, M. (1979). Childhood. In Smith p. 6.

Penman, C. (1986). The Quaker idea. In Quaker Social Responsibility and Education, pp. 76–7.

Prys-Williams, B. (1986). Jerusalem again! lovely. In Quaker Social Responsibility and Education, pp. 68–9.

Quaker Social Responsibility and Education. (1986). *Learners All: Quaker Experiences of Education*. Quaker Home Service. London.

Reps, P. (Senzaki, N. (trans)) (1971/57). *Zen Flesh, Zen Bones*. Penguin, Harmondsworth.

Robinson, E. (ed) (1978). *Living the Question*. The Religious Experience Research Unit, Manchester College, Oxford.

Rodgers, J. L. (1984). Is God a teddy bear? images of God. In Shelley, pp. 91–9.

Rutter, M. (1983). *A Measure of Our Values. Swarthmore Lecture*. Quaker Home Service, London.

Sartre, J. (1944). *Huis Clos*.

Schuurman, S. (1987). *Tristan: Physically and Mentally Handicapped – Socially and Spiritually Gifted*. George Ronald, Oxford.

Shelley, J. A. and others (1984/82). *Spiritual Needs of Children*. Scripture Union, London.

Smith, W. H. (1979). *W. H. Smith Literary Competition 1978: Children as Writers: 20th Year*. Heinemann, London.

Stevenson, Y. (1976). *The Hot-house Plant: an Autobiography of a Young Girl*. Elek/Pemberton. London.

Strommen. M. P. (ed.) (1980) *Research on Religious Development*. Hawthorn. Summary of Elkind; see Greer.

Tate, T. (1991). *Children for the Devil: Ritual Abuse and Satanic Crime*. Methuen, London.

Timms, N. (1964). *Social Casework: Principles and Practice*. Routledge and Kegan Paul, London. In Moran.

Westerhoff J. H., III (1980). *Bringing up Children in the Christian Faith*. Winston Press. Minnesota.

Winterson, J. (1985). *Oranges are not the Only Fruit*. Pandora Press, London.

7   Enter these enchanted tales

Enter these enchanted woods
You who dare (Meredith, 1912).

Myth and counselling

Once upon a time they all lived happily ever after. But not before a
sufficiency of trials and triumphs, achievements and come-uppances.
The human is addicted to narrative. Every event, however cosmically
immense or insignificant, may be confined, elaborated, communicated
as a story.

Physicist Stephen Hawking achieved fame by rendering *A Brief
History of Time* (1988) not only accessible to lay people but even
continuing to sell in hardback some years after publication. Explanations of space and time by physicists are as much retellings of myth as
any tale of Eden or Prometheus.

The earliest stories explore and 'explain' precisely the same matter
as every other story spoken, written, enacted throughout every
culture, every history; namely the insoluble mysteries of creation and
reproduction, 'the *single* poetic theme of Life and Death...the
question of what survives of the beloved' (Alun Lewis, in Graves,
1961, p. 21).

The idea of myth may seem distant from a social workers' office,
hospital ward or family centre playroom. Yet both workers and
children are involved with myth in many ways. Patricia Goldacre
(1980), teacher and educational therapist, found myth, legends and
fairy stories to be 'rich sources of universal experience of life and
death' and 'a comfort because they expressed and made familiar
feelings which were new to the children' (p. 39).

Every individual lives according to a personal myth, the idea of
myself, the story *I* am enacting. For example, I am relieved that I have
not been 'written' by Iris Murdoch (whose novels are deeply rooted in
myth, and whose characters suffer greatly); I favour J. B. Priestley
(because, also intricately connected with mythic foundations, he
allows abundance of life in every dimension to people over 25, indeed
over 60, who do not need to be heroic or beautiful or clever, who make
mistakes or suffer uncomfortable emotions and blunder about).

Myth is a great deal more than the production of one author. It is the
basis of values and beliefs which are expressed within the work of that

author, whether intentionally fictional or intended to be an exposition of 'fact'.

Myths are not changeless but are, rather, transformed by the retellings and actions which they have also influenced. *Black Orpheus*, sets that ageless story in a brilliant Caribbean carnival; *Orphée* by Jean Cocteau, creates a surreal black and white French nightmare, full of motorbikes and mirrors. Both films are completely themselves: to understand them does not require knowledge of the Orpheus myth. But each brings deep and new insight to the myth: the central truth is intact but illuminated.

Mircea Eliade (1975) notes that 'the diseases and crises of modern societies are rightly attributable to the absence of a mythology appropriate to them', suggesting that Jung in *Modern Man in Search of a Soul* (1933) 'implied that the modern world – in crisis ever since its profound break with Christianity – is in quest of a new myth, which alone could enable it to draw upon fresh spiritual resources and renew its creative powers' (Eliade, 1975, p. 25).

It is impossible not to live in the context of some myth, because myth is human-made and constantly reinforced or recreated. Let me refer again to my younger self as illustration. Brought up within a low church Anglican tradition, I learnt about strict morality and service within the context of inexplicable psalms and transcendentally beautiful language. I understood about suffering (the wrath of my father if I woke him on my way to early service) and duty (attending church weekly whatever the difficulties).

I also loved the stories of the Greek and Norse pantheons but was taught that these were fables while the Judeo/Christian story was fact. I believed in the myth espoused by *Woman* magazine – a girl protected her virginity against all odds; a man did not respect a former virgin, even one he had himself deflowered; a girl should be married by the age of 25 lest she become too old to attract *him*; a girl should be married; a girl should not have children out of wedlock (maximum shame); a girl should have children as young as possible (an elderly *prima gravida* risked a mentally handicapped baby – more shame).

In addition, according to the myth of the Prodigal Student, girls are bad news economically because they get married; girls who go to university should work for at least two years after graduation to 'earn' their grants: girls cannot expect to have careers because they will stay home to look after children. And so on. How, in all that confusion of superstition, expectation, prejudice and nonsense could a young person develop a sense of sense, of values? Yet we did, and must have been informed by deeper, stronger, more life-connected myths too.

Even in the 1970s, I blush to own, I was teaching the false myth which proposed that women in 'middle age' are finished, liable to depression, have nothing to do when the children have grown up and left home and do not need them anymore and husband may be seeking younger females for sexual purposes – owing to the inevitable decline in interest in such activities of the menopausal woman drifting irrevocably towards dotage.

'Adolescents' fared no better. A woman of my aquaintance told her estranged husband that he might expect their daughter on his doorstep when 13 as she would then become difficult.

These were some of the false myths of the 1950s–70s in middle-class England. What are they today? And what for children and young people in other countries and cultures?

In May 1991, Vlado (13) in Yugoslavian Macedonia sang me his favourite song, standing in the shadow of a ruined hilltop fortress: Yugoslavia was on the verge of civil war (already one Macedonian dead in fighting between Serbia and Croatia) and had lacked a president for weeks; the Republic of Macedonia felt threatened with imminent annexation by any one of four other countries – Albania, Bulgaria, Greece, Serbia. His school history book contained a succession of photographs and stories of great (and dead) patriots. With his friend Aleksandar he told many tales of famous fighters from many centuries, speaking with vigour and immediacy; his passion was for military aircraft.

His song expresses both his personal and his national myth, telling of a hero who calls to the patriots from his 'black and dark gaol', wishing that his mother knew so that she might dig his grave, out of the sun, with the inscription 'here lies one who has suffered, here lies Aleksandar of Ohrid'. The chorus follows every verse, sung twice: 'I swear on my dearest, I swear on my best, I swear on the cross and the candle'.

For these children, the interesting and pervasive literature is about the real threat to their country, the songs which express the call to arms, their post-school future in the army. They are surrounded too by an old and rich culture in the country which saw not only the birth of Cyrillic script, the Macedonian language and, probably the first European university (at Ohrid), but also knew Philip and his greater son, Aleksandar, the world conqueror.

Bookshops display the *Greek Myths* of Robert Graves in Cyrillic. But next door the kiosks are dripping with explicit girly magazines (no discreet top shelves here) and the cinema shows the worst American sex and horror. Despite this, for Vlado and Aleksandar there is no place for cartoon turtles, no mind-softening cacaphony masquerading as music; their myth is clear and deeply felt, reflecting the reality of life for them in their country. The tales of patriots are no romantic fictions; these boys may in time themselves take guns to the hills, fighting for freedom.

Myth is usually expressed in the form of a story which explains and/ or celebrates some fundamental phenomena of life and death and which may then attract some development of human behaviour focused on the event and/or participants. For example, the story of the death, burial and resurrection of Jesus may be seen as demonstrating the sowing of seeds into the earth and, after a period of apparent 'death' and inactivity, their germination and emergence into the light, transformed into the new life, essential for the continuing life of all animals. This story in turn becomes the focus for a succession of ceremonies including special words, music and actions.

Our personal, individual stories are enacted within the context of the myths of our local culture, family and the wider environment – political organization, dominant religious system.

Shirley Lowry (1982) identifies one common myth component with relevance to all ages and most cultures – the hero. She proposes a four-part pattern in which 'The hero enters the unknown, struggles with what lies there, finds something of value – a boon, and returns with that boon to his community' (p. 90).

The hero may not always attain parts three and four and is often 'so transformed by his experience in the forest that home is lost to him forever'. Lowry suggests that the possibility of loss and risk are essential to prevent the pattern becoming 'mere cliché' (p. 90).

She proposes that this 'pattern forms the basis of many stories, reflecting and enlarging the real experience of our own lives'. Continually meeting 'the unexpected, with its risks and opportunities…we either turn back or discover something that helps us to deal with it and with similar challenges in the future. Small wonder that we want stories about people under stress and that we follow their responses so eagerly. These stories help us to create and interpret our own lives' (p. 90).

Kathryn Allen Rabuzzi (1988) suggests that 'The hero who succeeds in his mythic quest achieves a very special gift' which, 'No matter what it is called in myth and fairy tale' is 'in a psychological context…"selfhood"'. Discussing the difficulty of defining 'self', she comments that 'For most individuals, self, one's own personal "I", is the starting point for any thought or action' (Rabuzzi, 1988, pp. 37, 38).

Bruno Bettelheim (1976) suggests that myth 'carries spiritual force; and the divine is present and is experienced in the form of superhuman heroes who make constant demands on mere mortals'. However much 'we, the mortals, may strive to be like these heroes, we will remain always and obviously inferior to them' (p. 26).

Myths (together with fairy stories and legends) can be interpreted to suit whatever model of life one chooses. Mythical heroes are 'of obviously super human dimensions, helping listening children to avoid being overpowered by any suggestion that they should copy the actions and achievements [often somewhat bloodsoaked] of the hero' (p. 4).

Taking a Freudian stance, he suggests that myths 'project an ideal personality acting on the basis of supergo demands, while fairy tales depict an ego integration which allows for appropriate satisfaction of id desires', accounting for the 'pervasive pessimism of myths and the essential optimism of fairy tales' (p. 41).

Rabuzzi (1989), presenting *A Mythic Analysis of Motherhood*, finds that 'To the extent that achievement of selfhood is construed as the result of successful heroic questing, it is implicitly masculine. Consequently, selfhood, as traditionally defined, is extremely difficult for women [and girls] to understand, much less experience for ourselves' (p. 37).

Bettelheim quotes Eliade who describes such stories as 'models for human behaviour [that] by that very fact, give meaning and value to life', suggesting that they 'were derived from, or give symbolic expression to, initiation rites or other *rites de passage* – such as metaphoric death of an old, inadequate self in order to be reborn on a higher plane of existence'. Eliade 'feels that this is why these tales meet a strongly felt need and are carriers of such deep meaning' (Bettelheim, 1976, p. 35; see Eliade, 1958, 1963).

There can be no doubt of the depth of meaning, but with myth – with legend, with fairy story, as with case study, court report, life-story book – the question must always be put *through whose eyes are people and their experiences seen?* Within my own small sample, Bettelheim and Eliade, Lowry and Rabuzzi offer commentaries of scholarly elegance and enchantment. But it behoves the reader to take care – interpretations of myths are themselves myths and using other myths in 'evidence' – these authors, for example, employ psychoanalytic theory, feminism, anthropology, religion.

My interpretation of a myth is made in the light of my own experience, the context of all the other stories of my life.

Use of the story of a Theban king to illuminate the experience of the Viennese bourgeoisie and, thence, to the dignity of defining a whole 'complex' depended on the interpretation by a white Austrian Jewish adult male of the nineteenth century, of a series of events dramatized within an explicitly religious context and theatrical convention, by an Hellenic adult male of the sixth century BC.

Oedipus Rex is amenable to many meanings and interpretations. In 1991, for example, director Jatinder Verma stressed the paradox of Oedipus' view of himself as a foreigner, an outsider, (reflecting the experience of the director and cast, as brown skinned residents in a predominantly white skinned community) when he comes to Thebes, becomes king and marries the dowager queen. Hubris (essential component of Greek tragedy) may, according to Jatinder Verma, be seen as Oedipus' pride in what he, as outsider, brings to his new city.

Conflict and catastrophe are found in the appalling revelation that, far from being a foreigner and therefore safely *not* who he is, Oedipus is a native of Thebes, son of the queen, his wife.

How would a black woman interpret this myth? A child might focus less on father-slaying and mother-wedding than on the behaviour of a family which could intend to murder an inconvenient son. Baby Oedipus had been exposed because of a prophecy that he would kill his father. Staking out on a mountain side had deformed his feet (hence his name) until he was rescued and fostered via a social working shepherd who placed him with the local royal family in Corinth. Here is a powerful reason for telling children the truth, however unpalatable, for Oedipus, believing the Corinthian king to be his birth-father, flees to avoid killing him, and meets and kills Laius, his unsuspected and unsuspecting father. What *does* an abused child 'owe' abusing and abandoning parents? (Sophocles, 1947).

A girl might wonder about the plight of Antigone and her siblings, children of an incestuous union. What is to happen to them when their mother commits suicide and their father, maimed and shamed, leaves them unprotected?

We know the answer. Antigone accompanies her self-blinded father over the world to Colonnus where he finds an expiating death. She will die horribly, walled up by her uncle in punishment for burying her brother's body during the civil war consequent on Oedipus' acts. The guilty father may suffer but the harm he causes his children will not cease with his death (Sophocles, 1947).

The use of myth as illustration or model must be approached with the greatest care.

With this in mind Bettelheim writes about the responses of individual children to fairy tales. He advises parents to be alert to indications that the child has become particularly interested in some story, which may in itself attract the parents' enthusiasm, and to be ready to move, with the child, to the next choice, so that the child may retain the belief that inner thoughts are private, until deliberately revealed. He advises that parents should not let children know if they have some idea of the reason for their interest. Even though the adult interpretation may be accepted, it is essential that 'We grow, we find meaning in life, and security in ourselves by having understood and solved personal problems on our own, not by having them explained to us by others' (pp. 18,19).

The myths, legends and fairy stories with which children born and/or educated in the British Isles become familiar derive from many sources, particularly Middle Eastern (notably the writings collected into the Christian *Old Testament* and Jewish *Torah*). Scandinavian-Teutonic (the great Norse Sagas) and the Classical periods of southern Europe (notably of Greece and Rome).

Additionally (and increasingly, I hope), the mythologies of the Indian subcontinent, Africa and the Caribbean Islands inform and enliven us. (Even in my junior schooldays in the 1940s I was acquainted with greedy spider Ananse and irrepressible monkey god Hanuman).

An exciting aspect of such stories is the similarity of theme found across cultural boundaries. Themes have trans-temporal vigour too.

Lowry discusses the story of Telemachus, son of Odysseus absent from home for 20 years (10 at the Trojan Wars, 10 touring the Aegean on the way back to Ithaca). The story represents Telemachus both as an individual and 'as the symbol of everybody's perilous, difficult move from childhood to adulthood' (p. 109).

Lacking satisfactory male role models, Telemachus 'has not taken up the tasks that would have helped him become an adult. He cannot afford the only actions by which he might grow up' (p. 110). Brought up by the brave and faithful Penelope and heir to his father, he is at risk from the many suitors who pester his mother to declare Odysseus dead and remarry. Penelope maintains the precarious balance (unpicking nightly the tapestry which, when finished, will signal her assent). He is the only child in a one-parent family, controlled by his responsibilities towards and emotions about his magnificently managing mother and ambiguously absent father.

Lowry suggests that 'Telemachus doubts himself so much and sees such a distance between himself and Odysseus that he wonders if he really can be the hero's son'. If his father should eventually return, may he find Telemachus unworthy? (p. 110).

Lowry links this with 'the modern child's silent question, "Am I adopted?" and his nightmares in which his father shouts contemptuously, "You're no son of mine"'. Homer's narration mirrors 'an experience that most readers, whenever and wherever they live, have shared. All parents seem to young children extraordinarily gifted, and the transition into effective adulthood seems impossible' (p. 110).

Telemachus is not left in limbo. An extremely exalted counsellor, the goddess Athena, helps him to 'toughen his assertiveness and confidence without tipping his mother into disaster or getting Telemachus himself murdered'. A particularly positive experience is the comment by Helen (formerly of Troy) that he resembles Odysseus, a comment which 'would nourish the boy's spirit: A total stranger sees Odysseus in me; so I *am* my father's son!' (pp. 110–11).

It is crucial that the apparently repressed, even frozen, boy is given the opportunity to make 'important decisions' and to find 'that impressive people respond to him with respect' (p. 111) (see Homer).

A story such as this helps recognition, at both heroic and essentially human levels, of the experience and needs of children and young people. Indeed, Telemachus might well add his name to that of Oedipus as the sponsor of a complex. Born in 1941, the child of a soldier whose post-war employment kept him from residence at home until about 1948, I know all too well the problems of a Telemacha. That myth, though focusing on masculine development within a male dominated society, has much to say to females and to today (whenever 'today' may be).

Old tales, new tellings

Notable in writing directed towards young people is *The Owl Service* (Garner, 1967), a telling in modern dress and with teenage protagonists of an ancient Welsh myth (from the *Mabinogion*, for example, Jones and Jones, (trans.), 1949).

Whatever the revelations about human relationships (including jealousy and possessiveness) this story is predominantly about ways of seeing. The owl service is a collection of crockery, patterned with what Roger sees as 'An abstract design in green round the edge, touched up with a bit of rough gilding'. But, says Alison, 'It's an owl's head'. Roger agrees, reluctantly – 'I suppose it is, if you want it to be. Three leafy heads with this kind of abstract flowery business in between each one' (Garner, 1967, p. 17).

Alison's interpretation and Roger's compliance will have dramatic, almost fatal effect on three young people and their parents. Only at the end of the book when Alison is nearly destroyed by the owl-power she has released, does a new way of seeing restore peace. The leafy heads and flowery business reveal a benign pattern. Roger *sees*: 'Not owls. Flowers...Gentle. Flowers...What made you think those plates could be anything else? Why didn't you cut the pattern into flowers right at the start, you silly girl?' (pp. 156–7).

Alison's way of seeing affects the interpretation of other people and releases the negative, destructive elements encapsulated in the old story. Roger can save only when he becomes free of someone else's interpretation and of his own investment and emotion. He must become himself.

The owl/flower design is reminiscent of the Gestalt double pictures of, for example, profiles forming and containing a vase. It is not possible to 'see' both faces and vase simultaneously – one form will always dominate.

Don Quixote asks Sancho Panza, 'Do you see what I see?' to which the bewildered but honest squire replies, 'I never know.' He learns the richness of understanding the interweaving of appearance and reality: which is which? and who would dare to say? The destruction of Don Quixote's books nearly kills him (Meyer and Martin, 1991: after Cervantes, 1605/15).

Our lives are influenced all the time by the stories which reflect and affect the cultural and psychic context. Linda Hoy (1987) explores a universal theme through two stories – one a play about an old man, the other the tale of a teenage girl. In course of taking several parts in rehearsals for Shakespeare's *King Lear* Rebecca gains understanding of her own and other peoples's responses to, in particular, the death of her mother. Anger with her father is eventually changed to reconciliation.

Fortunately Rebecca and her father need not experience the ultimate fate of Cordelia and Lear who are murdered. Rather, on

Rebecca's return from France, following in Cordelia's footsteps (but on a school trip, not as queen) she finds her father waiting, unexpectedly, on the quay and feels that 'Somehow it seemed to me that in the end we were going to pull through...to survive. I could imagine us both struggling a bit and tottering about and making fools of ourselves sometimes but, in my mind's eye, I could see us getting there in the end. Winning' (Hoy, 1987, p. 154).

This book draws on many stories; not only *King Lear* but also, for example, current ideas of normal responses to bereavement and mourning, the constitution of families, the expected behaviour of young people in general and of girls in particular. It draws, in fact, on a myth – the myth of adolescence.

Linda Hoy (1989) writes that 'What I'm really interested in...are crisis points – the events that change people's lives. A lot of these crises happen during adolescence' (Hoy, 1989, p. 3).

Both myths and fairy stories present pictures of young people no longer physically children but not yet entered into full adult powers. They are usually virgin and their stories frequently focus on the experiences – often in the form of ordeals – essential to attainment of mature sexuality, marriage and parenthood. Girls may have to wait at home or in durance vile, while boys achieve manhood by dragon slaying or treasure seeking.

Bettelheim considers that 'Even when a girl is depicted as turning inward in her struggle to become herself, and a boy as aggressively dealing with the external world, these two *together* symbolize the two ways in which one has to attain selfhood: through learning to understand and master the inner as well as the outer world' (p. 226).

My own experience is that, as a girl in the 1940s–50s I did regard stories about pretty passive princesses as appertaining to me and, without much confidence, (lacking, I thought, two of these qualifications) supposed that life would begin only when an active exciting hedge slashing prince would go to the trouble of rescuing me.

George Macdonald's view (1965/1863) accords with mine. His prince becomes separated from 'his retinue in a great forest. These forests are very useful in delivering Princes from their courtiers, like a sieve that keeps back the bran. Then the Princes get away to follow their fortunes. In this they have the advantage of the Princesses, who are forced to marry before they have had a bit of fun. I wish our Princesses got lost in a forest sometimes' (Macdonald, 1965/1863, p. 158).

But the maturing girl too may find an active role. Angela Carter (1990) in a worldwide collection of fairy tales, introduces a large cast of lively heroines, full of initiative and useful assertiveness. In Hans Andersen's *The Snow Queen* Kay, the boy, must passively wait for rescue by his friend Gerda.

Kay is abducted and imprisoned in her palace by the Snow Queen. If he can arrange blocks of ice bearing letters into the word 'Eternity' the

Queen promises that 'you shall be your own master, and I will give you the whole world and a pair of new skates'. But the blocks are in the lake of Reason and Kay cannot make out the word: 'stiff and silent he sat there, you would have thought that he was frozen' (Anderson, n/d, p. 343).

Meanwhile Gerda seeks Kay through many adventures, helped by humans and animals. A child at the beginning of her journey, she is seduced by an old woman who erases her memory and keeps her in a flower garden. 'I have often wished for a dear little girl like you', says the witch and combs Gerda's hair until the child forgets herself and her mission. The 'witch' is surely a mother who wishes to keep her daughter in a pretty unmotivated childhood, to delay the development of puberty, preventing the girl from pursuing her male friend and sexual relationship (p. 331).

This episode is reminiscent of the three encounters of the disguised stepmother with *Snow White*. First, as a pedlar, she tries to suffocate the girl with a stay-lace, (inhibiting normal development). Next, as an old woman, perhaps a grandmother figure, she combs the girl's hair with a poisoned comb (the act of motherly caring perverted by the poison of jealousy). Last, as a wholesome looking farmer's wife she offers Snow White the red, poisoned half of an apple, herself eating the green, innocent part to 'prove' its safety. As a result of all three encounters, Snow White falls at once into a deathlike sleep. The mother has delayed her maturation and the spell of prolonged childhood can be broken only by awakening into the next stage of her life, relationship with a sexual partner (Grimm, n/d, pp. 202–206).

Gerda's memory returns when she sees a rose (often a symbol of female genitalia and probably red, the colour of menstrual blood, like the red, poisoned half of the apple which causes Snow White's long sleep) (Anderson, n/d, p. 333). The developing girl leaves the cosy anxiety-free garden and walks over the world, suffering and growing, protected by her very vulnerability, her innocence and her mission.

Her adventures include encounter with a robber girl with whom she shares a bed. 'The robber girl put one arm round Gerda's neck and clutched the knife in her other hand. She snored so loudly that Gerda could not close her eyes all night, she did not feel sure whether she was to live or die' (p. 339).

Soon the robber girl helps Gerda to escape. Gerda has experienced adolescent homosexuality, shown in this incident as both loving and dangerous. She moves on towards heterosexual maturity, aided by the robber girl's gift of a fast running reindeer, which may be seen as the enhanced energy accompanying fulfilling and developing sexuality. The homosexual episode has been energizing. Gerda's whole personality is developing.

This episode may also, and not to exclude the above idea, be seen as representing the recognition by 'good' Gerda of other parts of herself, other possibilities. 'Naughty' Gerda releases the developing girl, helps her escape from the mother who would imprison her (the robber queen) – but empowers good Gerda with more energy, the newly invigorated girl pursuing, enriched, her journey.

We are all, as child and adult, constantly influenced by the stories we read and are told. We choose, for example, the newspaper whose stories best agree with our own views and which consequently confirm those views. Many people read newspapers not for 'truth' but for stories (and pictures) yet, knowing that, regard whichever version of an event they prefer as 'fact'.

Children (and adults) respond to and act out the stories to which they are all the time subject, becoming the people the stories tell them to become. Many television and cinema advertisements, for example, tell stories. I recently saw several directed towards young people. In one, a picture story, a boy with keys connected to a concealed battery taped to his hands, opens and drinks a can of liquid and dramatic electric sparks fly. Striding into a café he sees a pretty girl with another boy. Kissing her, while holding her head between his charged hands, the electrical excitement is conveyed as both inter- and extra-personal sparks fly.

Lesson: boys and girls in early to mid-teens expect to be interested in exciting sexual contact. Boys are good looking but shy. Girls are pretty and can be passively won from other boys, Boys with the aid of magic metals (and love potions?) gain confidence, sexual potency and girls.

I suspect that a similar ad-plot with roles reversed would be shown as funny.

I remember that I consciously believed the stories I was told in childhood about Jesus, a kind man who, said the vicar, with God (an additional and approving father) was especially helpful to children. We sang 'There's a Friend for little children above the bright blue sky'. As I grew through my teens, I began to worry about ceasing to qualify for heavenly special care.

Elizabeth Taylor (1988) represents the way in which the inescapable environment of story pervades and influences life through Oliver (about 10) who 'did not merely read books. He snuffed them up, took breaths of them into his lungs, filled his eyes with the sight of print and his head with the sound of words. The paper had personality' (p. 14).

He learns about love, going 'every Saturday morning to the Public Library to look at a picture of Lorna Doone' (Blackmore, 1869). If the book is not there he returns home 'wondering who had borrowed her, in what kind of house she found herself that weekend' (pp. 14–15). He learns about manly behaviour from Alan Breck (*Kidnapped*, Stevenson, 1886).

Oliver's life is intertwined with the people in his books. 'To discover how Oliver's life was lived, it was necessary,...to have an extensive knowledge of literature'. His impartial diet includes 'comic papers, encyclopedias, Eleanor's pamphlets on whatever interested her at the moment, the labels on breakfast cereals and cod liver oil, Conan Doyle and Charlotte Brontë' (p. 15).

To discover how anyone's life is lived it is necessary to have an extensive knowledge of the 'literature' on which that life is based and through which it is formed, a literature inevitably demonstrating models of behaviour and the expectations of other people.

Myths of childhood

At any moment, in any society and any group within society, there thrives a myth of childhood, the accumulation of stories and ideas leading to expectations. My own view of the myth current in the society within which I have grown up, work and live is that children are regarded as status objects and possessions. People will go to any lengths to obtain them, yet we learn constantly of abuses which in other situations would be described as torture: how weak the word 'abuse' has become.

Children may be expected to be expensive, demanding and difficult; they must be protected (although methods of protection may in themselves be harmful) and controlled (although methods of control may be punitive and lead to increased alienation from 'good behaviour'); they must be educated, (although 'training' and 'testing' are more productive); they must obtain employment (which is scarce, but failure to obtain employment indicates inadequacy).

Children are entitled to Easter without Good Friday and Christmas without Advent. In a 'take the waiting out of wanting' society they hear stories about princes and princesses successfully surviving ordeals which may entail a good deal of both wanting and waiting. How do children reconcile such confused messages?

Adolescence is portrayed as a land of the instant satisfaction of wants disguised as needs. What happens to the values, the essential health and growth of the young person, celebration of the exciting journey through the forest? Although today's Prince/ss may fly over the forest on a cheap package trip, there are abundant possibilities for adventure of both body and spirit. Is the will to adventure present?

The literature on which our children's lives are based is extensive; but is it a wise and loving library? acts of parliament, models of psychology, governmental and agency guidelines, court and school reports, advertisements, magazines, and so on.

It is difficult to describe a myth until it can be seen at some distance of time and/or space. And regarding former times and/or other cultures is an activity whose main constituent must be humility. In a talk broadcast on BBC Radio 3 (1990) Jeffrey Richards (Professor of Cultural History at Lancaster University) demonstrated the impropriety of accepting theory without query.

Discussing *Childhood in the Middle Ages* he reviews the assessment by Philippe Ariès (1973) that 'the Middle Ages had no concept of childhood' based, for example, on 'the high rate of child abandonment and infanticide and on the absence of that sentimentalisation of childhood that was a feature of later ages'. (Richards refers particularly to Shahar, *Childhood in the Middle Ages*, 1990, and Boswell, *The Kindness of Strangers* 1991).

One argument of Ariès depended on 'the absence of visual representations of children' since 'when they appeared it was as miniature adults'. But Richards draws our attention to what we already know, really, for there 'were many pictures of children as children in the Middle Ages' including and especially all those of Jesus as a baby. The image of Mary 'as a loving mother cherishing her child was widely popular and was clearly internalised by the population as something to be emulated'.

Didactic writers depicted children 'as a source of joy and a trust from God' and 'child rearing manuals and educational tracts abounded'.

Richards comments that 'The sentimentalisation of children can be seen in the popularity of paintings of the Massacre of the Innocents and the Flight of the Holy Family to Egypt' and 'in the developing cult from the twelfth century onwards of the Baby Jesus as an all-knowing, all-seeing, wonder working child and in the first appearance from the thirteenth century of the Christmas manger with the ox and donkey attending the Christ child'.

Processions of children were organized 'by communities in times of crisis in the confident hope that their angelic innocence would turn away the wrath of heaven'.

Richards presents two contemporary comments on children. Bartholomaeus Anglicus, a medical writer, in 1230, describes small boys:

> Living without thought of care, loving only to play, fearing no danger more than being beaten with a rod, always hungry and hence disposed to various infirmities from being overfed, wanting everything they see, quick to laughter and as quick to tears, resisting their mothers' efforts to wash and comb them, and no sooner clean than dirty again.

During the Black Death, Lapo Mazzei of Tuscany wrote:

> I have seen my two sons, the older and the middle one, die in my arms, in a few hours. God knows what my hopes were for the first, who was already a companion to me and a father with me to the others, and what progress he had made...and at the same time in one bed were Antonia sick unto death and the other boy who died. Think how my heart broke, seeing the little ones suffer and their mother not well or strong, and hearing the words of the older one. And to think of three dead.

Richards notes that 'These are not the words of someone who has emotionally distanced himself from his children and they are not atypical.'

He shows too how 'writers of medieval didactic, medical and theological works' distinguished 'various developmental stages in childhood' including '*infantia* (or infancy)', (birth–7), '*pueritia* (childhood)', (7–12), and '*adolescentia* (adolescence)', (12 or 14–adulthood).

Richards considers that 'what is striking about...people in the Middle Ages is not how different they were from us in the modern world but how similar' with 'a clear concept of childhood. They understood children, child care and child psychology', expecting 'children to go through a process of growth and development...much as they do today'. Both 'The closeknit affectionate family, cherishing its children' and 'the neglectful and selfish family, brutalising its children, existed side by side much as they do now'.

Particularly striking is his final comment. 'If anything it is the present rather than the Middle Ages which is eroding childhood, forcing children before their time to become mini-adults and depriving them of a vital stage of their development'.

This essay demonstrates an extensive knowledge of literature indeed, and also of graphic art. More, it shows the ability to realize children within their own society with a perspective and without that patronizing neo-classic attitude with which former times and distant cultures are still so often regarded and with which children are still commonly regarded in present-day Britain.

We suffer still from dissection, post-Platonic dualism (good/evil; dark/light; mind/body) and over-specialization (science/arts; industry/creativity). Richards refers to historians who 'may rely too exclusively on their inevitable fragmenting and partial sources'. People training for and practising in medicine, nursing, psychology, social work, teaching, learn about children and childhood from fact-and function-focused textbooks.

Here is an illustration. *Attending to Children* (Crompton, 1990) was, at the publisher's suggestion, intended to appeal to a mixed readership, crossing, in both material and relevance, disciplinary boundaries. In a university bookshop I noted some copies on the social work shelves. Shyly, I approached the counter and explained that my book would be equally relevant on the nursing display: it even quoted books currently on that shelf. Might a copy be placed there? My vision of doubled sales was dispelled. No no. To try it in another part of the shop would be unthinkable without other authority. The subtitle *Direct Work with Children in Social and Health Care* could not move the assistant. One book: one shelf.

Blue cheese, golden thumbnail

This is the way we see children too – in compartments and, often, without imagination. Yet the stories which inform us from our earliest youth require and provide for response by the whole person. David Pithers, quoted in an article about interviewing allegedly abused children, complains that social workers 'do not know anything about the developing relationship between fantasy and reality in a child's minds' (in Rickford, 1991, p. 26). My present concern is that we pay too little respect to the importance of fantasy – of image, metaphor and story – and the constant interweaving of 'fantasy' and 'reality' in all life and all communication.

A Quaker mother, for example, felt that police questioning her about her mode of religious worship (during an enquiry into alleged ritual abuse) responded as to something extremely strange. Yet, to a Quaker, nothing could be more ordinary than to sit in a silent circle for an hour.

Roman Catholics believe that the bread and wine they ingest during celebration of the Mass become the actual body and blood of Jesus; a high and holy mystery to a believer but a dangerous fantasy to many whose realities – and fantasies – depend on different stories, or even only a different version of the same story.

James Thurber's lovely story *Many Moons* (1965) demonstrates the dilemma. Princess Lenore (10, going on 11) becomes ill and prescribes for herself the moon which the King her father agrees to obtain. The Lord High Chamberlain (power/civil service) refuses the commission. The moon 'is 35,000 miles away and it is bigger than the room the Princess lies in. Furthermore, it is made of molten copper. I cannot get the moon for you. Blue poodles, yes, the moon, no' (p 179).

The Royal Wizard (magic/science) does no better: 'It is 150,000 miles away, and it is made of green cheese, and it is twice as big as this palace.'

The Royal Mathematician (academia) declines on the grounds that 'The moon is 300,000 miles away...It is round and flat like a coin, only it is made of asbestos, and it is half the size of this kingdom. Furthermore, it is pasted on the sky. Nobody can get the moon.'

Then comes the Court Jester (art/imagination) and the King says, 'Every time I ask anybody for the moon, it gets larger and farther away. There is nothing you can do for me except play on your lute'. The Jester asks about the estimates of size and distance, plays quietly on his lute, and concludes that, 'They are all wise men,...and so they must all be right. If they are all right, then the moon must be just as large and as far away as each person thinks it is.'

Only the Jester, lowest in the court hierarchy, thinks to ask the opinion of the Princess regarding distance and size of the moon. 'It is just a little smaller than my thumbnail,...for when I hold my thumbnail up to the moon, it just covers it' and 'not as high as the big trees outside my window...for sometimes it gets caught in the top branches.' To the third question, 'What is the moon made of, she answers, 'It's made of gold, of course, silly' (pp. 181–3).

A tiny golden moon is made for Lenore to wear on a golden chain and she recovers at once.

This leads to another problem, to which, again, the grand men propose elaborate solutions; but the Jester asks the child, 'how can the moon be shining in the sky when it is hanging on a golden chain around your neck?' The Princess looks at him and laughs. 'That is easy, silly...When I lose a tooth, a new one grows in its place...I guess it is the same way with everything' (pp. 187–8).

The child cannot be helped by the knowledge or planning which should serve the responsible parent. The King does not even bother to ask the Jester for help; what could he suggest when the great ones have failed? Only the Jester, whose profession is not much admired, is not too proud to approach the child herself, asking (low status) instead of telling (high status, authority).

More, the Jester listens to the answers and translates these into sensible, effective action (the necklace). When the great men panic about a further possible crisis – (a possibility which they entirely manufacture themselves) – the Jester calmly refers to the child herself. Again asking a brave and simple question, he learns that there is, ('That is easy, silly') no problem. The child is brimful of common sense. The adults suffer anxiety, rage and gloom and waste immense resources of energy, simply because they fail to do the simple things.

This story includes within exquisitely written and humorous fantasy, several sound lessons about both assumptions and communication, surely packing far more impact than any number of sober texts counselling 'listen'.

All formulations of human life and behaviour use story, whether to express and explain the creation of the world, death, the cycle of seasons, sexuality or parent/child relationships.

Myth in helping

Approaches to counselling are themselves stories, even would-be myths, and are brimful of the stories and myths from which they derive.

Two books I found useful compendia included, early in descriptions of each model, sections on 'Historical Context' and 'The image of the person' (Dryden, 1984) or a brief, lively biography of the founder (for example, Carl Rogers) and a summary of his (always *his*) view of 'The Nature of People' (Thompson and Rudolph, 1988).

To understand the approach it is essential to understand its genesis and to recognize its components. I particularly enjoyed learning that

Albert Ellis worked with his brother finding trousers to match unwornout suit jackets and was later personnel officer in a fancy goods firm (Thompson and Rudolph, 1988, p. 103).

I felt that the founder of Rational Emotive Therapy was a real person and that the essentially practical, even rather instrumental model, had one base in the no-nonsense world of commerce. The story of the revived suits appealed to my parsimony or, at least, hatred of waste. Here, then, might be a model of human behaviour which sought to make the best of apparently bad jobs. 'So your pants are worn through? Not the end of the world. Not even the end of the suit!'

Ellis was influenced by not only the contemporary (twentieth-century) myth of the USA – based on an ethic of work and struggle for achievement – but also the myths supporting psychoanalytic theory, with roots in ancient Mediterranean culture and flowerings in both drama (Oedipus) and philosophy (Epictetus). The story of Albert Ellis the individual is unique, comprising the interweaving of the myriad stories which formed his environment.

Many counsellors are deeply aware of the power of myth and fairy tale in helping, and not only children. Writing on gender-focused, work Jocelyn Chaplin (1989) notes that

> Counsellors can use images of famous or ordinary, modern or ancient
> people to help clients recognize the range of characteristics available
> to their gender. Many Jungian-influenced counsellors today use myths
> and stories of ancient goddesses such as Artemis and Innana to help
> women empower themselves both by re-enactiong the myths,
> visualizing or painting them, or simply learning about times when the
> female gender had more respect and value than it does today (p. 234).

She records that 'pre-historical mythology has provided many insights which have been integrated into the development of feminist counselling' (p. 10).

On pastoral counselling, Foskett and Jacobs (1989) consider that 'The therapeutic model which dominated pastoral care and counselling from the 1960s to the 1980s has been complemented by a new model which aims to integrate the theological and the therapeutic, through the common element of story and narrative'. They identify three stories, 'the client's, the counsellor's, and the religious story – and in pastoral counselling all three have to find their place and interaction with each other for the ultimate benefit of client, counsellor, and the religious vision (Foskett and Lyall, 1988: ch. 5: Bohler, 1987)' (Foskett and Jacobs, 1989, p. 262).

Reba Bhaduri (1990) found 'The perspective offered by the *Bhagavad Gita*' invaluable in work with a dying child and bereaved family:

> Dialogue between Arjuna and Krishna is the main theme. Faced with
> pain and and conflict Arjuna tells Krishna, 'My mind is overwhelmed

with pain. I do not see what could remove this grief of mine that is utterly drying up my senses'. Social workers are often faced with a similar story from a bereaved client. (p. 16).

A focus of the opening section of the *Bhagavad Gita* is the nature of life and death, and the continuation of the Spirit (see Mascaro, 1962).

In her work with Julia, 'a frozen child', psychotherapist Margaret Hunter (1987) describes how the stories of Snow White and Pinochio aided and informed Julia's progress from ice, through wood, to becoming a 'real girl at last' and discovering love (p. 30).

One picture is of Julia looking 'into the mirror chanting: "Mirror mirror on the wall, who is the fairest of them all? Me of course!" She vividly enacted the cruel stepmother's attempt to kill Snow White but told me: "Only in this story she doesn't win and Snow White is queen" (p. 28).

Snow White is one of the most powerful and universally known stories. What discussion of stepmothering could refrain from reference to the wicked witch queen? In 1979 I wrote an article whose clear intention was to de-stigmatize stepmothers (Crompton, 1979). To my horror the article appeared with an enormous and hideous illustration – the wicked stepmother to end all wicked stepmothers. The depicted stereotype was more powerful than my rational and well-informed discussion – a point of some importance when introducing or responding to stories within counselling interactions. My personal view of *Snow White* is that it is powerful propaganda against stepmothers; a child telling or enacting the story within a counselling context might be responding to the stepmother and offering a totally new and personal interpretation.

Bettelheim (1976) describes a child finding his own interpretation of a story, very different from the orthodox idea and helpful to himself. A boy (5) asked for *Rapunzel* to be read to him, on learning that his grandmother, who undertook much of his care, was to enter hospital. For this boy at this time, this story indicated that there was 'security from all dangers in which the substitute mother kept the child' and 'That one's own body can provide a lifeline. [Rapunzel's hair-ladder] reassured him that, if necessary, he would similarly find in his own body the source of his security' (p. 17).

Here the child found help through a story which he had chosen, being read to him by, I assume, an adult whom he had chosen and with whom he felt safe and comfortable, perhaps even the grandmother herself. He took from the story what he wished and needed.

Bibliotherapy

Use of literary material in such a way is sometimes termed *bibliotherapy*, defined by Margaret Marshall (1981) (writing for librarians) as 'a programme of planned and guided reading as treatment for emotional and other problems...the aim is to give support, and to modify behaviour' (p. 101). Within the context of counselling children, I would see the use of literature as more flexible in that, for example, only one book might be offered to – or by – the child, rather than a whole programme.

It is crucial that the counsellor should read whatever is either suggested to, or brought to the counsellor by, the child. I read *The Bell Jar* (1963), Sylvia Plath's wracking description of a girl's depression and suicide attempts, because one of my tutees anxiously asked me what I thought of the book. Although not my choice of bedside reading I felt bound to discover what the book was about but had to take care not to assume that my responses could mirror hers or that she identified with the central character – or with Sylvia Plath.

Herein is a central danger of *bibliotherapy;* 'identification' is used, to my mind, inaccurately. Margaret Marshall (1975) considers that teenage readers may experience 'the identification which is largely unconscious but which involves empathy and the recognition of similarities' with fictional characters and events. 'Following identification, the reader is likely to respond emotionally, perhaps anticipating the characters' reactions...'(p. 42).

I would feel happier with the idea that readers recognize similarities between themselves and aspects of fictional characters. It is, after all, said that the real-life people on whom authors base characters frequently fail to recognize their own portraits, even claiming kinship with completely different characters.

It is even dangerous to use the concept of identification in this context, for the stories in novels (and biographies) must come to some tidy conclusion – good overcoming evil, victims rescued, suffering leading to success or destruction. In real life it is rarely possible to write 'The End' and close the book. However happy and fulfilled life may be, none of us could write with total accuracy 'And we all lived happily ever after'.

The primary use of printed literature, in particular, is in offering a neutral, non-judging, non-pressing and enjoyable medium for the child to discover a range of ways of being. For example, a girl whose mother had died and whose relationship with her father was unsatisfactory would not identify with Rebecca (Hoy, 1987). However apparently close their circumstances, they would not identical.

Rebecca learns about feelings and relationships through involvement in drama workshops preparing for a production of *King Lear*. Acting the part of Cordelia or Goneril or Lear himself, she does not 'identify' with their characters but she recognizes, through her response to their behaviour and the feelings she attributes to them, her own so far unexpressed feelings. So a reader, meeting Rebecca in print, may learn, through the described experience of another person, something about her own feelings and some possible ways of managing.

As with the little boy who found comfort from *Rapunzel*, the characters with most importance for readers may not be those most obviously 'like' them. Deliberately to offer a book because it contains an apparently similar person may misfire, even be dangerous, for who knows what another reader perceives: only listen to the opinions of adult professionals for proof that one critic's genius is another critic's idiot. And remember the owl/flower ambiguity of *The Owl Service* and Princess Lenore's tiny golden moon.

I recently listened to a dramatized version of *Don Quixote* (Meyer and Martin, Radio 3, 1991) and felt, for the first time, interested in that story. Another listener, frustrated and irate, complained to a radio programme that the original book had been ruined by irresponsible adaptation. For me, the Don came alive; for her, he was murdered.

I deeply believe in the power and virtue of reading. One of the many benefits of using the pre-written word in counselling children is the opportunity to 'meet' other people on safe ground, at the reader's own pace and without the danger of interaction.

Linda Hoy's Rebecca may or may not speak to the condition of the reader but one may try out being Rebecca in private, as Rebecca tries out being Goneril and Lear and Cordelia in the security of the drama workshop. Whatever the response, the reader need not share it with anyone else.

Shapiro (1984) considers that 'A major part of bibliotherapy is the interactive discussion with parents, teachers, or other children that these stories stimulate (p. 51). In one-to-one counselling the essential element would be the availability and willingness of the adult to discuss but not to impose. (For further discussion of bibliotherapy, see Crompton, 1980).

Missy Red Riding Hood

It may be that the great power of fairy story and myth lies in that aspect of universality which is the shared knowledge of the story. Last year's heroes were Teenage Mutant Ninja Turtles. Will they be remembered by the time this book is published? But who has not heard of Jack and the Beanstalk, Cinderella and Snow White in some form? In April 1991, Heffer's children's catalogue *Choices* was devoted to 'Sound of Reading' – eight printed A4 sheets listing cassettes, including a number devoted to the tales of heroes ranging from Aladdin to Ulysses.

On a Greyhound bus riding from northern Texas to San Francisco, Vincent Leroy Power (9) entertained me with stories. I expected tales of the old plantation and legends of the West. But Goldilocks met

American bears and another familiar naughty girl was admonished by a beaming black finger-wagging wolf, 'Now Missy Red Riding Hood...'

In a ruined fifth century church in Macedonia a boy introduced himself, *Aleksandar*; our shared knowledge of the stories belonging to that name, the strength of the myth reaching even to this distant island, helped make a bond. None of us referred directly to those stories or discussed their different meanings for us, English adults, Macedonian children: we simply smiled and moved into a fresh place of understanding.

Summary

Myth is a deep part of every life with many aspects, interpretations and manifestations. We live individual myths in the context of social, national, religious, political, psychological myths. Contemporary and/ or individual interpretation of an ageless myth, for example, of **Orpheus**, **Oedipus**, **Telemachus**, **Lear**, may lead to new perceptions and **understandings**. Childhood itself is mythologized. **Approaches to counselling** are created by the individual amalgamation of myth by individual initiators, commentators and practitioners, many of whom are themselves deeply aware of the power of myth.

Bibliotherapy uses myth with other narrative and literature in counselling. It is important always to attend to the child's own **perception** and **interpretation**; blue cheese or golden thumbnail, goddess or space goal, the reality of the moon encompasses many myths and her myth encompasses many realities.

Link

Through surveying the deep impression of myth, fairy tale and story in many aspects of life, Chapter 7 ends with face-to-face telling and listening and sharing. This is the way in which we make stories our own and make our own stories – the subject of Chapter 8 is 'A Story of Life'.

References

Anderson, H. (n/d). *Fairy Tales*. Ward Lock, London.
Ariès, P. (1973). *Centuries of Childhood*. Penguin, Harmondsworth.
Bettelheim, B. (1976). *The Uses of Enchantment*. Thames and Hudson, London.
Bhaduri, R. (1990). Counselling with Karma. *Social Work Today*, 21, (33), 16.
Blackmore, R. D. (1869). *Lorna Doone*.
Bohler, J. (1987). The use of storytelling in the practice of pastoral counselling. *Journal of Pastoral Care*, 41, (1), 63–71.

Boswell, J. (1991). *The Kindness of Strangers: the Abandonment of Children in Western Europe from Late Antiquity to the Renaissance.* Penguin, Harmondsworth.

Carter, A. (ed). (1990). *The Virago Book of Fairy Tales.* Virago, London.

Chaplin, J. (1989a). *Feminist Counselling in Action.* Sage, London.

Chaplin, J. (1989). Counselling and gender. In Dryden, et al., pp. 223–36.

Crompton, M. (1979). Common needs and shared fears in 'non-natural' mothers. *Community Care*, 4 January, 20–22.

Crompton, M. (1980). Of books and bibliotherapy. In *Respecting Children: Social Work with Young People.* Edward Arnold, London.

Crompton, M. (1990). *Attending to Children: Direct Work in Social and Health Care.* Edward Arnold, Dunton Green.

Dryden, W. (ed.) (1984). *Individual Therapy in Britain.* Harper and Row, London.

Dryden, W., Charles-Edwards, D. and Woolfe, R. (eds) (1989). Handbook of Counselling in Britain. Tavistock/Routledge, London.

Eliade, M. (Mairet, P. (trans.)) (1975). *Myths, Dreams, and Mysteries: an Encounter Between Contemporary Faiths and Archaic Realities.* Harper and Row, New York.

Foskett, J. and Jacobs, M. (1989). Pastoral counselling. In Dryden, et al., pp. 252–65.

Foskett, J. and Lyall, D. (1988). *Helping the Helpers.* SPCK, London. Quoted in Foskett and Jacobs.

Garner, A. (1967). *The Owl Service.* Collins, London.

Goldacre, P. (1980). Helping children with bereavement. *Adoption and Fostering*, 4, (2), 37–40.

Graves, R. (1955). *Greek Myths Vols* 1 and 2. Penguin, Harmondsworth.

Graves, R. (1961). *The White Goddess.* Faber and Faber, London.

Grimm, J. and W. (n/d). (Marshall, B. (trans.)) *Grimms Fairy Tales: for Children and the Household.* Ward, Lock, London.

Hawking, S. W. (1988). *A Brief History of Time: from the Big Bang to Black Holes.* Bantam, London.

Heffers Bookshop (1991). *Choices* (catalogue). Cambridge.

Homer (Rieu, E. V. (trans.)) (1946). *The Odyssey.* Penguin, Harmondsworth.

Hoy, L. (1987). *Your Friend, Rebecca.* Century Hutchinson, London.

Hoy, L. (1989). *Kiss File JC 110.* Walker, London.

Hunter, M. (1987). Julia: a 'frozen' child. *Adoption and Fostering*, 11, (3), 26–30.

Johnson, S. P. (ed.) (1965). *A Book of Princesses.* Penguin, Harmondsworth.

Jones, G and Jones, T. (trans.) (1949). *The Mabinogion.* Dent, London.

Jung, C. G. (1933). *Modern Man in Search of a Soul.* quoted in Eliade.

King, A. and Clifford, S. (eds). (1989). *Trees be Company: an Anthology of Poetry.* Bristol Classical Press, Bristol.

Lowry, S. P. (1982) *Familiar Mysteries: the Truth in Myth.* Oxford University Press, Oxford.

Macdonald, G. (1965/1863). The light princess. In Johnson pp. 147–76.

Marshall, M. (1975). *Libraries and Literature for Teenagers.* Deutsch, London.

Marshall, M. (1981). *Libraries and the Handicapped Child.* Deutsch, London.

Mascaro, J. (trans.). (1962). *The Bhagavad Gita.* Penguin, Harmondsworth.

Meredith, G. (1912). Enter these enchanted woods. In King and Clifford, p. 52.

Meyer, N. and Martin, D. (1991). dramatization of Cervantes. *Don Quixote.* BBC Radio 3.

Murdoch, I. (1963). *The Unicorn.* Chatto and Windus, London.

Plath, S. (1963). *The Bell Jar.* Heinemann, London.

Priestley, J. B. (1929). *The Good Companions.* Heinemann, London.

Rabuzzi, K. A. (1988). *Motherself: a Mythic Analysis of Motherhood.* Indiana University Press, Bloomington.

Richards, J. (1990). *Childhood in the Middle Ages.* unpublished paper, read on BBC Radio 3.

Rickford, F. (1991). On record (child sexual abuse). *Social Work Today,* 21. 3 91, 26.

Shahar, S. (1990). *Childhood in the Middle Ages.* Routledge, London.

Shapiro, L. (1984). *The New Short-term Therapies for Children: a Guide for the Helping Professions and Parents.* Prentice-Hall, New Jersey.

Sophocles (Watling, E. F. (trans.)) (1947). *The Theban Plays.* Penguin, Harmondsworth, (442–441 BC), *Antigone,* (429–420 BC), *King Oedipus.*

Stevenson, R. L. (1886). *Kidnapped.*

Taylor, E. (1988). *At Mrs Lippincote's.* Virago, London.

Thompson, C. L. and Rudolph, L. B. (1988). *Counseling Children.* Brooks/ Cole, Pacific Grove, Calif.

Thurber, J. (1965). Many moons. In Johnson, pp. 77–88.

8 A story of life

Once I was a real turtle

In Wonderland the Gryphon brings Alice to meet the Mock Turtle who is 'sitting sad and lonely on a little ledge of rock' and 'sighing as if his heart would break'. Alice asks, 'What is his sorrow?' and the Gryphon answers, 'It's all his fancy, that: he hasn't got no sorrow, you know'. Alice is introduced as 'This here young lady...wants for to know your history, she do'. The Gryphon it seems is encouraging Alice to take the Mock Turtle's history with a pinch of salt, wise perhaps in Wonderland but a poor position for a counsellor (Carroll, 1982/1865, p. 88).

Perhaps the poor Mock Turtle would have benefited from the attention of a well-listening counsellor for his history begins, 'Once,...I was a real Turtle' (p. 48). Here is an echo of Julia whose playing-out of the Pinochio story included her saying, 'I want to become a *real* girl' and recognizing that the wooden boy would have 'to do something special' in order 'to become a real boy in the end' (Hunter, 1987, p. 29).

The sensation of being unreal or mock, even a mock-up model, is surely familiar to everyone. The Mock Turtle's sorrow was real, to him if not to that pragmatic observer the Gryphon (himself an unreal mock-up comprising components of eagle and lion). Telling our histories and being listened to with respect may be a considerable aid to attaining that sense of realness which is health.

Some models of counselling focus largely on narration and interpretation of the client's whole history. Others are concerned mainly with the immediate problem and recent events but here too the client's idea of self and story predominate.

Counselling sessions and the relationship with the counsellor are themselves part of the continuing history of the client. Equally the client is part of the continuing history of the counsellor. Every individual, every contact effects some change.

The counsellor's story, leading to and including the current interaction with the client, is as important to that interaction as that of the client. Murray Ryburn (1991) (lecturer in social work) considers that 'every statement made in an assessment report by a social worker is at least as much a statement about that particular social worker, in the wider context of her or his role and agency, as it is a statement about those who are being assessed' (p. 21).

He asks 'whether there is ever an objective reality that we can know of and describe as observers. Can we, in other words, exclude ourselves from the observations that we make of others and the world? A crucial question for any of us who are in an assessing role' or, I suggest, a counselling or any other interactive relationship (p. 21).

Ryburn is challenging 'the belief that it is possible for us to *know best*, through a process of assessment, the appropriate type of placements for children and young people who are to be adopted, and consequently who will be good enough parents for those children' (p. 20). The counselling approaches I have been studying emphasize the importance of not knowing best, of thoroughly attending to the client's own narrative, of not leaping to the rescue. But I wonder whether such objective, totally client-focused attention is always practised, especially when the client is a child.

Ryburn refers to a panel discussion on whether 'two children aged eight and nine, both of whom wished to be adopted, should continue to see their father after adoption'. They constantly expressed the 'wish to have regular contact with their father, who had cared for them for a good part of their lives' but although this was noted by the panel, 'discussion carried on as if this was almost an irrelevance' (p. 20).

Panel members were not indifferent to the children's wishes but were influenced by the belief that 'adults necessarily know better than children' and that 'through a process of thorough assessment it will be possible for social workers to know better than their clients what will be best for those clients' (p. 20).

I have been a social worker with and on behalf of children in a number of different guises and am convinced that Murray Ryburn is right. These perceptions may be transferred to such other disciplines as medicine, psychiatry, nursing and parenting. However objective, even instrumental the decisions and behaviour, the adult/helping/powerful person can operate only within her/his own history.

To refer once more to Ryburn: 'our conclusions will not be a reflection of any objective truth or reality. They will reflect only at one particular time the individuality and collectively held idiosyncratic views...about what the truth is' (p. 21).

A doctor working within the conventional medical framework may prescribe medication or surgery for a condition which may with equal or greater efficacy be treated by a distillation of herbs, acupuncture or homeopathy.

The many schools of counselling intend to aid clients to find ways of managing the problems of life in such a way as to release and focus otherwise wasted energy in order to have life and live it more abundantly. But no two approaches express these aims identically and no two clients consulting any two counsellors, even within the same agency, will be regarded either 'objectively' or 'identically' any more than any two clients will receive identical service from any one counsellor.

What do you wish to confess?

History – yours, mine, the world's – is being made all the time. Telling your history to me will change both you and me. The change may be immediate, even dramatic, as the telling alters the perception by the client of both self and outside world; but the listening counsellor too is changed, perhaps by the burden of knowledge and/or pain, perhaps by other resonances. The counsellor is changed by the experience of hearing the other person's story and by the story itself which now becomes part of the counsellor's own memory and therefore affects her/his future thoughts and behaviour.

Elizabeth Bowen (1983) narrates how a young woman is haunted almost to destruction by the suicide of a friend at school (she hung herself in an apple tree), because she has never been able to tell the dreadful story. Only a strong middle-aged woman is able to receive the story, courageously offering an intensive residential course of coun-selling. We are never told what happens during the weeks Mrs Bettersley spends with 'the haunted girl' but she eventually emerges 'possibly a little harder and brighter. If she had fought, there was not a hair displaced. She did not mention...by what arts, night and day, by what cynical vigilance, she had succeeded in exorcizing the apple tree. The victory aged her, but left her as disengaged as usual'. The counsellor has been changed but she maintains her client's con-fidentiality. Her client is changed too. Freed of her terrible secret and restored as, at last, a whole person to her husband, she 'disappeared into happiness, a sublime nonentity' (p. 470).

In *Coming Home*, Bowen conveys the multiplicity of emotions experienced by a girl (12) returning from school in excitement to tell her mother of the glory that her essay has been read aloud. Rosalind 'had understood some time ago that nothing became real for her until she had had time to live it over again. An actual occurrence was nothing but the blankness of a shock, then the knowledge that something had happened; afterwards one could creep back and look into one's mind and find new things in it, clear and solid' (Bowen, 1983, p. 95).

Excitement and glory turn to anger, then fear because her mother is unexpectedly out, so that, when she returns, Rosalind can tell the story neither of her glory nor her anger and fear. She can only hurt the hurting mother. Yet even as the girl reviews for herself the deprivation she believes she is inflicting on the depriving adult, she feels sadness for her mother and rushes to make all right. But her mother has already forgotten, wrapped in her own memories, the glory of her own afternoon.

The failure of the adult to be available (in any way) when particularly needed leads the overwrought child to the mercy of 'The sense of insecurity' which 'had been growing in her year by year...Safety and happiness were a game that grown-up people played with children to keep them from understanding, possibly to keep themselves from thinking...Anything might happen, there was no security' (p. 97). By failing to share any of their afternoon's stories, Rosalind and her mother lose not only the pleasure of communication but, more important, a crucial opportunity for intimacy and understanding. There is no security.

Mrs Bettersley was changed by her exposure to the story of the haunted girl Myra which thus became part of her own story. Rosalind and her mother are changed by their unshared stories, each making assumptions about the other, neither knowing, or caring to know, the truth.

Counsellors listen constantly to children's stories but how much do they recognize either those which are untold or those which are purpose built? Dolly, in the novel by B. M. Gill (1986) attends a convent boarding school and is about to make her first confession. The priest asks, 'What do you wish to confess?' Dolly has given the matter much thought and truthfully responds, 'Nothing' (p. 49).

The priest is not convinced and presses her, 'If you haven't done anything, you might have committed a sin of omission'. Dolly waits for some suggestions. 'He came out with several – including the sin of spiritual pride – and Dolly hotly denied all of them. She didn't even know what spiritual pride meant. They were both beginning to sweat' (p. 49).

Dolly tries. 'If she couldn't come up with a sin soon he'd come out from his side and thump her.' To her relief she recalls a sin. 'She'd told him a whopping big lie as soon as she'd entered the box. "Bless me Father, for I have sinned", she'd said. She'd told him she'd sinned when she hadn't'. She confesses. '"Well, thank God for that", Father Donovan said acidly...and curtly told her to say three Hail Mary's' (p. 49).

When the next child, Zanny, confesses truthfully that she had 'drowned little Willie – in the goldfish pond', giving full details of both this and her murder of Evans the Bread, the priest believes that she is telling not her story, but stories. 'You know, Zanny, that it's wrong to tell a lie...And you won't tell any more lies, will you, Zanny?' (p. 52).

Zanny responds, in some bewilderment, '"No, father". (How could you tell more when you hadn't told any?).' The priest continues. '"You know it's wrong to read the wrong sort of books. What sort of books do you read?" "Peter Pan", Zanny suggested cautiously. Taking grasshopper leaps after his mind was tiring her.'

The priest asks, '"Have you ever read any nasty comics belonging to boys...About people like Evans the Bread...?" "No Father". "And if no is a lie, you won't do it any more, will you, Zanny?" Zanny, totally confused, said she wouldn't and was given three Hail Marys' (p. 52).

From this encounter with her spiritual counsellor, Zanny concludes that lying (even when you haven't) is a sin of greater weight than murdering (even when you have). And Dolly learns that, 'You have to go around committing sins just so as to please Father Donovan' (p. 53).

Hasn't every parent said, 'Did you do it? No? Well don't do it again'?

This is reminiscent of those 'children who *tried* to tell' Leeds doctor Michael Buchanan and his colleagues about sexual assault. 'At one time if a child said "My dad put his hand in my knickers", people would say, "Filthy little liar"' (Campbell, 1988, p. 22).

And is there not a premonitory echo of the suggestion that children involved in certain allegations about ritual abuse had confused videos with real life? Why were they, allegedly, watching videos of such disgusting content? Tate's discussion of this topic is entitled 'Children's stories' (Tate, 1991).

Telling the tale, telling stories and similar phrases are often used as synonymous for lying, especially when applied to children. Gill, Campbell and Tate demonstrate the disastrous effects of mistaking the kind of story and making assumptions about children's stories themselves – indeed, the children's histories.

Zanny, like Mary Bell whose attempts to reveal her story were also unheard (Sereny, 1972), commits several more murders before she is taken seriously, just as many children would be sexually abused before attempts to tell were heard.

Counselling is an invitation to present one's autobiography, a favourite human activity but in everyday life usually lacking the totally attentive listener, focused for a protected time and over a substantial period on the autobiographer. Even a written autobiography cannot be guaranteed that even a single reader will stay to the end.

The counsellor is a captive, however willing and/or paid. How well the counsellor listens to not only the main plot but also the sub-plots and hidden themes and how well the metaphors and references are recognized and understood is of first importance. You can listen to a broadcast story with one ear and a cup of coffee while opening the post and ordering the coal. You may miss the subtlety of characterization, the glowing language, even the twist at the end but you can at least follow the plot. Counsellors need to tune the radio carefully, switch on the answerphone and listen to and behind every word.

Memory is so oblique

It is usually not easy to distinguish between story (fiction) and history (fact) in even one's own narration. As I talk about some event of my childhood I wonder, blushing slightly, if I remember actually doing or saying this or that or only being told about it.

Bowen (1986/1934) recalls of her school days that. 'Lessons must have occupied a good deal of our time, but I remember very little of this' (p. 19). She considers memory to be 'so oblique and selective that no doubt I see my schooldays through a subjective haze. I cannot believe that those three years were idyllic; days and weeks were no doubt dreary and squalid on end' (p. 21).

Even to our diaries we are not totally truthful, expecting no readers but ourselves to criticize either record or interpretation.

Sophie, in Elizabeth Taylor's novel (1985), anticipates prying eyes by writing, 'Anyone who reads bad things about themselves in this book have been spying and therefore deserves it'. She uses her diary for a fine collection of intimate notes beginning, 'Pliny about Vesuvius this morning' (p. 78).

She comments on the pregnancy of a resident relation. 'I pray I shall never have a baby. Of course, not everybody dies or else they wouldn't take the risk': her own mother had died giving birth to her (p. 78).

She records visiting her mother's grave with her 'sort of half-cousin' Tom (in fact her father) who 'asked me wouldn't I like to go to boarding school...I said I would drown myself if they made me and he sighed heavily. But it will stop him saying any more about it if he knows my life is at stake. It makes me quite sick even speaking about it so I know I should die because I should cry every night if I had to go' (p. 78).

The day's events, impressions and reflections are combined with a worry about her (adoptive) father and new governess: 'What are they saying about me? I hope they decide nothing horrible' and a record of '*Marks for the Day*' including 'Goodness. Fair...Industry. Made bed. Learnt vocab...Bravery. Not...Honesty. OK.' Taylor comments that 'it had been a good deal of writing for a little girl and had all to be gone through again the next evening' (pp. 78–9).

Sophie is also writing a novel in an exercise book. '*The Lost Girl*' (p. 134). Taylor is teasing the reader; Sophie's mother is dead and her birth father is her adoptive father's cousin, residing in the same house. Sophie is lost in a confusion of adults' relationships, emotions and unresolved problems. She will soon be lost forever, crushed to death by a falling statue as she waves to her cousin-father Tom (p. 148).

Is the novel within a novel fiction or the reflection of the facts of Sophie's life? And how is it different from the 'factual' diary invented by the author of the 'real' novel?

To ponder this for long opens doors into long corridors of literary criticism. But it raises important questions for all who listen professionally to stories. The dilemma can be illustrated by reference to *Oranges are not the Only Fruit* (1985). This is a novel, on bookshop fiction shelves. But it is also, we are told, based on the actual childhood of the author Jeanette Winterson. The girl in the book is named *Jeanette* and the central character in fantasy sections is *Winnet Stonejar* (anagram of the author's name). So is it autobiography? Which events are 'true'? Which characters 'really lived'? Which words were 'really' spoken?

With historical novels we may check dates, customs, furniture, language. We know that we can not know what Alexander really said to Hephaistion but we are content with an *as if* portrayal. Reading autobiography we pay the author the respect of assuming that truth is being told, recognizing that events are recalled after many years and through the perspective of many experiences. But then, fiction is the distillation of 'real' experience. For example, when I was writing an (alas, unpublished) novel about young people I found myself deeply involved with the 'naughty girl' whose life and behaviour could not have been more different from my own, yet who became some projection of myself.

Autobiography is the raw material of counselling, clients bringing, telling and re-shaping their life stories.

A published autobiography which speaks to me for its directness and modesty is that of novelist Elizabeth Goudge (1974). She considers her mother and herself, seeing that

> she, who if she had been a well woman would have been a wise mother of many children, was in illness the reverse. Whenever I sneezed she sent for the doctor...And so the child was and is with me still. All my life I have been waging war with her. I have a dim hope that I may get rid of her before I die, but it is very dim.

The mature accomplished woman, with clear-eyed humility recognizes the child in her, and the courage to seek her own idea of adulthood (p. 76).

Her father too gave unwanted succour to the unwanted 'child'. At 10 she 'decided that I no longer wanted to be called Beth. I told my family that it was a babyish name. I...must now be called Elizabeth. Having declared my ultimatum I banged the door shut on my childhood and thought it gone. But my father opened the door again. He obstinately refused to call me anything but Beth' (p. 93).

In two paragraphs the author offers apparently authentic glimpses of herself from several angles at once: the mature adult looking back, her present feelings, her memory now of feelings then and even prediction of future feelings, for she concludes that if she and the 'neurotic selfish little beast' have not parted company before death and, 'I...find that she is with me still, the starting of the battle with her all over again will be my purgatory', (where I hope that some counsellor hears this history and helps Elizabeth and Beth declare peace) (p. 76).

It would be interesting to know how Elizabeth Goudge felt when she had completed this book, owning such feelings in her own name instead of incorporating aspects of herself (houses in which she had lived, people she had known, emotions) in her novels.

If your kids had to know all about you

I suspect that biography (case studies and client vignettes) is more common than autobiography in the literature of counselling theory and practice but counsellors cannot avoid constantly compiling their own autobiographies; some may do this more consciously/honestly than others – I think of Rowe (1987) and Mearns and Thorne (1988).

I have found no accounts of counselling written by counsellees and only a few accounts by the recipients of intervention by, for example, psychiatrists, doctors and psychoanalysts. Almost all these were by adults, some with reference to themselves as children or to their own children.

The only exception to hand is the material written especially by young people for inclusion in *Adolescents and Social Workers* (Crompton, 1982).

Dorna (16) with long experience of the care system, chose her own pseudonym and collected writing from several friends. She regarded a social worker as someone who 'reads reports by other voices in authority and what is said on file paper – it *must* for some unknown reason be the real you'. The danger of the biography compiled by adults and following the child around, 'a piece of paper saying, "Beware, this child is violently aggressive"' could be avoided by workers 'If they never looked at your files and decided to find out for themselves what you're really like...To be able to say to your kid; "Listen, I've never read your file so it's up to you to tell me!" they would get a lot further on' (Crompton, 1982, p. 9).

Dorna had found that 'Some social workers already use this line but they forget every kid knows they have to read their files before they've even met them. If it was true and they hadn't read their files that's where the trust and respect starts' (p. 9). She wanted to tell her own story in her own way to an adult she could trust and respect, not feel that whatever she might say would be at best half heard by someone who already 'knew' what she was like from a file report and the opinions of other adults.

Counsellors receive children who have been referred by other adults – teachers, doctors, police, parents – already labelled as having some problem, displaying some disturbing behaviour. Only ChildLine, university/college counsellors and the organizer/counsellor of a small voluntary youth counselling centre, of those I met, could take their callers at their own valuation without preliminary comment from an adult. Others had first met their clients via referral letters and reports.

In no agency could children select their own counsellors or see a file before contact. 'Social workers', wrote Dorna, 'forget to think what it would be like if that particular child knew their life story – how would they feel towards them? I mean if it was compulsory that when you became a social worker your kids had to know all about you' (p. 9).

Perhaps this is why I respond so warmly to the brief and lively vignette of Rogers, Jung, et al. by Thompson and Rudolph (1988). Knowing a little about their backgrounds, interests and quirks, I recognized them as fellow humans and could receive their teaching as having connection with real life.

I relish the picture of William Glasser who 'loves to day dream and has little use for intellectuals who make understandable ideas difficult to grasp' and 'has a great sense of humor, which he uses skillfully in his teaching and counseling'. Knowing that he enjoys *Peanuts*, I meet Charlie Brown anew (Thompson and Rudolph, 1988, p. 48).

I checked the *Preface* to see if the authors offered some equivalent introduction to themselves. 'This book is our way of sharing with readers the ideas and methods we have found useful for changing children's ineffective behavior and helping them to become more responsible and fully functioning persons' (p. vi). I can expect a personal book not a chilly detached study.

Having acknowledged the help of colleagues, editors, secretaries – (I feel better about my own, short book when I see that Thompson and Rudolph had six secretaries) – and spouses, here is the sentence that sends me over the page happy: 'To our children, now adults of whom we are very proud, thanks for being patient with our attempts to use you as test cases for our counseling techniques' (p. vii). The authors are real people too.

It is not that the counsellor's life history should be told; if I want to know all about Fritz Perls I should seek his biography, not a book on children and counselling. But counsellors are giving messages about themselves all the time, telling their stories in appearance and manner, the atmosphere and furnishing of the office or playroom, the behaviour towards the client.

Jo (15) was disgusted that the psychiatrist to whom she was introduced for help with what adults feared to be anorexia nervosa

> sat with his feet on the desk and smoked 'to put me at my ease'. But the putting at ease does not seem to have extended very far. Jo loathes cigarette smoke but although he did ask if she minded, 'because it was the first thing he said to me, I didn't feel I could say "Yes, please don't". It was obviously his room and who was I to stop him smoking?' (Crompton, 1982, p. 10).

The psychiatrist was giving a great deal of information about himself, even without benefit of a file.

How many clients feel, 'Who was I to stop him smoking'? How many could ask the counsellor to remove his feet from the desk, or place their own feet beside his? A student on a counselling course commented on the information given by tutors, including rejecting body language of one who turned away from the speaking student, half covering her face, refusal to give any detail at all about their lives, even though the course served a fairly small local community in which both staff and students lived, and tutors required students to 'reveal all'. Do counsellors imagine that they are invisible and inaudible?

Book about me

Nursery nurse 'Nancy Mint' experienced no difficulty sharing completion of worksheets with 'Lucy', counsellor and client each making her own *book about me*. Nancy regards this as encouraging openness, fun and truthfulness, showing that she trusted Lucy.

The idea of compiling a *book about me* is not new but appears to be increasingly popular. Vera Fahlberg (1981) provides extensive advice about the compilation and use of a *Lifebook* which 'should be developed through the child's time in care and should accompany him into permanent placement, whether that be back to the child's biological family or to an adoptive home'. The Lifebook 'can be used as a tool to help the child understand his past, what is happening to his family and what it means to be in care' (p. 51).

Helping a child to create a life story book can be a tremendously positive experience for both child and adult – and in my view should be undertaken only if it is seen as such. There can be no virtue in a mechanistic collection of sheets with a few facts and photographs.

The main purpose of a tangible life story book is in the making. Just as the book I am presently writing is alive under my pencil, so the child's autobiography must *be* life as well as a record of history.

To be regarded as needing an autobiography of this kind is as terrible as to be an evacuee with a label around your neck in case you are mislaid, in case you forget your own name, in case you are nothing more than a case.

So-called senior citizens are encouraged to engage in reminiscence work, recovering, valuing and having valued memories of life long past. Children compiling life story books have few years to recall and record but, as much as for an 85 year old, the whole of life is there.

Connor, et al. (1985) write of some difficulties and mistakes. 'Some social workers form the view that they have no time or skills to carry out life story work and therefore it should be left to "the experts". Others regard it as a purely technical exercise to go through the motions of recording chronological information' (p. 32).

For other workers the aim seems to be 'to complete the work in record time to get it out of the way, while at the same time hoping it will answer the child's questions and salvage a placement or lead to a better one' (p. 32).

The authors fear that 'In our anxiety to complete the exercise, which we may have undertaken reluctantly on instructions, we can lose sight of the effect this has on the child. Rushing life story work is a recipe for disaster, leaving both worker and child angry and frustrated with the exercise and each other' (p. 32).

Among negative effects of poorly conceived work are that 'The worker may end up viewing life story work as a medium he has no feeling for and pass it off as yet another failed social work fad. The reader can draw his own conclusions about the effect on a child who already has a life filled with failure' (p. 32).

These comments relate not only to creating a book but by extension to all components of counselling practice. I am particularly struck by the reference to frustration, anger and failure experienced by both adult and child. To feel a failure even in telling one's own life story!

A social worker described life story books which were 'full of photographs without feelings' and Helena Allen (1986) writes of such work 'sadly often divorced from its roots, becoming a simple cognitive exercise undertaken without casework skills'. Allen regards child clients as 'captive' and suggests that 'The only escape from intrusive adults who threaten defences will be for the child to arm him or herself emotionally, developing a veneer of "understanding"', which 'leaves chaotic emotions inaccessible and the child much harder to reach at a later stage' (p. 66).

The bear cave

When I was employed to help 'Luke' (6) make a life story book I had no clue how to begin and was prepared to spend several sessions helping us both to feel at ease together. The object of the work was partly to draw together the many strands of his already complicated history and numerous moves. He was, it was suggested, a 'frozen' child but I found him to be fog- rather than ice-bound.

Perhaps because I was not hampered by a predetermined plan, Luke himself gave the clue. He showed me his treasured possessions in his bedroom, including his birthday presents, and suddenly I heard the crucial word *present*. We were looking at some books together at the time and it was natural to ask if he would like to make a book about himself and to start with the present presents. The first story and pictures were of the birthday party, the large table surrounded by friends and foster family.

Recording the present was constantly of course recording the past which would soon become distant in space, too, as he was to make two moves before 'permanent' placement.

Luke always chose the subject of his drawings, recording happy life-enhancing experiences in a situation which was to observers not satisfactory. Although the foster placement in which I first met him was not happy, he could remember and retain some concrete evidence of things that had gone well for him. His perception of the foster home was different from that of worried social working or rejecting fostering adults.

We moved backwards to draw pictures of lost houses and relations and babies, and forwards to draw more houses – potential 'forever' homes.

Using a ring binder we could store souvenirs of special outings. He also had a photograph album which we put in order together. Particularly moving was the sole picture of his mother, very blurred, with another person whom Luke did not know.

While we sought to discover and record the past and work towards the future we also recorded and kept the many stories Luke composed during our sessions. He would snuggle up to me on the floor or lie on the settee, very relaxed and happy while I remained on the floor near his feet.

Talking very fast, this child, who achieved little at school and had apparently poor language facility, would contrive lively and exciting tales of seaside adventures and encounters with monsters, always featuring himself as hero. These always ended with some garbled formula which I eventually unravelled as 'And they all lived happily ever afterwards', a wish for Luke's own future held as fervently by all who knew him as by himself.

Between sessions I would set out in my best printing the words I had just managed to scribble, using a number of different coloured pens and illustrating with stick figures.

Next week we would read the stories together and the delighted Luke would sometimes add more pictures, I still relish the huge grinning monster with monolith teeth dropping almost onto the head of a little escaping boy. This picture in itself represented a small but important chapter in Luke's story for one aim of the work was to help him experience and express a range of emotions; although his monster grinned, the boy was afraid.

I hoped through the writing-out and illustrating to help Luke gain a stronger, more positive view of himself, for example, in that his rapidly spoken words and lively stories were of enough value for an adult to listen to, write out and return to him.

At that time he could not read them himself although some time was spent time with Luke reading a few of his own words. He appreciated that the pages of clear colourful writing were his and enjoyed the little pictures of himself, his relations and his favourite teddy bear.

To help both record the painful and bewildering past and anticipate the unknown and bewildering future I made up stories based on Luke's favourite characters. A little engine experienced adventures not unlike those of Luke himself and a familiar bear faced dislodgement from his foster-cave and placement with a new but as yet undiscovered family of foster-bears. His present foster-bear was recognizably kind, loving and sensible. I word-processed a short section per page so that Luke could draw pictures on whichever page he chose. I illustrated the bear book myself and he added figures and coloured in my outlines.

Nina Bawden (1987) includes a description of a stepfather comforting a bewildered little boy with just such a story. Billy is a beloved fluffy purple hippopotamus carried round by Barnaby with a bear and a monkey in 'a green Marks and Spencer plastic bag'. Barnaby talked 'to them when he was alone in his bedroom'. His mother has never read to him and he is entranced by his stepfather's reading – and unsure what is expected of him (pp. 77–8).

One evening the narrator asks:

'Do you think Billy liked that story?' He frowned. I said, 'Shall we ask him?' I picked up the animal and whispered in its purple ear. I said, in Billy's voice, holding my nose and producing an adenoidal squeak, 'No, I'd rather have a story about a brave hippopotamus. I don't like stories about silly old cats who get rolled up in pastry'. 'I don't know any stories about hippopotamuses', I said. 'Then you must be a very stupid old man', Billy squeaked back.

Barnaby laughed...I advanced on a somewhat randomly constructed tale about a purple hippo and a bear and a monkey who lived with a boy whose name I couldn't remember, who spent the day in a green bag and came out at night when everyone was asleep, to have fun and adventures and play with the toys the boy had in his bedroom.

Barnaby said, in an awed voice, 'Is the boy's name Barnaby?...Do you think the boy has a Daddy?'

Inspiration deserted me. I muttered, oh, yes, most probably, but this was a story about Billy, the hippo, and that seemed to satisfy him. Or he respected my innocence. He said philosophically (or it may have been drowsily, because his eyelids were drooping), 'I forgot for a minute, hippos don't have Daddies, do they?' (pp. 78–9).

I find this story appealing for several reasons, not least that it recalls part of my own story, for my first article about working with children was entitled *Hippopotamus or Cow?* (Wardle, 1975). This article had been stimulated partly by an afternoon spent with a bewildered little boy not unlike Barnaby. I had told him a story about a little boy whose home and recent experiences were similar to his own. After narration of 'all the events of Jo's past 24 hours, I said, "And then he went home. I don't know what happened next". Jo sat up brightly, "I think he went to bed". I had been careful not to use Jo's name for the hero of the story and not to insist on any overt response' (p. 431).

One thing I found difficult when Luke moved to the new foster home was that his new carers appeared to show no interest in the life story file. When I visited to say goodbye he seemed to me already to have changed, cut off from that portrait of his life which he and I had compiled through so many life-filled sessions together. Luke had laughed and cried and created and grown and I had loved him. He had,

I thought, begun to emerge from the fog; the book was a tangible record of the real boy.

I supposed that his new carers disliked it because so much of his past had been painful. They wanted him to forget his own story and be reinvented from the moment he entered their home. Almost a year of helping him to learn about the bright and the dark and the reality of his life seemed to be rejected. Unhappy things should be forgotten. Yet his memories of events which were to those of us who had loved him unrelievedly painful, were often happy, for example, the party and holiday he had with such vigour drawn and narrated and constantly referred back to, enjoying the records in his life story book, his autobiography. By rejecting his sadness, I felt that they also rejected his happiness. I feared that the fog might close in again.

But when much later, I submitted my draft of this account to Luke's regular social worker, I was delighted by this comment: 'I thought it would be important for you to note that Luke is very well settled...and his "book" is regularly referred to by both himself and his carers'. This is part of my own story: I find parting particularly difficult and I had not dealt well with my own investment in the work and relationship with Luke. The counsellor needs counselling, especially at times of meeting and parting.

One other thing I did for Luke. I bought him a box, a smart carrying case to keep and transport his fragile treasures – birthday and Christmas cards, birth certificate, photograph album and the folder. Like Barnaby, he had previously kept his life in a plastic supermarket carrier.

River cards

Work with 'Mark' (10) was also intended to help a child in a fog gain a sense of self. Like Luke he had moved several times but unlike the younger child retained clear memories of his parental home.

As for Luke I bought a set of equipment for his sole use and when our work together ended, I gave him everything – pencils, rubber, punch, sharpener, paper for both writing and drawing (a good quality pad) – and an attractive sturdy carrying case, all in his favourite colour. He told me on several occasions that moving between homes his things got lost; people and his sense of self got lost too.

Where Luke made up stories Mark drew pictures. He narrated events of the recent or more distant past and read my carefully written out accounts the following week. Sometimes some piece of information was missing and could be supplied later or he caught me in an error which I cheerfully corrected. It is important to acknowledge when children are right and adults wrong and to apologize.

Thus we both caught his present – which would become precious when he had to leave a happy but essentially temporary placement –

and tackled difficult areas from the past, particularly the reason for his placement in care at all. Approaching this in narrative form was helpful to us both.

The most sustained use of this approach occurred during and following a day revisiting places which had been of significance in his past – the maternity hospital, the court which had made the care order, several home addresses and some special private places including a museum, the venue of a recent school outing. During lunch after the earlier visits we reviewed the events and wrote/drew. I compiled the whole into a story with a separate chapter for every event. The combination of history with the story of the day itself (which included several adventures) created an impressive and attractive contribution to his autobiography.

Another approach to telling and recording Mark's story was through picture postcards. We realized that all his homes had been within either a few yards or a few miles of a particular river. Indeed our later meetings took place beside it. One of his most lively and vivid stories of life with his birth family involved the throwing of a treasured possession into it by an enemy-boy; retribution was exacted by throwing one of the boy's possessions into the water too – a story of almost mythic form and power.

We arranged pictures of various places on the river in a separate display folder, augmented by pamphlets and maps in an envelope in the main life story ring binder. I hoped that Mark would enjoy the image of the river representing some continuity in his fragmented life. He was certainly pleased with the cards and attractive, sturdy display folder and responded to the idea of geographical links between the several sites of his life.

In *The 2000 Pound Goldfish* Betsy Byars (1982) describes another way in which postcards may record and play an important part in a life story. Warren's mother Saffy is on the run, a violent peace protester. Saffy keeps contact with her two children only by occasional telephone calls to a public box and equally rare postcards which become 'dark with fingerprints, limp from many readings' (p. 43).

Warren hoards the cards and at times of stress reads them, keeping out of the way of his grandmother who has disowned her daughter: 'It was night, the light was poor, and he was in the bathroom, sitting on the side of the tub, reading by the streetlight. The poor light didn't matter. Warren knew the words by heart' (p. 43).

These cards are all Warren has and he begins to realize that they are unsatisfactory – 'post-office cards – no pictures of palm trees or mountains or monuments to linger over' or to identify his mother's whereabouts 'Dears – That was the way she always started. He wished just once she would use his name. Dear *Warren* would mean a lot to him.' Reading through the old cards which represent his mother's autobiography and his own, passive, relationship with her, he begins to see the flaws in the messages: 'He felt betrayed' (pp. 43,44,45).

He remembers Saffy's last visit and his belief that 'his mother had to do these things. She was Joan of Arc. She alone could save the troubled world. But now...He glanced down at the postcards.' Warren has realized, scrutinizing the cards, that 'it did not really seem like she was saving the world. Marches and bumper stickers didn't seem like a Wonder Woman struggle. He felt a faint stirring of guilt as this unsettling thought took root and grew.' There is no one to help with these confusing feelings. Worse. Grandmother enters the bathroom and stands on the cards – both symbolic and very concrete: 'It was as if she were defiling something sacred' (pp. 47,45,50).

With Mark and Luke the stories written and told by both children and adult were the property of the children, kept safely within both that relationship and the strong attractive folders. They were shared with other people only by choice of the boys themselves; for example, Luke liked to show his drawings to his foster mother.

The stories, pictures, photographs and cards were valued and protected. As social worker employed only for this work with the children, I was free from involvement in the past and with other members of the families. As a social worker at all I should have no personal feeling about the other family members.

In contrast Warren's grandmother had a great deal of feeling about her daughter and little imagination to spare for the hurt boy. His sense of self, his life story were not safe with her. She stamped on not only his cards but also on his ability to express his anger and fear. Just as he begins to discover betrayal and guilt and the possibility of growth, he is forced back into defence and illusion: 'My mother is alive and she cares about me and she wants me and she'll come and get me when she can!' (Byars, 1982 p. 48).

A complete sense of self

Kathy Randell (1989) comments that 'We have an obligation to put the past into perspective, to ensure that the child has a clear understanding of it'. I am not sure that any adult can put the past into perspective or ensure that anyone else has a clear understanding of their own past. She considers that 'In a strong and stable environment children can, and do, bear the pain. It is we – the adults – who have difficulty'. The counsellor will help children 'be aware' that their life stories are 'precious,...private' possibly 'painful' and causing both sadness and happiness (p. 22).

Helping children learn and recapture the stories of their lives can be done only within a relationship. Why should a child share memories, bewilderment and secrets with a stranger? Connor, et al. (1985) write about Ben (9) who was '"Stuck" around two years of age'. If he 'was unable to have his own way his behaviour would regress and become wildly erratic resulting in frequent and prolonged temper tantrums' (pp. 32–3).

The keyworker considered that 'life story work would be a useful focus to begin to help Ben understand his past, present and future'. Crucially, 'little could be achieved until he had first helped restore Ben's trust in adults, second helped him understand and control his negative behaviour, and third helped him understand that relationships between children and adults are built on emotional, not material rewards'. In order to help Ben 'to share perceptions of his life experience', it would be essential 'to establish a trusting relationship with the adult working with him'. Building such a relationship included the keyworker sharing 'something of himself, and his own experiences,...not intimate details but sufficient to show the child he was human and had a life outside social work' (p. 33).

Chris Lightbown (1979) writes from experience as a social worker that 'the greatest resistance people feel to embarking on a life story with children is fear of the pain it may involve. This is usually rationalised by the worker in terms of the great anxiety a child will feel if faced with the true facts of her situation' (p. 14).

She recalls foster parents who 'were afraid to mention the existence of a natural mother to a child'. She helped them 'to piece together a life-story together with John'. They were astonished by 'The ease with which he accepted rather uncomfortable reasons for his being in care' and 'at last, with great relief, they accepted that John had been able to face up to things far more easily than themselves'. Lightbown adds that 'A sympathetic, simple and realistic account always seems to prove best' (pp. 14–15).

Phillida Sawbridge (1990) shows how the recognition and interplay of all feelings and experiences are essential to health and integrity. From experience of post-adoption counselling she writes of Helen (29) who was not clear about whether or not to seek her birth mother.

During five sessions, Helen was helped 'to go back over her life-history, and to explore what she knew and how she felt about mothers' including her adoptive mother, mother-in-law, friends' mothers, mothers in general and her birth mother, and 'Helen's expectations of herself as a parent. The counsellor used charts and lists as ways of recording and illustrating what Helen was saying, and Helen always wanted to take these away with her and go over them again on her own' (p. 32).

Joan Wheeler, born Doris Sippel (1990) writes from first-hand experience of adoption and the shortcomings of the counselling available to her in the 1970s in the USA. 16 years after reunion with her birth family she told her story – the story of her 'sense of lost childhood with my siblings' and 'of betrayal toward both sets of parents'. Learning her true story was crucial to her development of a 'complete sense of self', including '170 years of genealogical history, tracing my birth family from Germany, France, Poland, and Switzerland to the old American West to Buffalo, New York, where they intermixed with my adoptive family 90 years ago. My ethnic and medical background are now known to me.' The author herself regards 'the most important lesson, for me as well as for others,...knowing the truth, no matter how painful, is always better than not knowing at all' (Wheeler, 1990, p. 27).

Joan/Doris learnt and faced and managed the truth and by interpreting the many 'lost' details of her story, became a strong and mature person. She and her many relations would have been saved a great deal of pain if clear-minded and truly attentive counselling had been available. Such counselling as there was tended to be counter productive, obscuring rather than empowering.

No life is lived in isolation, no action taken without consequence, no story told without impact. 'To light a candle' says a wise wizard 'is to cast a shadow' (LeGuin, 1971, p. 56). To invite a confidence is to undertake a burden. To speak of one's life is to give, to make oneself vulnerable. Counsellors and client are joined in trust, in confidence, in vulnerability. Like the snake holding its own tail in its mouth, if one should bite and one be bitten, both would be bruised.

Summary

Storytelling, particularly personal narrative, is a universal human activity. Telling stories is explored in contexts of **history, facts, reports** and **assessment**. A major role of counsellors is to act as attentive **listeners** and this may entail strain. **Failure really to attend** whether to another person's need to narrate or to the meaning behind words **inhibits communication** and may lead to **disastrous misunderstanding**. The boundary between **truth** and **fiction** is blurred even, or especially, in memory, as illustrated in **autobiography, novel/fictionalized auto-biography**. Children referred to counsellors have often been preceded by a **file** and/or **report** but have no reciprocal prelimary clues to the **counsellor's story**. Counselling may include making a **lifebook** or **life story book**; this may be fraught with problems but approached with love and care, is rewarding for both child and counsellor, creating and recording 'A Story of Life'.

Link

Exploration of communication and self-expression through various media turns in Chapter 9 from oral to visual context, with a variety of pictures including 'Roses, Pagodas and Owls'.

References and Further Reading

Allan, J. (1988). *Inscapes of the Child's World: Jungian Counseling in Schools and Clinics*. Spring Publications Texas, ch. 10.

Allen, H. M. (1986). Life story with a difference. *Adoption and Fostering*, 10, (2), 66–7.

Bawden, N. (1987). *Circles of Deceit*. Macmillan, London.

Bowen, E. (Wilson, A. (ed.), (1983). *Collected Stories of Elizabeth Bowen*. Penguin, Harmondsworth, Coming Home, pp. 95–100 The Apple Tree, pp. 461–70.

Bowen, E. (1986/1934). The Mulberry Tree. In Lee, pp. 13–21.

Byars, B. (1982). *The Two-thousand Pound Goldfish*. The Bodley Head, London.

Campbell, B. (1988). *Unofficial Secrets; Child Sexual Abuse – the Cleveland Case*. Virago; London.

Carroll, L. (1982/1865). *Alice's Adventures in Wonderland*, Chancellor Press, London.

Connor, T., Sclare, I., Dunbar. D., Elliffe. J. (1985). Making a life story book. *Adoption and Fostering*, 9, (2), 32–5.46.

Crompton, M. (1980). *Respecting Children* Edward Arnold, London, ch. 5.

Crompton, M. (1982). *Adolescents and Social Workers*. Gower/Community Care, Aldershot.

Crompton, M. (1990). *Attending to Children*. Edward Arnold, Dunton Green.

Fahlberg, V. (1981). *Helping Children When They Must Move*. BAAF, London.

Gill. B. M. (1986). *Nursery Crimes*. Hodder and Stoughton, Dunton Green.

Goudge. E. (1974). *The Joy of the Snow: an Autobiography*. Hodder and Stoughton, Dunton Green.

Hunter, M. (1987). Julia: a frozen child. *Adoption and Fostering*, 11, (3), 26–30.

Lee, H. (ed.). (1986). *The Mulberry Tree*. Virago, London.

LeGuin, U. (1971). *A Wizard of Earthsea*. Penguin, Harmondsworth.

Lightbown, C. (1979). Life-story books. *Adoption and Fostering*. no.3. 9–15.

Mearns, D. and Thorne, B. (1988). *Person-centred Counselling in Action*. Sage, London.

Oaklander, V. (1978). *Windows to our Children: a Gestalt Therapy Approach to Children and Adolescents*. Real People Press, Moab, Utah.

Randell, K. (1989). The luxury of knowing who you are. *Social Work Today*, 21,(10),22.

Richards, J. (1991). *Childhood in the Middle Ages*. BBC Radio 3(unpublished talk).

Rowe, D. (1987): *Beyond Fear*. Collins, London.

Ryburn, M. (1991). The myth of assessment. *Adoption and Fostering*, 15,(1), 20–27.

Sawbridge, P. (1990). Post-adoption counselling: what do we actually do? *Adoption and Fostering* 14,(1), 31–3.

Sereny, G. (1972). *The Case of Mary Bell*. Eyre Methuen, London.

Tate, T. (1991). *Children for the Devil: Ritual Abuse and Satanic Crime*. Methuen, London.

Taylor, E. (1985). *Palladian*. Virago, London.

Thompson, C. R. and Rudolph, L. (1988). *Counseling Children*. Brooks/Cole, Pacific Grove, California.

Wardle, M. (1975). Hippopotamus or cow? on not communicating *about* children. *Social Work Today*, 6, (14).
Wheeler, J. (1990). The secret is out. *Adoption and Fostering*, 14,(3),22–7.
Winterson, J. (1985). *Oranges are not the Only Fruit*. Pandora Press, London.

9   Roses, pagodas and owls

Smiling Me

In *Talking Pictures*, my chapter on art in *Respecting Children* (1980) I quoted: 'After the battle over who is to clear up has been finally resolved and the picture or model is the only reminder of the glory and frustrations of the afternoon, remember that it contains something of your child's vision and something of his growth. Respect it' (Pluckrose, 1974, p. 10).

It seems right to begin a new chapter on the use of art where I had finished – achievement and the encapsulation of the child's vision and growth. This was beautifully represented in 'SMILING ME', an embroidered picture of a smiling sun made for and given to student counsellor 'Ria' by 'Lou' who had, with her help, grown through difficulties and sadness to full 'smiling' and to be able to express that new vision in a work of art.

Through her gift (in the sense of both *present* and *talent*) Lou not only communicated gratitude for the counsellor's help but also demonstrated how she had been helped to develop motivation, tenacity and skill.

Lou's embroidered picture represented the non-verbal conclusion to a series of mainly verbal interactions with her counsellor. Pictures may sometimes themselves be the main medium of communication or a means to real verbal exchange.

All material in this chapter is drawn from creative activity – children drawing, painting, modelling. Chapters on story and music include discussion on responses to printed literature and live/recorded performance. I have found no reference, however, to therapeutic employment of pictures and sculptures, for example, to dominant colour or use of calming landscape or stimulating pattern. I assume that this gap is due largely to my verbal/musical leanings but wonder if workers with children are conscious of the effect of the visual environment and possible use of response to graphic and plastic art.

Polish pagoda without cloud

In an infants' school in Warsaw, little girls taught me Polish as they drew (slonce), cats (koti) and flowers (kwiati), naming them for me to repeat.

I spent half an hour on the floor with Piotrek (6) and his friends as they drew (for Women's Day) women in a variety of countries. Piotrek's was a Japanese lady who must be precisely placed on the page in relation to obligatory pagoda, bush, pool, fish, tree and cloud. Piotrek and I, enjoying his painting, felt fine together. I thought the picture lively and good.

But the teacher intervened, Piotrek might think he had finished but where was the cloud? Piotrek (and I, privately) thought the cloud unnecessary but pictures of Japan must include clouds: one white, top, right. The communication with me, almost completely non-verbal, had felt warm and expansive. Piotrek was pleased with his picture so felt good about himself and confident with this stranger adult. The teacher's criticism felt to me to be humiliating; it required the child's creation to conform to a rule, not to express his view of the subject.

Although this took place in a classroom, it has relevance to interaction within a counselling setting; the cloud may be missing because there is, simply, no cloud: but the cloud-expecting counsellor may seek for a little mare's tail, imagine impressive (but repressed) cumulo nimbus or interpret the absence of a never-existent fog.

Leave trouble here

Art as a means of communication is universal and discussion in this chapter will be broadly based. But it is essential to acknowledge the specialism known as 'Art Therapy'. Ann Gillespie, (art therapist at the Catholic Children's Society 'Familymakers'' Homefinding Unit, Gravesend, Kent) described the basic principle of her work thus: 'through the use of simple visual and tactile media such as paint, crayons and clay, people (not just children) can explore their unconscious conflicts and fantasies in colour, marks and images', a way of 'getting it out' within 'a natural creative process which in itself is therapeutic' and from which 'symbolic material emerges which speaks from the unconscious to its creator, and which sometimes, but not always, provides a basis for verbal exchange with the therapist' (Gillespie, 1986, p. 19).

She describes her purpose as 'to give each child a space in which to explore those feelings and sensations which have no words, which are undifferentiated, because they are too painful, too confused, or are memories from pre-verbal years' (p. 19).

Importantly:

> Children have very little time in which they are allowed just to *be*, without questions, criticism, help or expectations, especially children in care. This space is valuable for that alone. The presence of a non-directive and accepting therapist, who acts as a mirror in which they can see themselves as they really are, lends a special symbolic quality to the therapeutic hour to which children respond (p. 19).

Referring to 'this natural form of self-expression', she writes 'Doing it is what counts, not the result' (p. 19).

In a letter to me responding to an earlier draft of this chapter, Ann Gillespie (for whose advice I am very grateful) wrote:

> It is important to take into account the power of images made in the presence of an art therapist, who is usually an artist herself, and therefore attuned to the subtleties of visual symbolism. The relationship built up between client, therapist and image within the art therapy hour can take the child into areas of deep unconscious feeling, through which they must be 'held' by a strong and trained therapist. Without this the child cannot explore safely and therefore no therapeutic growth can happen.

The essential component of *containment*.

She explains the distinction between art therapy (for which special training is essential) and the use of art

> with children by other workers who are not qualified art therapists, but who use drawings with children in other ways and for other purposes. It is important because many people do not appreciate the difference, falling into the trap of simplistic and maybe dangerous interpretations or of seeking certain results from the children when they ask them to draw.

'Joe' (art therapist in a hospital-based child and family unit) says that children referred to him 'may think they should be "doing art" but the important thing is to introduce it as an idea, leaving the children to find it for themselves'. Like Ann Gillespie, he regards the prime consideration to be 'giving children time and space for themselves with an individual adult and choice between, for example, speaking, playing, drawing'.

In her article, Gillespie comments that while several of the children in the unit 'have folders of drawings and paintings and shelves full of models', some 'have none' and that she has 'learnt to appreciate the "art" of some of the others who conduct battles, burglaries, trials, murders, funerals and dinner parties all without touching the art materials at all' (p. 19).

However, 'the children all call their sessions "Art Therapy" even if they never do "art" and never feel they have to' (p. 23).

Joe, negotiating with children about the use of their time and space with him, may suggest that, through talking about or drawing problems, it may be possible 'to leave trouble here'.

The troubles which may be brought to, expressed, explored and even left with the individual adult, whether entitled art therapist, counsellor, nurse or social worker, are legion and may relate to any number of circumstances and settings. The following sections describe the application of art-assisted communication in a number of settings and with a variety of adult practitioners.

A lion like a mummy: psychiatrist and social worker with residential care staff working with bereaved children (after murder)

Drawing pictures played an important part in joint work by a psychiatrist and social worker with four young Egyptian children who had witnessed the horrendous murder of their mother by their father. The children spoke no English and no 'language that an interpreter could understand, having developed their own personal language' although they could 'understand two foreign dialects' (Isaacs and Hickman, 1987, p. 32).

The oldest, Anna (7) was 'the one who looked after the others, and it was said of her worryingly, "It is as if she has not been affected". She proudly claimed that she had not cried much and was clearly conveying that it was her job to hold herself and the others together' (p. 33).

A month after the murder, Stephen Isaacs and Sally Hickman arranged their first regular monthly joint meeting with all four children. 'Anna was tense and frozen' during play re-enactment of the scene. At one point she 'drew a lion which looked like an Egyptian mummy but denied any connection with her mother' (p. 33). (I am not clear whether this refers to verbal punning and if so, if Anna had sufficient command of English for this.)

During later meetings she 'drew more and more pictures of houses with trees and grass under the tree, often with a cross over the grass. She euphemistically talked of her mother as "under the ground" and we understood her to be struggling with the concept of her mother being dead' (p. 34).

There was an attempt to use drawings as a means of communication with the father during a visit to him in prison six months after the murder but he 'rejected their approaches and offers of drawings and was almost totally uncommunicative' (p. 35).

Mahmoud's reponse was to struggle 'with the disappointment, trying to maintain an idea that his father could come back with him and repeating that his mother was alive'. Encouraged to draw a picture of where he thought his parents were. 'Mahmoud drew his father in a room with a key on the outside, then his father outside the door as well, as if he were free to come and go as he pleased' (p. 35).

Referring not only to drawings but all kinds of communication, the authors comment that 'We feel it is apparent that it is not always easy to understand what is being communicated, there may be several meanings to each communication and one can never be certain of having comprehended them' (p. 35).

Another form of visual art was effectively used. Staff in the residential home were encouraged to display photographs of both parents. 'When the photograph of Mrs R. did appear, the children jumped on the bed and described how their father had jumped on their mother's stomach' leading to further indications of their understanding of what had happened. For example, Mahmoud said 'that his mother was only asleep. If he shouted loud enough perhaps he could wake her' (p. 34).

Seeing the photograph also stimulated the children to cry for the first time since the funeral.

A drawing of sunshine: voluntary counsellor with bereaved child (suicide of father)

This material was contributed by Joan Cooley in the form of an unpublished article, for which I am very grateful: to be published subsequent to completion of the present text in *Bereavement Care*, Spring, 1992.

Sam (nearly 7) was introduced to Joan Cooley (a volunteer counsellor with *Cruse*) following the suicide of his father. Another counsellor worked with Sam's mother. He was 'having violent dreams, fantasies, was bed wetting, a nervous tic had reappeared, and the school reported lack of concentration and withdrawn behaviour' (Cooley, 1990).

From Sam's mother, with whom she established 'a trusting relationship' and who fully supported Joan Cooley's article, the counsellor learnt that his

> beloved Great Grandma had died six months ago, that his father's
> disturbed personality had prevented him from bonding and showing
> any affection for Sam....that Sam had been witness to violence to the
> mother and had tried to stand protectively between them. Later Sam
> had to cope with change of home, school and his mother's continued
> distress, migraines and stay in hospital for investigation.

A combination of many varied activities included a number of drawings. An early self-portrait is a lively depiction of *Sam walking a tight-rope* in full clown make up with a huge, exaggerated, smiling mouth.

The self-portrait from Session 4 is also smiling. From the right side of his head (left of picture) floats a balloon enclosing *Pleasant thoughts* – 'If I am good I will get a reward. Going to my new house. Looking forward to Joan coming. My mummy giving me cuddles when I am unhappy.' Sam's eyes turn towards these thoughts. On the other side are *Unhappy, worrying thoughts*. 'Bad dreams. Horrible films and going to bed afterwards in the dark. Dean Taylor. Sometimes I get hurt. Sometimes I fall over'.

The counsellor found the early sessions 'bland'. He 'accepted my visits, and mother reported that he looked forward to having me to himself. The details of his drawings 'showed flair and maturity'.

The squiggle game proved to be a successful aid 'to loosen Sam up', revealing 'strong aggression in manner and content; and, usefully, his understanding of the permanence of death, which we talked through'. Squiggling 'became a firm favourite, demanded as a reward to finish future sessions'.

The activity is straightforward and shared. One partner draws a free squiggle which the other turns into a picture, then vice versa. Detailed description of squiggling is given by D. W. Winnicott through, for example, work with Ruth (8) who 'was able to remember and relive the distress that belonged to the time of her becoming a deprived child and she was able to illustrate this in drawing. The experience was a therapeutic one for Ruth, and the changes in Ruth benefitted the whole family' (Winnicott, 1971, pp. 317ff.). I have found no accounts of the meaning and benefits of squiggling to the adult participants: I enjoy the game and my own efforts usually turn into flowers.

While Sam was away on holiday Joan Cooley, who was feeling anxious about the contact, found the work of Claudia Jewett (1984) to be a 'lifeline' and was also greatly helped by the local Cruse consultant, a child psychiatrist. A new artistic activity was introduced, to aid 'the recognition and naming of feeling'. Joan and Sam made faces 'at each other to represent inner feelings of sadness, anger, loneliness, happiness and anxiety. These Sam translated, drawing on to cardboard with intense care, then cut out'.

The back of each face was labelled with a variety of words to link the appropriate expression/feeling, for example, 'sadness, anger, loneliness, happiness and anxiety'. Puppets representing significant people in Sam's life had been made, and 'Sam suggested that snips at the side of each face plus a rubber band would fix these on to the puppet and could be changed appropriately. He raced in to tell his mother. "You can tell how people feel by the look on their face"', an enormous discovery for him. Sam's involvement in the activity, and ease with his counsellor, enabled him to take a very active and imaginative initiative.

Drawings focused on 'comparative pictures with written examples of *Daddy happy Daddy angry* or *Sometimes I miss Daddy* and *Sometimes I don't*. For the latter he could now illustrate with detail his father throwing boiling hot coffee in his mother's face. Mother weeping, Father in profile (considered to be a symbol of a child's maturation) and all in black'. The counsellor's comment that the father '"must have been in a black mood"', gave Sam satisfaction, and he wanted this inscribed'.

In the last session Sam 'completed his last two highly expressive comparative drawings *Sam anxious* and *Sam no longer anxious. He can tell his fears and worries to someone who can listen*'. As Joan Cooley was about to leave for the last time, Sam gave her 'a drawing of sunshine and a tree reflected in water and a card inscribed "Thank you for being my friend"'.

Monster with trees: counsellors with dying children

In *Inscapes of the Child's World* John Allan (1988) devotes a chapter to *Spontaneous Drawings in Counseling Seriously Ill Children* including a case study of the art work of Caroyl, a little girl dying over several months of leukaemia (pp. 93ff.).

The main theme of both chapter and work is the endeavour to help terminally ill children 'to live each day more fully in spite of emotional turmoil' (p. 93). Such writers as Susan Bach (1969), Myra Bluebond-Langner (1978) and Elisabeth Kübler-Ross (1983) have contributed to understanding that children may be clearly aware of approaching death. 'Those who learned to know death, rather than to fear and fight it, become our teachers about LIFE. There are thousands of children who know death far beyond the knowledge adults have' (Kübler-Ross, 1983, p. xvii).

Myra Bluebond-Langner identified stages of awareness, passing from being seriously ill (1) to dying (5) (1978). John Allan suggests that arrival at each phase of awareness may stimulate such reactions as denial and anger. Counsellors can help children to progress perhaps towards acceptance, allowing feelings to be experienced and expressed through drawing (pp. 94–5).

Susan Bach (1969) documents in detail sequences of paintings and drawings of two 8 year old children dying of cancer in a Swiss hospital. Caroyl, the artist in Allan's study, was in Canada but difference of continent and verbal language do not seem to affect the kind, and possible meanings of, the images chosen.

Only a few examples can be described here but the first I choose because Allan refers to it as emphasizing the value of drawing for children. One day Caroyl was too ill for lessons at home but agreed that she would like to draw a picture. This shows a little girl whose heavily drawn, downturned mouth and tears are echoed by a face in her stomach (p. 105).

An example of the picture leading to discussion of the child's feelings is entitled *Monster* (pp. 108–10). The description demonstrates not only the detail of the picture itself but also of the counsellor, Jodi's, care in finding possible meanings.

Caroyl draws two evergreen trees (the subjects of an earlier picture and possible interpretations by the author). Between these trees is a monster who 'at first appears to be frightening to the tiny person who calls for help. Is this death calling for her?' The figure is framed in a window within the gable of a house, a small window which recalls to me the 'soul windows' which appear in the Swiss houses drawn by Susan Bach's children.

The monster is drawn in dotted lines which to Jodi 'suggest the breaking down of her own body boundaries due to the leukemia'.

Detail about the position and colours of the monster are given, including that the 'mouth is blood-red and seems smeared, possibly signifying the need for an infusion of healthy blood'. Jodi wonders whether the person is in fact 'calling to the monster for help'.

Responding to the prominence of the written word 'help' flowing from the person's mouth towards the monster, Jodi 'asked Caroyl if she ever felt like that figure'. This led to 'a long discussion about how her family was coping, her wish to talk more, but wanting to protect them from more distress'. Jodi considered that 'The lack of windows on the ground floor and the sketchy front of the house could have told us that she had to keep something hidden or could not be "up front"' (pp. 109–10).

In his conclusion to this chapter, Allan comments that Caroyl 'benefited greatly from the ongoing love of her parents and family, from the counselor's support and from the opportunity to release through drawings and discussions' (p. 113). He proposes some guidelines, including that the counsellor should respect and accept all work without judgement and being careful not to make interpretative comment. Counsellors' responses should be 'open-ended and tentative, giving the child options in responding' (p. 114).

He encourages the use of drawings in work with a range of practitioners, including medical staff, school counsellors and teachers, suggesting, too, that grieving relations may be comforted by sharing their children's work. While knowledge of psychology and symbolism aid 'skill in interpreting content', Allan concludes that 'basic caring and a willingness to be open to the child's view will enable many to be effective in aiding a child on a journey through life' (p. 115).

A divided house: nursery nurse in a family centre with an unhappy child

'Renata' telephoned the police from a call box: 'My Mum's going to kill me.' Investigation showed that this was not so but that telephone call was taken seriously as a cry for help and Renata was referred to a family centre. Nursery nurse 'Nancy Mint' found her to be 'a very inward child – it was difficult to understand how she'd been triggered to make that flamboyant telephone call'. Renata's constant response to any question was 'I don't know really' and work to make any kind of real contact with her was 'a really long slog'.

The abuse of Renata was not physical but emotional, the unconscious deprivation by adults who were 'too busy' to recognize the little girl's unhappiness and desperate need to be noticed. Her parents regarded her as 'just naughty' and at school she was seen only as a disruptive element, often waiting outside the classroom from which she had been rejected, when Nancy called for her. In school Renata's need to express powerful feeling was constantly 'squashed' but in the Family Centre she did not respond to opportunities 'to thrash about and be boisterous'.

However Renata drew amazing pictures, especially of houses, 'very disjointed, drawn brick by brick, very monotonous' and using space confidently. Nancy noticed that she never put her family inside the house, which would be distinctly divided down the middle. Beside the house on one side she would draw herself and her younger brother, Rex, and on the other her father and stepmother. One member of the family was always omitted – her baby half-sister; Renata said that she would like to be the baby. Nancy hoped that Renata might become able to put the figures within the house.

Rex, it appeared, was Renata's only chosen companion, drawn as the sole other occupant of a desert island. The two children were close in age and Rex seen by his mother as 'perfect'.

The island drawing was prepared by Nancy Mint with the caption '*Your very own island! Would you have anyone there with you?*' Two palm trees, a sturdy log cabin and peaceful bay make the prospect of shipwreck attractive. Among her other drawn work sheets are '*A delicious, hot, steaming pie. What would you do with it, when, and why?*' – these words surrounding a good-enough-to-eat sketch. A sheet bearing a large, enticingly blank and open book invites the child – '*IF...you could write a book, what would it be about? See if you can design the cover today? What would you call your book?*' A sturdy telephone suggests '*phone someone*'.

Because it can fly: art therapist with an unhappy child in care

Jackie (11) was introduced to Ann Gillespie, an art therapist working in a residential homefinding unit, as 'like a caged animal, climbing the walls – loud, aggressive, hostile – gets picked on, fights with everybody, does dangerous things to smaller kids, strangles if she hugs, bites and scratches, and swears from morning till night'. The residential staff 'were desperate. I wondered what magic I was supposed to have' (Gillespie, 1986, pp. 19, 20).

Sessions were 'infinitely varied' and Jackie's involvement very intense. 'Initially she tried out the materials and made windswept, agitated drawings in felt pen or charcoal, splodges of fingerpaints, and numerous animals in clay' (p. 20).

The speed and urgency with which Jackie worked are described below. Clay figures of horses 'seemed to represent her struggling to create some form in her life' and 'she began to express some of the chaos in large drawings that we did together on the floor', following the squiggle model of D. W. Winnicott (1971); 'one person makes a free "squiggle" on the paper, giving it to the other to complete or adapt into what they will' (p. 20).

Jackie, however, 'could never play this game as it was intended, but would take over constantly, wildly drawing, adding, and talking, talking, talking, as the marks spread like wildfire over the paper, accompanied by streams of barely intelligible fantasy, bossing me about at the same time and leaving me out of breath and confused' (p. 20).

Ann Gillespie recorded what she had remembered one day:

> There was a house with a fence round it and my squiggle was a worm or a snake that wasn't allowed into the house – then there was an old lady's house with no fence round and he went in there and ate her up. Someone came and cut the squiggle in two and there was black blood. Another squiggle came and was cut in two and there was green blood. There were rivers out of which all these things came, and the rivers flooded, but the people got on the roof and there was black blood everywhere...
>
> I never figured out what any of this meant. I just knew this frantic stream of confusion and destruction had found a safety valve (Gillespie, 1986, p. 20).

At this time, Jackie's keyworker left with no immediate successor. Sessions with the art therapist were times when she could let go of the tensions and battles of the rest of the week and begin 'a friendship with an adult on a non-authoritarian and non-parental level' (p. 21).

On one occasion, Jackie and Ann 'drew round each other on large sheets of paper. Amazed at the sight of her outline on the floor, Jackie 'painted it in with her usual dash and became horrified as the paper tore again and the figure looked like some monstrous animal in clothes' (p. 21).

At the next session Jackie 'Resilient as always...Coloured in my outline with enormous care, concerned for each little blemish, showing that she could learn from experience, but also rather sadly, how tattered was her own self image and how perfect she wanted to make mine' (p. 21).

The advent of her new keyworker helped Jackie to move away from 'her babyish reliance' on Ann Gillespie, beginning 'to construct more complex models, taking more time, talking about them, and no longer so locked in herself, but looking outwards towards the world' (p. 21).

When Jackie had been seeing Ann Gillespie for a year, she made 'an aeroplane which fell apart so many times, that she announced that as there was such a lot of work to be done to it, it would have to stay in the hangar until 12 September'. This date had dual significance as Jackie's birthday and the return of therapist from holiday, being 'so obviously about herself that I knew now she had some non-verbal understanding of the meaning of her own images' (p. 21).

Model-making concludes the account of Ann Gillespie's work with Jackie, who 'finished what she says is a Firebird and what to me looks like a battered Spitfire, both apt images of her. This one, she says, "Is ready to be launched now, because it can fly"' (p. 22).

The turtle portrait: social worker with child in care

'Mark' (10) had been committed to care some years before when another child in his family had been sexually abused by their stepfather. As part of preparation for what was hoped would be a permanent placement I was asked to work with Mark alone, seeing him once a week. An important aim was to help him again a stronger sense of self, to increase his self-esteem and confidence.

Not being very energetic, I was nervous about my ability to keep up if a 10 year old wanted to express himself too vigorously. It proved easy, however, to find interests and activities which we (as individual people, rather than as 10 year old boy and 50 year old woman) could share. On a walk during our first meeting (after the introduction) we had an adventure with a goose which not only gave us much to talk about but also material for a written story and illustration.

These were made in a café since we could not easily meet in the foster home and there was no social services department office within 20 miles. I would meet Mark from school and we would walk to our café, where the waitress thought we were doing extra homework, giving us every help to gain as much privacy as possible, even letting us stay after the café closed.

I bought Mark a bird book, a ring binder and equipment for drawing, choosing everything possible in his favourite colour. I kept everything in a large shopping bag so that I was responsible for bringing the 'Markbag' to each meeting; it would have been difficult for him to keep everything together and to carry it all to school for our meetings.

The first picture was of the goose. First Mark told me the story of our adventure, then drew a magnificent goose, copying from the bird book. He started from a webbed foot, drawing the outline accurately and confidently filling the centre of the sheet. He has considerable talent and deserved every word of my praise.

A pattern developed from this, Mark telling me a story, usually an account of some recent event, while I scribbled down in writing about which he was justly scathing. He would then draw (in coloured pencils) some illustration which we carefully added to the folder. During the week I would write out the story, often using different coloured pens, which he liked, and showing the result to him at our next meeting. Although hardly 'art work' this visually demonstrated that Mark's life and words were important enough for an adult to use time and effort to record, preserve and present attractively. He would read very carefully, gently correcting errors.

Under Mark's guidance I drew my first bicycle. He rightly thought it would be a kindness to pass on some of his own skill and my effort, now in his folder, does him credit as a teacher. It may sometimes be difficult for a child to find opportunity to teach the adult, especially in such time- and space-limited contacts as, broadly speaking, counselling. I could, for example, have benefited from swimming lessons too but management of that activity would have been impossible. For drawing, the simple equipment was easily to hand and portable.

A drawing which I particularly enjoyed was of a single mallard's feather. The accompanying story, *The Shiny Feather*, was beautiful and Mark drew diagonally across the whole page one large and delicate feather. My own copy was made for sheer pleasure.

My last Mark-tutored drawing led me to much thought. Sitting on a river bank, he invited me to follow his drawing lead, not telling me the subject. I realized that my pencil was beginning to outline a Teenage Mutant Ninja Turtle (a popular cartoon figure). I did not want to continue this picture. I felt sorry that Mark was reproducing an existing figure instead of creating something imaginative and I disliked the violent reputation of the film characters.

Since I did not want to hurt or reject Mark, I continued to draw and solved my own problem, I thought, by wreathing the sword with flowers.

But communication does not cease because the adult has become confused. Mark recognized my withheld response to his work – the first time I had been other than genuinely approving. I tried to recover the situation by praising the colouring. But Mark knew. When he narrated that day's story he said, 'Margaret didn't like my drawing'.

This was all about *my* problem, mixing my own principles with Mark's freedom – which I had, explicitly, given to him. I had no right to censure his choice and I muddled my own response. My very fear and dislike of violence led me to do violence to the child himself.

Far from doing anything to earn my disapproval, he had followed lines which had before achieved pleasure and approval: I had encouraged him to copy existing pictures (for example, of the goose), I had enjoyed being taught to draw subjects of Mark's choice, and I had never before introduced my own feelings. Months after this, for me, painful episode, I realized that my righteous disapproval of the Turtle had probably been communicated to Mark as bewildering disapproval of himself.

It is artistic justice that beside me as I write is a grinning green shelled monster, a portrait of a Turtle, by Mark.

Owls and elephants: on interpretation

Susan (13), responding to Violet Oaklander's 1978 invitation to create her own world on paper, 'took up only half the sheet with her drawing, leaving the other half blank' She was invited to talk about the picture and then about the blank part. 'That's for my life that I will grow up into. I don't know what it will be, so I didn't put anything there.' The counsellor commented, 'There's a lot of room there for all kinds of things' and Susan said, 'Right!' (p. 21).

Oaklander comments on this as 'a good example of the importance of not doing interpretations as such'. Response to the drawing might have been 'Aha, this child is obviously constrained and constricted. She is fearful and keeps herself tightly closed, or she is unbalanced in some way'. Whatever the truth of such analysis, 'after Susan's experience of visualizing and drawing her world, and then sharing and elaborating on her drawing with us, she was able to look at the white expanse and offer the possibility that there was more to come in her life'. The girl's voice and expression 'showed optimism, hope, an opening, a reaching out for life' (p. 23).

A constant and fundamental theme in the literature and practice of counselling is the need for caution and reticence in interpreting, whether behaviour, creation or words. Had Oaklander told Susan her view of the unfilled space, before or after the girl explained it's purpose, the chance for the verbal and facial expression of optimism and hope would have been lost and, with that, the opportunity for Susan to feel her face smile and her voice sound confident.

In a letter to *Community Care* Amory, et al., (1986) a group of art therapists wrote:

In our experience most social workers find it hard to facilitate a spontaneous drawing from a child because they are so frightened of drawing themselves. This can lead to a kind of 'I can't draw either so don't worry' approach which puts a drawing down before it is started.
...
...because the task of social workers is so often to obtain information about how a child is feeling in order to make decisions, a pressure must be felt even in the request for a drawing. Those drawings that appear especially meaningful run the risk of being overanalysed, whereas it is the manner and the context in which the child produces the drawing that holds the subtler messages. On the whole, the urge to pin down, to demand or extract a meaning, deadens what should be a living. changing, shifting process.

Unless this process has been experienced, and is re-experienced regularly, the worker cannot share and facilitate in a child the joy and pain of visual creativity which is in itself perhaps the most therapeutic act of all. It heals and enables growth of self-esteem, whether or not we or the child understand it. The 'meaning', if there must be one, is often so complex or so unknown that only at a deep unconscious level does it mark a movement in a child's progress.

It requires great faith and ability to bear this unknowingness. It is
also essential to value and respect the child and his products, thus
building in him trust in his own creative powers. It is a time-consuming
task and needs specially sensitive and trained antennae to feel for the
coded and concealed messages the children themselves are searching
for.
...
There *is* a mystery about art, and social workers are right to be afraid
of its power. Drawings can be obtained on demand, but they tend to
end up as lifeless diagrams with stereotyped explanations attached.
They should not be a means to an end, a way of getting a child to talk;
they are an end, or rather a process, in themselves (Amory, *et al.*
1986).

In the playroom with Ann Gillespie (a signatory of the above letter),
Jackie (11) 'never talked about her drawings and models'. Working
fast, 'Clay lumps were thrown together to make horses, hamsters,
cats'. Such was the urgency of her creating that 'When paint was
applied, it also went on fast, probably obliterating any drawing
underneath, or dripping carelessly over the model' (p. 20).

The therapist was careful not to intrude or interfere 'As far as
interpretation went. I could speculate to myself about the content, but
said nothing to her. In answer to a tentative question which might be,
"And what could the horse be thinking now?", I would get, "He's too
busy eating grass", in a tone which clearly told me to keep off' (p. 20).

More important than interpretation, translating symbol into (apparently) jointly understood verbal language, is respect for the children's
choices. Ann Gillespie writes (in a letter) 'the important thing about
the choice to do what they will is that the child is thus given a position of
self-direction and control throughout, which helps them to build a
sense of autonomy and self-esteem. This is an important experience
for children in care who are so disempowered in their everyday lives'.

Inaccurate interpretation may be at the least embarrassing and at
worst dangerous. Nancy Mint recalled the bewilderment of a child
whose picture she pinned to the wall upside down – a not unfamiliar
experience for both adult and child. Most of us, I imagine, have made
at least one '*That's* nice dear – what is it?' *faux pas*.

Even more humiliating is the confidently expressed, wrong interpretation. Antoine de Saint-Exupéry recalls that 'Once when I was six
years old I saw a magnificent picture in a book...of a boa constrictor in
the act of swallowing an animal'. The narrator made a drawing himself
which he showed to the grown-ups, asking 'whether the drawing
frightened them'. The adult response was, 'Why should anyone be
frightened by a hat?' But the drawing 'was not a picture of a hat, it was
a picture of a boa constrictor digesting an elephant'. To aid the foolish
grown-ups, he drew an explicit 'X-ray' picture, the elephant clearly on
view within the snake whose long body, naturally, it distends: 'Grown-
ups never understand anything by themselves and it is tiresome for

children to be always and forever explaining things to them' (de Saint-Exupéry, 1974, pp. 7, 8).

But grown-ups deserve some sympathy, for the first picture does look like a hat! Context is all. From their experience with the young Antoine, one hopes that the adults learnt to ask questions before giving opinions. (I am indebted to Claire Seymour (1990) for drawing my attention to this material in her unpublished thesis.)

The positive danger of mis-interpretation is illustrated in the novel *The Owl Service* (Garner, 1967), based on a tale from the *Mabinogian* (for example, Jones and Jones, 1949). In brief, the owl service is a set of china dishes decorated with an ambiguous design. Interpreting this as stylized owls' heads affects the behaviour of three young people, leading to fear and violence.

> Look at the pattern!...Don't you see what it is?' An abstract design in green round the edge, touched up with a bit of rough gilding.'
> ...It's an owl's head...That's the body. If you take the design off the plate and fit it together it makes a complete owl. See, I've traced the two parts of the design, and all you do is turn the head right round till it's the other way up, and then join it to the top of the main pattern where it follows the rim of the plate'...
> It was an owl: a stylised, floral owl (Garner, 1967, p. 17).

Peace and health are restored only when an alternative interpretation of the design is recognized as a garland of flowers.

'Blind analysis of a child's artwork is dangerous. It is imperative to have the child actively explain the meaning of the picture' (Allan, p. 146). If, indeed, there must be interpretation. But Ann Gillespie asks, 'Do we have to?' (p. 22). Do we need to know? If we suspect, if we are told, we must beware. Empty spaces may await the fulfilment of life, hats may hide undigested elephants and owls in reality be flowers.

Rosebush

One flower especially flourishes in several studies – the rose. Based on the work of J. Stevens (1971), John Allan, Violet Oaklander and Claire Seymour describe use of the rosebush fantasy. Children are encouraged to imagine themselves as rosebushes, visualizing roots, stems, branches, leaves and flowers. They may be asked to describe and/or draw their visions.

Allan describes study of the pictures and words of children, reflecting whether emotionally healthy or suffering inner turmoil, concluding that 'For counselors, the rosebush strategy may be a useful screening device for detecting children who have been or are being sexually abused', advising strongly that such techniques must be employed with great caution and with specialized training and supervision (pp. 82, 83).

Oaklander asks the children 'to open their eyes when they are ready' after relaxing 'and draw their rosebushes'. Drawings are later described in the present tense and in the first person. Thus Carol (10): 'I'm just beginning to bloom. I'm all different colors. I'm magic...Since I'm magic I don't need anybody to help me....I'll never die'. But when the counsellor 'read each statement back to her, Carol said of herself, 'I'm just beginning to grow. Sometimes I don't need anyone to help me. Sometimes I feel alone. I know I'll die' (p. 33).

Gina (8) said, 'I can grow easier if I don't have roots; if they want to replant me it will be easier. I always have buds.' Her adoptive parents had separated and she 'had many uneasy feelings about her situation – much anxiety about what would happen to her' (p. 35).

Working with Trevor (10) who had experienced removal from home at the age of 3 because of neglect, and ending of adoptive placement at 6 or 7, followed by a period in children's homes awaiting 'a permanent family', Claire Seymour used the Rosebush guided fantasy. Like Gina, Trevor had no roots – they 'would not grow, because nobody took care of it'. There were, however, 'lots of thorns on it so that it would hurt anyone who tried to touch it' (Seymour, 1990, pp. 1, 10).

This dissertation includes a number of rosebushes: Laura's (nearly 4) is a spherical squiggle with twigs; Chris's tall and slim with many bare branches is 'in space – it is dead because there is no oxygen'. Chris also contributes a whole landscape – soft rolling hills, a reed-fringed pond with frog and winged insect and a bare rosebush which is 'young it take care of its self it lives near a pond were the weather is fine' [sic]. Adam too provides two images, One 'is on the back of a motor bike being delivered, for the queen. It's alive and well' and Adam, driving the regal bush, looks out of the picture and smiles. The other 'is in the woods all by itself growing very bushy'.

Monsters, cake and concern for the soul

> it's a funny thing, but if you just scribble a pattern, then look at it
> hard, you can see figures and faces in the scribble, so then you black in
> the lines that make those faces and – it's hard to explain.

Josephine, one of the young residents in *The House of Mad Children* in Rosemary Timperley's novel, (1980) has been describing to Anna, a (very) temporary helper, how the six children, all with appalling histories, had collaborated to decorate the Family Room wall in secret. Reg

> did most of the monsters, creatures with people-legs and animal
> heads, or people-heads and animal legs, and the horrible insects with
> human faces. May did the background landscape, and I added the

witches' arms to the trees and put eyes in the middle of the flowers. Clive did the little black devil-things and the instruments of torture and the gallows, although I did the naked man on the gallows, and Ahmed did his 'thing' (p. 59).

This may sound far-fetched, a work of fiction. But I still recall vividly the chalk on blackboard drawing in the locked unit of an assessment centre – the skull, the weapons, the blasted tree, the anger and hatred and frustration captured in so innocent a medium.

Only Vanda, a wise woman, faces the problem of the mural. 'Their fancies go to their heads, which already are mixed-up. You should not deliberately fill them with new fancies...They should be shown that they are as ordinary as anyone else. Each of them is encouraged to think he is extraordinary. It is wrong. I am afraid for their souls' (Timperley, 1980, pp. 59, 35, 36).

Anna's response to Josephine's explanation is, 'I know what you mean', followed by, 'Where's the cake?' (p. 59). Reading the novel it is easy to ask, 'does she really understand?' or perhaps to applaud her common-sense diversion of attention to the mundane task of setting tea. Cake may be an antidote to monsters but fear for the soul still lurks.

Summary

Roses, pagodas and owls and many other images illustrate this depiction of sharing **art assisted counselling**. The activity itself may be helpful, providing opportunity for protected **time** and **space** and **choice**. Children's behaviour during, for example, drawing, may offer clues to feelings but, as with the products (pictures, models and so on) the greatest care must be taken with **interpretation**. Owls may be roses, but roses may be owls.

Link

Exploration of communication and self-expression through various media concludes with the least discussed form, music. Chapter 10 acts as a sequel to my chapter in *Respecting Children* (1980), 'Notes on Notes'; and continuing the present theme of telling our own stories in our own ways, it is entitled 'A Sound of Their Own'.

References

Allan. J. (1988). *Inscapes of the Child's World: Jungian Counseling in Schools and Clinics*. Spring Publications, Dallas, Texas.

Amory, C., Gillespie, A., Halliday, D. and Skaife D'Ingerthorpe, R. (1986). Letter In *Community Care*.

Bach, S. (1960). *Spontaneous Paintings of Severely Ill Patients*. Geigy, Switzerland.

Bluebond-Langner, M. (1978). *The Private Worlds of Dying Children*. Princeton University Press, New Jersey.

Cooley, J. (1990). Searching for a Way Through: an account of bereavement work with a seven year old boy. Unpublished article. (Later published in *Bereavement Care*, Spring, 1992.)

Crompton, M. (1980). *Respecting Children: Social Work With Young People*. Edward Arnold, London.

Garner, A. (1967). *The Owl Service*. Collins, London.

Gillespie, A. (1986). 'Art therapy' at the Familymakers Project. *Adoption and Fostering*, 10, (1), 19–23.

Gillespie, A. (1991). Personal letter to Margaret Crompton.

Isaacs, S. and Hickman, S. (1987). Communicating with children after a murder. *Adoption and Fostering*, 11, (4), 32–5.

Jewett, C. (1984). *Helping Children Cope with Separation and Loss*. Batsford/BAAF, London.

Jones, G. and Jones, T. (1949). *The Mabinogion*. Dent, London.

Kübler-Ross, E. (1983). *On Children and Death*. Macmillan, New York.

Oaklander, V. (1978). *Windows to our Children: a Gestalt Therapy Approach to Children and Adolescents*. Real People Press, Utah.

Pluckrose, H. (1974). In *Every Side of the Picture*. The Save the Children Fund, London.

de Saint Exupéry, A. (Woods, K. (trans.)) (1974). *The Little Prince*. Pan, London.

Seymour, C. (1990). Counselling Children. Unpublished dissertation. University of Durham.

Stevens, J. (1971). *Awareness: Exploring, Experimenting and Experiencing*. Real People Press, Utah.

Timperley, R. (1980). *The House of Mad Children*. Robert Hale, London.

Winnicott, D. W. (1971). *Therapeutic Consultations in Child Psychiatry*. Hogarth, London.

10   A sound of their own

An expensive frill?

A considerable disappointment in writing *Attending to Children* (Crompton, 1990) was the shortage of material about music in working with children. That shortage, together with anxiety about the length of the manuscript, led me to include only one very short section, in the chapter, *Talking Without Words* (p. 96). Given a further chance in preparing the present book, I can draw on no material from my contacts with practitioners in a number and variety of agencies.

No one who wrote to me mentioned music either, although correspondents represented parents, teachers, social workers and counsellors.

Both in spite and because of this I am so convinced of the importance of this form of expression and communication that I offer this chapter, based on a number of texts and my own experience. The literature on which I draw includes only one of the texts focused on counselling children mentioned elsewhere. In all the texts on counselling I studied, words predominate and art and drama find their place. Only Shapiro (1984) describes a musical interaction.

Material is drawn mainly from the education section of a university library and some from my own shelves. A mind-survey of English literature (for both adults and children) could supply very few examples of music described as playing an important part in the lives and interactions of the characters.

The 'professional' literature available to me focused on either education in school or on music therapy for children and young people with special needs, usually physical and/or mental handicap. There was very little attention to the employment of music in service of people whose special needs are social, emotional and/or spiritual, without other disability. Is music regarded as of use only to people who are so incapacitated that they cannot communicate verbally? Can would-be helping adults communicate only with words? 'Trying to ensure that I have understood or will remember, or to reflect back to a child, I am all too likely to seek too many repetitions or force some delicately, quietly offered flight of words into a four square paragraph...Can I be sure that you are really feeling your feelings unless – and until – you tell me? All about it. In words' (Crompton, 1991, p. 31).

Perhaps we regard music as either protectedly personal or for public performance. A musical 'purist' might regard the idea of 'using' music as abusive of art. But we have no trouble in employing the language of Shakespeare as a means of self-expression and interpersonal communication. Bach and Schubert hold no exclusive rights in melody and harmony (nor would they, whole and life-loving people, have wished so to do).

To the musician, music is the supreme art, the language of being. But in many situations it is both un- and de-valued. Donald Hughes (1985) (a former music advisor and head of a college school of music) found that a Department of Education and Science document 'did nothing to discourage those who, faced with the brutal necessity of making cuts, chose an "expensive frill" like music as one of the most palatable ways of achieving their aim', leading to cuts in specialist staff at all levels of teaching and training (Hughes, 1985, p. 7).

If the value of music can be so disastrously overlooked within the broad field of education, it is of no surprise that (to my knowledge) it is hardly recognized within mainstream social and health care and welfare training.

The crevices between words

'What does a musical communication communicate?' asked Brian Newbould (1981) in his professorial inaugural lecture at the University of Hull. He proposed that

> it communicates a psychological state [which] has spiritual, emotional, and sensual components; and it is something that neither words nor any other medium can communicate. Music fills in the crevices between words. It seeps between the dictionary-fixed symbols of everyday communication, touching those parts of human receptivity that verbal utterances cannot reach...Words, for all the ambiguity, resonance, innuendo they may display especially in a poetic assemblage, are neither as flexible nor as wide-ranging as music. When words are spent, music will encourage a battalion in battle, a baby to sleep, a Shakespearian Duke to love, a criminal...to repent, a production-line worker to produce, a dairy cow to yield; it will help to purge the grief of a mourner, to concentrate the devotion of a worshipper, to rally the loyalty of football spectators, to ennoble the rituals of divine service, Olympic games, festival of remembrance, degree congregation (p. 11).

Music is constantly around us, used often insidiously to manipulate our behaviour. At quiet times in the supermarket, pleasant soothing muzak may encourage me to feel relaxed, to linger waltzingly, to treat myself to a little luxury, to try something new. At busy times when the store aims to move hordes of shoppers swiftly from entrance to check-out with laden trollies, the muzak is brisk, encouraging quick even urgent decisions, the temptation now not to revel in tantalizing treats but to pass Alice-like along rabbit holes lined with tins demanding 'take me', filling the basket with too much for fear of missing something in the hectic quickstep. Even more sinister is the political use – or abuse – of music. Newbould mentions the encouragement of a battalion in battle; what of the patriotic music accompanying filmed pictures of war, of martial music at political rallies, stirring the emotions into irresistible fervour? What is the effect on young people of constant voluntary exposure to the sounds drummed into their ears through personal stereo sets? I first saw one of these in a London park after some weeks abroad and thought the boy must be afflicted in some terrible way, thinking the apparatus to be of some clinical significance.

Since then, I have not been surprised to learn that use of headsets can lead to the affliction of deafness. But may they not also signify another kind of affliction – that of inward migration, flight from contact with not only the outside world and other people but also one's own inner world of thought, response and silence. Constant exposure to other people's sound, however objectively excellent, prevents attention to that music of the spheres which sings both beyond and within.

A sense of belonging

Music is an integral and universal part of life. 'There is no phase of man's struggle for existence that has not been accompanied, communicated, and extended by music. From the most primitive to the most sophisticated of cultures, music has been central to every ritual; every significant event in man's personal life has its accompanying musical expression' (Bergethon and Boardman, 1979, p. 3).

Eunice Bailey (1958) in her beautiful account of working with young children finds that even if 'we are not all "musical",...we are all responsive to some aspect of musical experience' (p. 16).

Music is 'a vital force in the shaping of culture – revealing an understanding by many segments of society of the power of music to enrich and enhance the quality of life' (Rinehart, 1980, p. 140).

It is 'a powerful force in bringing a child and his heritage together. All of us need a sense of belonging, of continuity, and of history. To the young child, the cohesiveness of family can be a bulwark against fears, intrusions to security, and inroads in self-esteem and positive image' (Bayless and Ramsey, 1982, p. 179).

Mike Mennell (1986) (a social worker) notes that the (white) foster mother of James (5) of mixed race parentage helped him to develop positive self-image and 'to counter racist taunting' by introducing 'music, food, magazines and "ethnic" comics into the home' (p. 131).

Bergethon and Boardman describe music as 'the history of mankind...a record of how man has reacted in his struggle with the environment, of what individuals have held dear, and of what they have seen as important to their wellbeing' (p. 3).

These and similar beliefs held by other writers, may be summarized in the title of, and introduction and preface to *Music: A Way of Life for the Young Child*: 'Music is a vital part of daily living', 'a necessary and vital dimension in the lives of children' (Bayless and Ramsey, 1982, pp. vii, ix).

Biffs, bangs and miserable trombones

One of the great powers of music is evocation of memory.

> Music when soft voices die,
> Vibrates in the memory (Shelley).

Vibrates is a powerful, carefully chosen verb, evoking itself *resonance* and *resonate*.

The diary of Nigel Hunt (1982) a young man with Down's syndrome, is alive with bands, songs and pop music as he recalls adventures in England and Austria. In the village of St Johann,

> every Sunday and Thursday the village band formed in front of the post office and they played one tune. Then they marched all the people down to the bandstand.
>
> There they gave this concert, and guess what they played! 'Mein schönes Innsbruck' and my father said 'oh, listen', then he began singing like a thrush. Then came the full swing when they began swinging in time to 'The Austrian Waltz', it was very funny. Up the back of the band was a comical old man with his flat chin upwards and he was clashing it [the cymbals] enjoying himself saying 'Hoi up, hoihup maxitswell', and when they had finished they all lined up and then marched the entire people right round the village.
>
> Then my mother ordered a table for three for a Tirolean evening at the Hotel Klausner and what an evening! They did a lot of *Schuhplattlering* having a wonderful time at Hotel Klausner. We both enjoyed it very much, then after back to our hotel for a night's rest (p. 54), (reparagraphed and my italics).

Nigel Hunt had 'wanted to make this book all about pop music, but my Dad says people will be more interested in my adventures'. However a whole chapter is devoted to *The Pop Music* (pp. 59–62).

Another irresistible evocation of a band must be included for its sheer glory. 'I heard a terrific throb and my ears were lifted and with a Biff biff bang the band came along, and when they turned the corner up came their oompahs and the miserable trombones and blowed me in the middle of nowhere' (p. 40). Here is a boy whose circumstances might by outsiders be regarded as sad, demonstrating through his response to music exuberance, abundance of life and a magnificent grasp of language.

But the memories evoked by and associated with music may, too, be sad, disturbing. Do not the lullabies sung by our mothers cause us in adulthood to weep? Elizabeth Goudge in the musically titled *A City of Bells* (1936) writes of Henrietta, a child whose only memory 'of the days before she went to the orphanage was a memory of music. A woman in a blue dress had sat at the piano singing and Henrietta had danced as she sang' (p. 44).

Henrietta can 'only remember what the woman had looked like,...the sound of her, her singing and her laughter and her deep, ringing voice'. Henrietta has been rescued and adopted. 'The memory of this woman and her music had become almost submerged at the orphanage'. Only in the quiet of her new, private bedroom 'it came back to her very vividly' (p. 45).

Music is a key to memory which had been locked up, frozen in a crushing, inhibiting environment where neither music nor memory were valued. When working with children to identify and unlock memory, how aware are we of both the environment and the possible keys which are rusting on some hidden hook?

The musical setting

Written within the context of education, the comments of Bergethon and Boardman on the *psychic setting* are transferable to counselling. When the teacher finds 'the increased noise level in the classroom, the messiness of the room, and the apparent confusion irritating and disturbing...the students will also feel frustration and learning may not occur' (p. 3).

Progress may depend on the teacher's acceptance of 'the new role as facilitator, rather than controller, of learning' when 'these seemingly insurmountable problems will gradually disappear and the teacher will see beyond them to the vision of learners actively engaged in music learning' (p. 4).

Eunice Bailey found that the problem arising in connection with making music could help the child/adult relationship: 'as the teacher and children get to know one another and share one another's interests, a solution can generally be found, and the children's understanding deepens as they recognize that adults too have to deal with problems'. Importantly, 'a teacher, as her children gradually discover, is only an ordinary person' with 'real likes and dislikes, prejudices, desires, hopes and fears' (pp. 96–7). The psychic environment enables increased communication – musical, verbal, emotional.

Music may itself provide an environment in which development can flourish. The Jester who obtains the moon for Princess Lenore gains inspiration through strumming on his lute. The music creates an atmosphere of calm and, rather than filling in the crevices between words, holds obfuscating words at bay (Thurber, 1965. p. 182).

I am reminded of 'Laurel' (15) whom I met first in the secure unit of a local authority assessment centre. To say *I met her* is not accurate. I saw her as I was shown over the establishment, clearly, since she was held in such legal and locked security, a Very Naughty Girl of whom I felt some fear and with whom I expected little communication.

But later Laurel and I were marooned together in the sitting room of an ordinary residential unit on the same site. She had been de-carcerated. I was between appointments. We both felt spare, anxious and awkward.

The Very Naughty Girl had shrunk. She sat huddled on a settee, playing and re-playing one record, rather wistful and wailing: I forget the words and tune but I remember clearly how the music expressed the lost girl and how she used it to create a sound environment – to fill up silence, maybe to control our conversation, but principally, I think, to show how she felt.

We had no responsibility towards each other and expected never to meet again. But during that half hour we made some contact, enabling me to meet a real girl instead of constructing a monster.

As we left the room she was even able to express anxiety over some matter for which I could obtain help from a staff member. In the dining room, restored to her peers, Laurel returned to brash, notice-me-but-hold-off behaviour. The music, and her freedom to choose, play and listen to it, had helped her to drop, even for a few minutes, a tough veneer. (At one point she had even offered to make me some coffee.)

Some secret power

It may never be possible to know the effect of particular music on individual children and it is in the nature of such experience that the very attempt to translate into words alters, even destroys, the true response.

Alvin (1965) describes how 'a child in revolt and full of ugly feelings may experience sublimation through music, and feel great relief in the contact with something good and beautiful'. A girl (14) in residential care who was intelligent but 'thought of herself as "a horrible and nasty girl not worth bothering about"' wrote 'after attending a concert in which she was enthralled and behaved exceptionally well: "After the concert when I went to bed, the sweet lively tunes kept on repeating in my ears. What a lovely day full of *goodness* and *beauty* it has been"'. The girl, who was described as disturbed, 'had a terribly low and pessimistic opinion of herself. The unexpected feelings of beauty and goodness she experienced may have helped her to revaluate herself and given her hope' (pp. 98–9).

Experiencing nothing good confirms that I am worthless. To experience goodness and beauty without cost or retribution may contribute to the birth of self-esteem. If I can feel like this, even for a few minutes, perhaps I am not all bad.

From here it is a short step to self-expression and the development of discovery, confidence and achievement.

Music helped to release 'fair-haired, shy, awkward Bertie' when he took part in Eunice Bailey's class. 'Blushing a bright and sudden red, he stumbled over to Catharine, who was the princess, and stuttered. "C-can I b-be your prince to s-save you today?"…And just for one day. Bertie forgot his gawky legs and arms, and leapt towards his princess, sweeping the goblins aside, and dancing triumphantly round the hall at the end' (Bailey, 1958, p. 84).

Following Lawrence Abbott's belief that 'music has some secret power to tap the very well-springs of our emotions', Eunice Bailey comments that 'As adults, we are sometimes scornful of this emotional appeal in music', imposing 'a sincere effort to appraise the value of music with intelligence'. But 'With young children this feeling self is constantly finding some way of expressing itself'. They 'welcome this emotional release through music and dancing, and gain from it a growth in self-confidence and stability' (pp. 103–104).

And not young children only. When, as I hope, I am 90 I shall still feel that I have never danced enough, never had enough music.

Grace for several weeks wrote stories 'about greedy witches who ate up naughty little girls – most of [whom] apparently disobeyed their mothers' but she was unable to join other children in 'building a wooden witchy house in the corner of the classroom…until they first made up a witch dance'. Grace was gradually 'drawn into the dance, and before long was dancing as wildly and fiercely as the rest. The content of her stories developed and her interests widened'. It does not appear that any adult directly accosted Grace about her cannibal witches, or fussed her about dancing. Her preoccupations and activities were noticed, evidently with care and concern. She was attended to, never coerced. In time she made important discoveries of which, it seems, she had no need to speak (pp. 105–106).

For Catharine, a song enabled release of 'anxiety and strain during the illness of a close relative'. In discussion of *My Bonnie is over the Ocean*. 'She suggested that the girl in the story had to go back home and look after mother who was ill, leaving her new friend behind'. Acting this part (from choice) she called, 'I can't come back till my mother gets well'. Other children said, 'It's very sad when she sails away isn't it? and 'I wanted to cry'. For Catharine, 'it was right, and she had played out the worry and the fear' (p. 105).

'Later she danced the part again: this time the mother in the story recovered, while the girl returned to her friend'. Bailey comments that 'Catharine could not have told me of her anxiety, she probably did not recognize its existence, but her feelings overflowed into the story and inspired her dancing, giving her both release and satisfaction' (p. 105).

Hearing this song in my mind I think of the repeated refrain 'Bring back, bring back, oh bring back my Bonnie to me, to me', the sadness of the implied separation and loss mitigated by the gentle positive tune in a major key. Perhaps Catharine was helped to feel hope, even as she expressed sadness.

A secret sound

A child's response to music may, even if not obvious or amenable to interpretation, be of considerable significance. Paul Bailey (1973), for example, watched very closely Sandra (8) during the music period in her class of mentally handicapped children. Her teacher described her as 'a complete write-off'. When the other children played (simple percussion music) Sandra 'just doodles in her copy-book' (pp. 19–20).

But Paul Bailey 'noticed that when the music was soft she made small circles on the paper [which] gradually became larger as the volume of the music increased, and reduced in size when the music became softer. Her pencil also moved faster or slower as the tempo of the music varied'. The teacher was astonished: 'although Sandra had been in her group for two years, she had not noticed that the child was really paying close attention to both the tempo and volume of the music' (p. 20).

To discover response and the ability to respond is crucial in much work with the children. Yet often, as with Sandra's teacher, it is easy to overlook or misinterpret some simple or delicate action or expression. The despised doodle may represent some actually tremendous act of creation or communication.

Response may be deeply secret and uncommunicable. Paul Bailey describes Ronnie (4): 'As soon as he heard music of any kind he immediately went under the nearest table, undressed completely, and sat listening quite intently, and apparently with great pleasure...As soon as the music ceased he dressed himself and emerged from under the table'. This mentally handicapped boy showed himself to be aware of and responsive to non-verbal, aural stimulus (pp. 7–8).

Because they could not, apparently, communicate verbally, Sandra and Ronnie were free from probing into what they felt and why they responded in their particular ways. Bayless and Ramsey refer to music as 'a natural and very personal language...accessible to the slow learner, the gifted, the handicapped, the young, and the old – it is truly universal' (p. 78).

Alvin (1975) writes that 'Primitive man has often believed that every being, dead or alive, had his own secret sound or song to which he would respond and which might make him vulnerable to magic'. The medicine man might try 'to discover the sound or song to which the sick man, or the spirit inhabiting him, would respond [giving] contact with and power over the evil affecting the patient' (p. 10). We are familiar with the idea of response to particular composers, compositions and instruments as individual, even unaccountable. Newbould notes that Einstein described the 40th Symphony of Mozart as 'heroically tragic' while Schumann found in it 'the poised gracefulness of Greece'. Newbould comments that 'Both responses are doubtless honest and doubtless true. Both qualities are in the music, and the ability of listeners to identify them varies according to their personality and experience' (p. 11).

The important point would seem to be the impossibility of *knowing* how any other person feels with and about any musical experience. In word-terms, I compare the little boy who found the story of *Rapunzel* comforting because he identified an aspect of being closely held and cared for when for most people this story seems to be about developing and frustrated sexuality and the desire to escape from captivity (Bettelheim, 1976, p. 17). (This point does not negate the discussion of the deliberate manipulative use of music, above.)

In counselling work with children, music may be involuntarily as well as deliberately involved. Who knows what apparently unexpressed responses are evoked? A visual comparison may be made with colour: when buying writing equipment and stationery for 'Mark' I took care to learn his favourite and least favourite colours. Partly because his choice coincided with mine, I usually wore this when we met and avoided the colours I knew he disliked.

I thought that the visual environment of our meetings would be aided by focus on acceptable, and avoidance of unliked, colours. If I am placed in a room with unrelieved white walls and ceiling and glaring light, or brilliant geometric migrainous patterns, my ability to see at all let alone respond sensibly and sensitively to another person may be inhibited.

Alvin (1975) quotes a psychoanalyst Hildemarie Streich (1970): 'the voice represents the hidden person, his individuality, his uniqueness. To be born means to become sounding, to have a voice means to be something which has its own growth, its own development.' Alvin continues, 'The sound of a voice is supposed to be as unique as a fingerprint' (p. 20).

The voices of both child and counsellor are unique, personal and capable of not only enormous range of expression but also of deception, misrepresentation and secrecy. The meanings of words intended and interpreted (by no means always identical) are far from being the sole communication of the speaking voice.

Intonation, timbre, accent, rhythm, variety of vocabulary, construction, spoken melody. Of his daughter Cordelia, Shakespeare's King Lear recalls:

> Her voice was ever soft,
> Gentle and low, an excellent thing in woman.

We are invited to learn from this posthumous description a great deal about both the woman and the feelings of her grieving father.

Adults speaking to children, especially babies, often adopt sweetly pretty tones, the equivalent perhaps of shouting at foreigners in the hope that unnatural timbre and volume will effect instantaneous translation.

Mark's foster parents and social worker were worried because he often substituted an extensive repertoire of grunts, animal noises and silly voices for acceptable speech. This menagerie rarely invaded our sessions together largely, I think, because when we first met, he was becoming ready to dispense with his verbal disguises.

However, another important factor was that our verbal interaction was, with very few exceptions on either side, straight. He did not need to import the voices from other parts of his life to a relationship which existed in so time- and space-limited a context as that of counsellor and child, and which focused entirely on him, with no rivalries, anxieties or distractions. If anyone's voice went silly it was that of the counsellor when she had to tell the boy of the unexpectedly imminent end of their contact. Then, unsure of myself and ruled by my own uncomfortable mixture of emotions (including anger) I heard my voice become 'false' at which Mark withdrew: 'Can I go now?'

The sound of healing

The voice in particular and sound in general are deeply important in healing. Alvin (1975) writes of the sound or song personal to the sick man to which he or 'the spirit inhabiting him, would respond' (p. 10).

The personal sound or song may be contacted by, and a healing result of, music. 'And it came to pass when the evil spirit from God was upon Saul that David took a harp and played with his hand: so Saul was refreshed and was well and the evil spirit departed from him' (1 Samuel 16:23).

There is no need to analyse the event, to know the exact nature of the evil spirit or the notation of the music. But it is important that the healing was interactive. David and Saul knew each other; David understood Saul, Saul trusted David. The music was played for, and only for, Saul, at the time of his affliction, perhaps, in Alvin's terms, offering and reaching his personal sound and song.

It is interesting too that the younger man, perhaps still a boy, counsels, through his love and music, the older. The association of children and counselling is by no means exclusively in terms of reception.

Dirge for an owl

The healing aspect of counselling is important in circumstances of affliction other than illness. Valerie Georgeson's story *Sophie's Blues* (1980) portrays the encounter between Sophie (8) and Joan. After a pop concert in a field beyond her garden, Sophie seeks, and finds dead, the owl she has loved. She meets Joan and blames her for this death. The woman helps her to express grief and they arrange a funeral. Joan composes a special dirge while Sophie builds a cairn and, as they bury the owl, Sophie, 'howled, while tears rolled down Joan's cheek. Then Joan took up her guitar and began singing' (p. 161).

The song, like David's playing for Saul, made especially for Sophie and the owl, for a particular person at a particular moment in the lives of both sufferer and singer, client and counsellor, captures the emotions of that moment and looks into the future, helping to change the ways of seeing of both individuals involved:

> Sophie watched the black face, listened to the black voice, soft and low, sad, beautiful, then the child's heart soared as the dark voice reached out of the chorus, higher and higher, until it danced and shouted on the mountain tops and she thought the dark sound must have snow on it when it came down again. Then she knew that the owl had to die, but at least it had flown, as Joan said, on planes of light.
>
> She also knew that she, Sophie, would never suffer in silence again, no matter what her dad said. Joan's voice went on playing games with the sounds her fingers made on the strings and Sophie danced and howled round and round the cairn, until at last the voice stopped and the fingers dropped from the strings and Sophie flopped down on the grass beside her friend. They lay feeling the sun on their skins and thinking of the cold bird under the stones.
>
> 'Did you know my owl?' Sophie asked.
>
> 'Not personally' answered Joan.
>
> 'Oh, I thought you did.'
>
> 'No. You can still be sorry about something that's died, though, can't you?' (pp. 162–3).

Sophie, having expressed her grief, wants to sing the song again. Joan, understanding the difference between spontaneous and shared expression, and performance, refuses. 'That bird's dead. Right?...And we're alive...so we've got to get on living now...It's done...dead and buried' (p. 164).

Released, Sophie discovers that she is hungry. She invites Joan home for breakfast but this woman is wise about more than grief and music. 'I don't think your parents would entirely appreciate seeing me so early in the morning and all'. The engagement has been focused, time limited, perfect. It is not transferable to another place. It has no past and no future. Sophie and Joan have been together. They have given to each other. This song was for one singing only (p. 104).

The secret nightingale of China

No story of music and healing is more exquisite than Hans Christian Andersen's *The Nightingale*. The Emperor makes captive a little wild bird who is displaced by a bejewelled clockwork replica. But the machine breaks and the Emperor becomes so ill that he is on the verge of death. His good and evil deeds pass by, looking him in the face, 'while death sat heavy on his heart'. He cries for 'Music! music! sound the drums and gongs to drown their voices!' He entreats the mechanical nightingale, 'you little golden bird sing for me now! I have loaded you with jewels and presents; I have hung my golden slipper round your neck. Sing to me now!' (Andersen n/d, p. 59).

But Death remains 'staring at the Emperor with his hollow eyes through the dreadful stillness'. Until 'Suddenly a burst of song trilled through the open window – it was the living nightingale who sat outside on the branch of the tree. She had heard of the Emperor's need, and was come to sing of hope and consolation'. At last the Emperor is saved. He offers reward but the nightingale asks for only one thing. 'Let no one know you have a little bird who tells you everything: it will be much better not' (p. 60).

The elephant song of Thuy Dang

Sophie and Joan share music which crosses racial and cultural boundaries and gain not only healing (for Joan too, is shown as in distress, tired, strained) but also learning, experience which leads to change in both participants. The Emperor is healed by a counsellor who is not human.

Starting from the context of education, North American teacher Pamela Griffith (1977) describes how sharing the music of two cultures aided not only the education of, but also, almost literally, unfroze a little girl. The extract, taken from a letter included in Bayless and Ramsey, 1982, is given in full.

> Thuy Dang was a first-grader in my class. Her family were Vietnamese refugees who had come to town in August. Only Thuy's father spoke a little English. Thuy was very attentive in class, but she never participated in music. Of course, her speaking was *very* limited, but she usually shyly tried. However, whenever we sang, Thuy just sat.

She didn't even tap, sway, or move to the various rhythms. Because I wanted her to enjoy music and because I realized that in singing Thuy would begin to speak aloud, I decided to find a Vietnamese children's song and have *her* teach it to the rest of us.

My search for a song proved fruitless. One Oriental lady even told me that I wouldn't be able to find one because Oriental children were taught to be quiet and respectful. I just couldn't believe that this bright-eyed happy child didn't sing! In desperation, I visited her home and discussed the situation with her father (who explained it to her mother). Thank, Thuy's dad, volunteered to tape a favourite children's song and encouraged Thuy to teach it to us. This began a lovely friendship between our families. Thank not only taped the song but wrote out these copies for us. He was both happy to help and very talented.

Thuy both played the tape and very hesitantly began to teach her cute little song. The rest of our class liked learning the foreign-language song that Thank voluntarily sent us, the *Elephant Song*. As Thuy taught us the song, we taught her a song about a dog – she began to sing, speak aloud, and participate in all the music. Music broke the ice and began a very warm and happy year for all of us (pp. 181, 184).

The words of the *Elephant Song (Con Voi)* seem particularly appropriate:

Look an elephant
He stands on the grass
He twiss [sic] his body and he's happy.
He invites another elephant come to his place and play with him
(p. 182).

Thuy Dang's elephant helped her to invite and give friendship. A child who might have become withdrawn and alienated was helped not only to communicate verbally but also to make a unique and valued contribution to her colleagues. Other important aspects of this story are the care of the teacher who formed a real relationship with the child, and the contact with and involvement of the family.

I am reminded of Mark teaching me to draw and of teaching Polish children *The Taylor and the Mouse: (Krawiec i mysz)* with its universally nonsensical chorus 'Hi diddle um tum tarum tantum, through the town of Ramsey', (inscribed by us for all time in the honoured guest book of that Krakowian school), a fair exchange for the 'Abracadabra mara BENZ' of *Pan Twardowski*.

I cannot, at this moment, remember sharing singing with a child client since, as a student in a residential nursery, I made up personal-name songs for bewildered under-fives – bewildered by their circumstances and not, I hope, my songs.

The swan tune

Juliette Alvin (1965) and George (10) developed contact through the medium of an instrument and a tune. George 'was not happy, although nothing seemed to worry him particularly. He did not remember his father, who died when he was an infant, and he got on quite well with a half-brother born from his mother's second marriage'. He 'was intelligent, above the average, very nervous and unstable, unkempt and disorderly' also 'physically incredibly awkward' (p. 6).

At school he was 'always at the bottom of his form, and got increasingly bad reports which were a source of conflicts with his family' and was 'careless [and] inattentive, and seemed unable to pull himself together. He was going a bad way and seemed not to care' (p. 6).

This is a not unfamiliar picture of the suffering child whose behaviour does not attract the intervention of health or welfare services, partly, perhaps, because this child appears to belong to a family in good material circumstances.

Swan Lake changed his life. Hearing a recording of Tchaikowsky's ballet, he 'was reached in an extraordinary way by the 'cello part in the score...identified himself at once with the tune and asked if he could learn the 'cello'. Alvin, meeting him in her role as teacher 'learnt so much from him about his life' that she 'tried to hide from him the fact that he was quite unfit to play a musical instrument 'having' no ear, no rhythm, no motor control' and always moving the wrong way (pp. 6–7).

What became clear, however, was 'that he suffered from loneliness', referring to his 'cello as 'my best pal' which he kept in his room, in order to see it on waking (p. 7).

Despite poor musical progress, George 'never lost his initial motivation...looking for some kind of satisfactory relationship through which he could express himself' and which he found with his 'cello. He described a dream: 'he was in an orchestra and played "that tune" [from *Swan Lake*]. The same dream occurred several times, and each time he was in a different orchestra' (p. 7).

The teacher continued 'with much patience and understanding' and gradually learned all about the difficulties of George's life. 'He had given up the idea that he could ever be good at school: there was a family crisis every time the school report arrived, and he was becoming quite callous about it. But he thought he would be good at playing the 'cello' (p. 7).

Taking this cue, Alvin 'made his 'cello become a means of rehabilitation', sending termly reports commenting on 'some of his good features such as eagerness, goodwill, punctuality, and so on, which gave a true and better picture of the boy, [which] helped to ease the family relationships' (p. 7).

George used this help, the relationship with the teacher, and his attachment to the 'cello, 'to evaluate himself and face his shortcomings'. The boy who 'was careless' and 'had no standard in anything' responded to 'the demands made on him by a teacher he respected and admired, [feeling] that she respected him and had confidence in his ability to do better' (p. 8).

Through this he became stronger, more stable, lost his indifference and regained self-respect, which aided his move to secondary school where, becoming a member of the orchestra. 'He felt he had something valuable to offer...and he started to form happy relationships through his music first with the pupils and masters.' Alvin, from a perspective of some years on, could report that 'From that day he never looked back, and his personality developed normally' (p. 8).

I read this story as one of courage on the part of the boy as well as devotion by the adult. I am moved by the evidence of patient care as Alvin, week by week, found her purpose as teacher of music subserving her role as counsellor, attending to the unhappy child's needs for expression, achievement and approval. Yet, also, he did learn to play, and well enough to join the school orchestra.

George recognized his own personal song and strove to release it through the strings and sounding box of his wooden friend. Alvin recognized that the boy's life was bound into that melody, those sounds, and that George must pursue his quest for that secret as surely as any hero of fairy tale. Gritting, no doubt, her musical teeth from time to time, she held him, giving experience of a positive, approving (but not colluding) relationship with an adult as he unlocked his tune.

New worlds

Beams, who suffered so grotesquely at the hands of child psychologist Mrs Winterschladen (chapter 4) eventually finds help, unexpectedly in a hospital – 'no toys on the lawn' – where 'they made me do a lot of intelligence tests which were extremely boring' before leaving her in ' a nice waiting room with comfortable chairs and a desk and a gramaphone and a fire and an old man asleep on a sofa. I pottered about a bit and started messing with the gramophone, and out burst the New World Symphony at the top of its voice'. Beams has been referred because she can't read. But, as the old man (in fact the doctor) points out, she has just read the record label. Soon, released and motivated at last, she can read perfectly and avidly (Gardam, 1973, p. 82).

Drum duel

Music based aid for Jacob (9) from psychologist Lawrence Shapiro

(1984) developed through neither voice nor instrument. Jacob, in a class for learning disabled children with behavioural problems, was driving his teacher mad with perpetual tapping.

Shapiro reports that 'When I saw Jacob by himself, he showed none of the recalcitrant behaviours that his teacher had described, but on the other hand, he was not thrilled to be seeing me' (p. 135). After some attempt at careful conversation, Shapiro decided that

> Being circumspect wasn't getting me very far, so I decided to be blunt:
> THERAPIST: Well, I guess you know why you're down here seeing me, don't you? Mrs B says that you're not very happy about being in her class and she's not very happy about all the trouble you gave her.
> JACOB: Yup. I know.
> THERAPIST: And she thinks that I might have some ideas to turn the situation around.
> JACOB: Humph.
> THERAPIST: Do you know what you do that really bugs the hell out of her?
> JACOB: (interested) No – what?
> THERAPIST: This! (I tap out a complicated beat).
> JACOB: (giggles) Oh, that!
> THERAPIST: Yup. This! (Another rhythm).
> JACOB: (smiling) You mean this? (He beats out about 30 seconds of a syncopated beat.)
> THERAPIST: That's it! (I repeat the rhythm.)
> We went on like this, beating out rhythms back and forth like a drum duel between two hot-shot drummers in rival bands. Although the mood was competitive, there was also a feeling of mutual respect. We got into a pattern of copying each other's beat and then adding another flourish. When I couldn't quite get the rhythm that Jacob had given me, or vice versa, we showed each other how to do it. We kept this up for the remainder of the session, and at the end of our time, I said, 'See you next week' and beat out the rhythm of the words. Jacob did the same (p. 136).

Building on this, Shapiro told Jacob about such other uses of tapping as American Indians' drum beats, Morse code and blind people tapping with canes. Jacob's teacher cooperated in allowing him to use tapped codes in class, for example, 'I need help'. Jacob was in due course referred to a music therapist.

Shapiro attended first to the teacher. Whatever happened between counsellor and child during the time-limited sessions, Jacob's teacher would have to continue enduring the maddening tapping in daily classes. Counselling in a vacuum is potentially productive of more harm than good.

Having learnt what behaviour makes the teacher really mad, Shapiro engages with this very behaviour in Jacob's contact with himself. Instead of trying to fight the tapping, Shapiro draws attention to it in order to use and thus control it. Attracting the boy's attention to the wider world of tapping, the counsellor helps to relieve pressure in the classroom and finds a focus for further therapeutic contact. Jacob's all too obvious personal sound, properly attended to, offered a clue to the means of focused self-expression and communication. Without however the careful attention of the counsellor, it was perceived only as a source of extreme irritation. I am reminded of Sandra whose drawn responses to music were dismissed as just doodles until Paul Bailey took time really to look, and of Ronnie, stripping and withdrawing into his own table cave (Bailey, P., 1973, pp. 2–8).

Life supporting singing

Although I hope that the points of my comments and illustrations are received as transferable between situations and settings, I am aware that I have made no mention of the use of music in working with children in hospital. In *Attending to Children* (1990, p. 96) I quoted June Jolly's memory of a boy (6) whom she had nursed for many weeks making 'his first conscious movement in response to his favourite record' (Jolly, 1981, p. 68).

Perhaps the hospital ward is not the place for extra noise and I do not know what happens musically in children's ward playrooms. But Hinekahukura Barrett-Aranui (1989) writes of the experience of a Maori family whose daughter spent six weeks in a deep coma on life support machines. 'She was constantly massaged, talked and *sung to*, and attended to by the immediate family'. When she was taken off the machines, 'The care given by medical attendants and family began to revive her muscular movements and she began to respond to the *singing* and constant chatter of her nieces and nephews' (pp. 102–103) (my italics).

Singing is deeply important in Maori life. For example, 'In pre-European times when children were born, each one was designated a task and they were sung to by their parents'. A girl might be given such tasks as 'weaving, reciting genealogy, or caring for people. All these concepts were sung to them' (p. 105). It would be natural for singing to take its place in the care and cure of the sick girl and, clearly, far from disapproval or restraint within the hospital. Do mothers sing even lullabies to their children on British wards?

Since music is in all cultures and across all boundaries of education, so personal and universal a means of both expression and communication, how sad it is that, in the British Isles at least, it has so little place in the repertoire of the ordinary skills of counselling.

Song-assisted counselling

At this point I must test myself. How could I use music in counselling a child?

In meeting and beginning relationships with children I might learn their favourite and least favourite music. When I had asked Vlado to tell me the words and melody of his local national song *Biljana*, he proceeded to offer his own favourite song, singing it, writing it out, and translating it on his own initiative. Thus I learnt a great deal about his feelings (the song was powerfully nationalistic, passionate and sad), his abilities (musical and verbal), and preferences. Also that he was generous with time and ability, able to concentrate and keen to communicate. (I did not at the time, of course, think of all this; then I was, simply, happy.)

Had Vlado been my client, we could have continued to enjoy sharing music (for I 'gave back' songs). Choice of and response to songs might give both further clues to a child's feelings, and opportunity for expression. Catharine, for example, in Eunice Bailey's account, evidently found *My Bonnie Lies over the Ocean* helpful in providing a context and opportunity for focusing on her feelings about her mother's illness. Later, the anxiety passed, she could use the music to express her new feelings.

I might, with a well-equipped playroom, play recorded music which I had chosen, to offer perhaps calming sound. But I should be very careful in this, remembering the unforseeable variety of responses available to every individual on every separate occasion to every stimulus.

I should have musical instruments available for children to select – at least percussion, a piano and easy blowing things. If a child already played an instrument I should possibly introduce this into sessions, remembering, for example, George and his 'cello (Alvin, 1965, pp. 6–8).

Music for many people provides the opportunity for achievement. George, though never, it seems, particularly proficient, attained membership of a school orchestra and through this success, greater ease of interpersonal communication. A number of the children described by Alvin (1965, 1975), Philip Bailey (1973) and Nordoff and Robbins (1971a, 1971b, 1975) were, although severely handicapped, enabled to participate in music making by the careful adaptation of some instrument. Counsellors are interested in helping the development of self-esteem and every opportunity for achievement is important.

I should try to learn about the importance of music in the child's home and background, particularly if problems included separation from birth family and/or the child's place within the family. The foster mother of James (Mennell) and teacher of Thuy Dang (Griffith) were sensitive to the cultural significance of music and thus its role in the sense of identity of the children.

The preferred music of home and background might, however, be rather than interestingly 'foreign', in some idiom which I would find at least difficult and at worst appalling. I hope that I would endeavour to learn from children in what ways their music was significant, for example, representing memories of a parent, stimulating movement, arousing aggression or blanking out thought.

I hope too that I should allow the child privacy to respond to and express the music, without the need to interpret into words. I should try to distinguish between my reactions and those of the child, keeping before me the musical equivalent of *Rapunzel* (Bettleheim).

I should try to notice the sounds my speaking voice makes and the other noises in the background.

I should enjoy shared fun and relaxation, for example, singing 'silly' songs and nonsense words. We could make up our own songs.

Indeed, creating personal songs could be very useful, choosing poems or writing one's own words and at the very least singing a melody. Just as we write out children's life stories and make up other tales together we could write down their tunes. A five-line stave can easily be ruled on plain paper if manuscript sheets are not standard counsellors' issue.

A sound of their own

Which brings me once more to that important point of Juliette Alvin's – the personal sound. The counsellor is seeking the personal sound of the child, a sound which is in itself, perhaps, a signature tune.

Nordoff and Robbins (1971b) write of Pernilla (10) who, unable to speak, could respond to a tune based on the 'three or four most recognizable sounds' which she could make. When her name was sung to this tune, 'she smiled and made sounds of pleasure' (pp. 20–21).

This very tune (G EA GE; in rhythm Da Dadi da da) was sung by my neighbours' children only yesterday, playing in their garden. Personal to Pernilla, it is also a universal children's tune.

A central aim of counselling children is surely the discovery of their own tunes, the personal sounds which match their names, identifying them as individuals, both unique and connected and connecting with the world. How can music be regarded, even for an instant, as an expensive frill?

Summary

The immense potentialities of **music**, which is a vital part of daily living, as a means of communication and self-expression in the context of helping, including counselling, may not be widely realized, although **music therapy** is well established and respected in many contexts. Several characteristics of music have been discussed, including as evocation of memory.

Descriptions of children and adults sharing music in many situations illustrate the power and importance of the art and include discussion of the individual, personal **secret sound**. The sound of the speaking voice is important as, for example, part of the aural environment and means of communication.

Music is a means of healing, too, including at times of **bereavement** and **anxiety** and through, for example, **song** it may aid communication between people of different cultures. The story of George and his 'cello illustrates the power of music to release a child from emotional suffering, leading to motivation to succeed and developing self-esteem – plus enjoyment of the music itself, and essentially within the context of relationship with a sensitive and caring adult. A less familiar form of musical expression, raw **rhythm**, similarly released finger-tapping Jacob.

All the children introduced in this chapter found and were helped by 'A Sound of Their Own'.

Link

Everyone in this book – child, adult, client, counsellor, patient, author – has, in one way or another, told something of an individual and personal story, contributing to the total story which is this book. No one has been perfect; no single approach to counselling is ideal, no counsellor helps everyone who comes for help, no child is happy as the day is long, a perpetual source of parental satisfaction and beloved of teachers, friends and siblings without interruption. The aim of living, of counselling, is to achieve not perfection but, following D. W. Winnicott, 'Good Enough Being', the subject of the Conclusion.

References

Abbott, L. (n/d). Approach to Music. In E. Bailey.
Ahmed, S., Cheetham, J., and Small, J. (eds) (1986). *Social Work with Black Children and their Families*. Batsford/British Agencies for Adoption and Fostering, London.
Alvin, J. (1965). *Music for the Handicapped Child*. Oxford University Press. London.

Alvin, J. (1975). *Music Therapy*. Hutchinson, London.
Andersen, H. C. (n/d). *Fairy Tales*. Ward Lock, London.
Bailey, E. (1958). *Discovering Music with Young Children*. Methuen, London.
Bailey, P. (1973). *They Can Make Music*. Oxford University Press, Oxford.
Barrett–Aranui, H. (1989). Nga matapihi o te waiora; (windows on Maori well-being). In Munro, et al., pp. 97–106.
Bayless, K. M. and Ramsey, M. E. (1982). *Music: a Way of Life for the Young Child*. Mosby, St Louis.
Bergethon, B., and Boardman, E. (1979). *Musical Growth in the Elementary School*. Holt, Rinehart and Winston, New York.
Bettelheim, B. (1976). *The Uses of Enchantment: the Meaning and Importance of Fairy Tales*. Thames and Hudson, London.
Bradley, A. and Jamieson, K. (eds) (1980). *Dandelion Clocks*. Penguin, Harmondsworth.
Crompton, M. (1980). *Respecting Children: Social Work with Young People*. Edward Arnold, London.
Crompton, M. (1990). *Attending to Children: Direct Work in Social and Health Care*. Edward Arnold, London.
Crompton, M. (1991). Invasion by Russian dolls: on privacy and intrusion. *Adoption and Fostering*, 15, (1), 31–3.
Gardam, J. (1973). *The Summer after the Funeral*. Hamish Hamilton, London.
Georgeson, V. (1980). Sophie's blues. In Bradley and Jamieson, pp. 156–64.
Goudge, E. (1936). *A City of Bells*. Duckworth, London.
Griffith, P. (1977). Personal communication. In Bayless and Ramsey, pp. 181–4.
Hughes, D. (1985). The Importance of Music. In *Music in Action '85*. UK Council for Music Education and Training in association with Able Children. Caxtons, Knebworth.
Hunt, N. (1982). *The World of Nigel Hunt: the Diary of a Mongoloid Youth*. Asset Recycling, Norwich.
Johnson, S. P. (ed.) (1965). *A Book of Princesses*. Penguin, Harmondsworth.
Jolly, J. (1981). *The Other Side of Paediatrics: a Guide to the Everyday Care of Sick Children*. Macmillan, Basingstoke.
Mennell, M. (1986). The experience of Bradford Social Services Department. In Ahmed, et al., pp. 120–31.
Munro, A., Manthei, B. and Small, J. (1989). *Counselling: the Skills of Problem-solving*. Routledge, London.
Newbould, B. (1981). *Music to an Unpurged Ear: Inaugural Lecture*. University of Hull, Hull.
Nordoff, P. and Robbins, C. (1971a). *Therapy in Music for Handicapped Children*. Gollancz, London.
Nordoff, P. and Robbins, C. (1971b). The Children's Tune. In British Society of Music Therapy, *Individual Music Therapy*. British Society of Music Therapy, London.
Nordoff, P. and Robbins, C. (1975). *Music Therapy in Special Education*. Macdonald and Evans, London.
Onion, N., (1991). Nordoff–Robbins Music Therapy Centre. *Music Journal*, Incorporated Society of Musicians, July 1991, 51.
Rinehart, C. A. (1980). The state of the art. Music: a basic for the 1980s. *Childhood Education*, 36, (3), 140–145. Quoted in Bayless and Ramsey.

Shapiro, L. (1984). *The New Short-term Therapies for Children: a Guide for Helping Professions and Parents*. Prentice-Hall, New Jersey.

Shelley, P. B. (c1820). *Music When Soft Voices Die*.

Streich, H. (1970). Unpublished paper read at the Institute for Analytical Psychology, Zurich. In Alvin 1975.

Thurber, J. (1943). Many moons. In Johnson, pp. 177–88.

Conclusion: Good Enough Being

A Glass of Marbles

Lennie, at the beginning of this book, wanted acting lessons on being a person. He found it very difficult to feel real. Julia, through help from Margaret Hunter, felt, at last, that she was a real girl (Byars, 1976: Hunter, 1987).

One of the themes explored above has been the difficulty of recognizing, acknowledging and balancing the many aspects of life, and some ways which we can help and be helped to achieve a sense of reality and to live abundantly.

This dilemma, so often a theme in children's books, is of the greatest importance for everyone who works with children. The story of Lennie and his flight into television soap fantasy may be charming and funny but there can be other flights whose landings, like Icarus falling from the sky, may be dangerous if not fatal. Tim Tate (1991), for example, writes of 'a number of heavy-metal rock groups who use satanic imagery in both their song lyrics and their stage presentation. Many are extremely popular, generally among late teenage boys' (p. 106).

He refers to 'thousands of young men and women across Europe and America whose dabbling [in satanism] started within the context of satanic rock music and led to a criminal record', citing the case of Welsh schoolboy Carl Hughes who enjoyed 'the notoriety of being a teenage satanist' and in an interview in 1989 said 'I was into all heavy satanic rock bands then, and I dressed all in black..., wore a pentagram and an inverted cross...and looked up all the rituals I could find in the local library' (p. 107).

Counsellors who believe in empathy may have to tread dangerous terrain, holding firm to their own balance and reality.

A vivid image of the shifting nature of reality is offered in *Charlotte Sometimes* (Farmer, 1969). Indeed, the title itself is such an image, for Charlotte, a schoolgirl during the 1939–45 war, alternates night by night with another girl, Clare, who attends the same school during 1914–18. Charlotte's sense of herself is disrupted and remade as she learns to live in two times at once.

In her 1914 life, she sees a tumbler full of water in which several marbles have been immersed:

> The marbles looked huge in the tumbler, huge and shiny and defined.
> But they looked part of the water too, as if by some alchemy it had

formed itself into solid bubbles, these veined with colour, not
reflecting colour, like soap-bubbles…But when she put her fingers into
the water and pulled a marble out, it was small by comparison with
those still in the glass, and unimportant too. It was like the difference
between what you long for and what you find (p. 152).

The marbles eventually appear in her 1940 life and help her to make
connections, to understand her own reality. She places the tumbler of
marbles in water on her school chest of drawers where

It looked individual. It belonged to someone. It seemed odd that it
belonged to her more as Clare than as Charlotte. But she had begun to
realize that she could never entirely escape from being Clare. The
memory of it, if nothing else, was rooted in her mind. What had
happened to her would go on mattering, just as what had happened in
the war would go on mattering, permanently (p. 190).

Charlotte's life story is represented in the tumbler of marbles. Far from
escaping into fantasy and concocting a false world, she integrates all
aspects of her life, having learnt very young that the sense of reality
depends on perception.

Good Enough Being

Another point with which I wish to conclude *Children and Counselling*
is the difficulty of being good enough.

I thought of this as I walked through the Inns of Court in London.
Acre upon acre devoted to the administration of justice, to laws and
rules, to ordinary people in trouble or trying to obtain their rights or
seeking revenge. I passed the enormous Land Registry building,
sitting four square and ornate on a great area of land. And a stream of
law people, uniformed in smart suits and British warm overcoats,
carrying black document cases and red gown bags, walked importantly
along pleasant paths past ancient beautiful buildings and immaculate
gardens.

The relevance of this for counselling is the sense of constriction by
rules and expectations. Even though most people may hope to escape
the law courts, the law is always with us and, while it is intended to
protect, may sometimes be foolish or oppressive in conception and/or
implementation.

Young children may not be aware of the legal restrictions on their
behaviour, but as the age of criminal responsibility is very low, few
years of innocence are allowed.

Rules are there in plenty from very soon after birth, rules within the
home, at school, in sport.

Children are always having to satisfy someone's expectations and
requirements, emotional, social, educational, physical. They must try

to satisfy parents and teachers; if the family follows a religious tradition there will be a minister or priest, some idea of the divine. The peer group and individual friends will be powerful.

Every aspect of life exerts pressure: for example, clothing. A little girl's mother may wish her daughter to be pretty in frills, or unisex in dungarees. School may require uniform which parents wish to see kept in good order for economy, schools expect to be kept smart for discipline, and peers require to be distorted in the interests of self-expression. If the girl belongs to a particular cultural group, she may be required to wear some distinctive form of dress, perhaps a veil or trousers. This may conflict with the girl's sense of self in Western industrial society. Who is she to please and how can she develop her own sense of self, and of reality?

A great pressure of life in this society is management of all the complexities of economics, relationships, education, employment, sexuality and so on and so on, and to be self-fulfilled into the bargain. I remember the relief I experienced in the film *Ghandi* when Mrs Ghandi tells her husband that not everyone even wishes to be as good as he is.

I am back to the **feminist** approach and my development from that to a **childist** approach to counselling, (to life). D. W. Winnicott brought relief to many women when he introduced the idea of *good enough mothering*. No need after all to be perfect, or even to try to be perfect, or even to wish to be perfect.

The philosophy of Albert Ellis's *Rational Emotional Therapy* is useful here, focusing on the negative effects of *musts* and *oughts* and the irrational belief that 'It is a dire necessity that I be loved or approved of by everyone for everything I do' and 'should be thoroughly competent, adequate and achieving in all the things I do and should be recognized as such' (Murgatroyd, 1985, p. 74).

I think we want our children to be perfect, entrapping them in musts and oughts (including that they ought to love their parents and siblings) and then punish them for, inevitably, failing, first to be perfect children and then to be perfect adults. How many perfectly sensible adults who live apparently successful *good enough* lives feel like imperfect children when they are in contact with their parents?

Comedian John Cleese tells a story on the lines that he meets his mother at the station. He is driving his first Rolls Royce, symbol of at least competence if not success. She asks, is he sure he has enough petrol?

A problem inherent in the idea of counselling is that the client, having learnt to solve problems, to manage the difficulties of life, to become assertive or loving or self-reliant or responsible, may then live happily ever afterwards. Brenda Mallon (1987) reminds us that the counsellor bears no pouch of happiness dust.

One of the greatest services one person can render another, and a counsellor can offer a child, is release from the search for unattainable perfection and recognition of the ability to be *good enough*. This also, of course, implies that the counsellor must accept the concept of *good enough counselling* and not lose sleep because of a sense of *failure*.

To feel *good enough* we have to feel recognized and respected as individual persons, not denigrated for what we are not but celebrated for who we are. Only then may we make *good enough* relationships, at best enhancing, and never harming, the lives of other people.

A Childist Approach to Counselling

In *Children and Counselling* I have introduced a collection of connections. I have looked at some ideas about children and some approaches to counselling and selected some themes for further exploration.

An important thread is the idea of **story**. We all not only live our own but also are part of other people's stories. Alice in Looking Glass Land after the noisy incident with the Lion and the Unicorn, realizes that she 'wasn't dreaming after all...unless we're all part of the same dream. Only I do hope it's *my* dream, and not the Red King's! I don't like belonging to another person's dream' (Carroll, 1982/1872, p. 200).

Belonging to another person's dream is very frightening and children are particularly at risk of being drawn into the wrong stories. Through considerations of **myth**, **story**, **music** and **art** I have considered some ways of narrating **life stories** and communication between adults who hope to help children adjudged to be in need.

For the time spent by adults and children together in the roles of counsellor and client to be fruitful, it is essential that a number of elements of relationship are clear, including the complex concept of **empathy**.

It is important too that *respect* for the individual child as a whole person is shown, not least in attention to the right to **privacy** and the contribution of **silence** to communication.

As the whole person of both child and counsellor are totally involved, the **spiritual** element of life, whether or not connected with religious belief and practice, is indivisable from healthy development.

> And how shall we be able to administer help to others without the Faith of the Counsellors? (Halmos 1965, p. 194).

References

Byars, B. (1976). *The TV Kid.* The Bodley Head, London.
Carroll, L. (1982/1872). *Alice Through the Looking Glass.* Chancellor Press, London.

Farmer, P. (1969). *Charlotte Sometimes.* Chatto and Windus, London.

Halmos, P. (1965) *The Faith of the Counsellors.* Constable, London.

Hunter, M. (1987). Julia: a 'frozen' child. *Adoption and Fostering,* 11,(3), 26–30.

Mallon, B. (1987). *An Introduction to Counselling Skills for Special Educational Needs: Participants' Manual.* Manchester University Press, Manchester.

Murgatroyd, S. (1985). *Counselling and Helping.* British Psychological Society/Methuen, London.

Tate, T. (1991). *Children for the Devil: Ritual Abuse and Satanic Crime.* Methuen, London.

Appendix ChildLine:
an example of child – focused counselling

Material in this appendix has been drawn from a visit to ChildLine Midlands (I thank Director Alison Seymour and Administrator Carolyn Broadhurst for their help and courtesy), from ChildLine literature (I thank ChildLine for permission to quote) and from an article in *Social Work Today*. [This chapter has been read and amended by staff of ChildLine.]

- ChildLine is the free national helpline for children in trouble or danger.
- ChildLine offers a confidential counselling service for any child with a problem.
- ChildLine listens, comforts and protects.

Getting through

'Our nightmare is the image of a child alone and terrified trying desperately to call for help and unable to get through': a powerful image calling to the deep fears of us all, those familiar nightmares of paralysis, the appalling inability to run, to cry out, to get through.

It is very difficult to be both emotionally and chronologically a child, alone and terrified and unable to get through. The dream of ChildLine to counteract the nightmare image its leaflet describes 'is that every child who needs us gets through first time'.

Getting through requires two conditions – a telephone line to get through on and a receptive adult to get through to. Getting through first time would require a large number of lines, so that no child caller need wait, and numerous counsellors of considerable ability:

> a child rang the line after taking an overdose. For three hours, a single counsellor kept talking to the child, who was fading in and out of consciousness. They did not know where the child was ringing from; all the child would tell them was the name of his/her school.
> While the counsellor kept talking, other staff tried to trace the school. Eventually they found it, and the headteacher searched the

school records for the child's address. With the child still talking on the phone to the counsellor, an ambulance arrived (Eaton, 1990, p. 40).

This child was rescued from death by the intervention of ChildLine counsellors. Once she was in hospital, other counsellors, (for example, a hospital based social worker), would be needed to continue the rescue from whatever nightmare had led to the suicide attempt.

Giving for control

'Rescue' may properly be applied to a situation of such dramatic physical urgency but ChildLine counsellors are usually wary of the idea. Alison Seymour, Director of ChildLine Midlands, considers that

> if you want to rescue people, you're not going to be a good counsellor because you will be wanting to push children into action. ChildLine counsellors aim to protect children, working with the child so that any action that is taken is with the child's full understanding and agreement. This can take time.

Being pushed into action is what happens to most children most of the time and especially those whose distress has led them to the telephone. They are, for example, suffering physical and/or sexual abuse, bullying, problems with parents, anxiety about school. The world of adults or other children is intruding, forcing them into fear, into collusion, into flight.

In one way or another the problems which stimulate the telephone calls involve and reflect lack of control by the children over not only their own lives and behaviour but also the outside world:

> Annie, aged eight, rang ChildLine because she was worried that her parents were going to split up. She had overheard them talking about legal separation. Annie was phoning from a friend's house and said she did not want to go home. She felt very sad and insecure. The counsellor explored ways of helping Annie feel more secure. After talking to ChildLine Annie decided to go home and talk to her parents about her feelings and what was going to happen. This call lasted eight minutes (ChildLine, 1989, p. 6).

Within a very short time the counsellor enabled a young child to change from flight to fight, to take an initiative, to feel at least a measure of control. It is important to note that the counsellor 'explored ways of helping Annie to feel more secure'.

Annie was not *advised* to go home. 'She and the counsellor talked through her problem and Annie was helped to take action that would lead to her telling her parents how she felt' (Seymour). ChildLine believes that the majority of young people and children are able to make good decisions about themselves. The role of the counsellor is to help to create and protect space for choices to be identified and decisions made. Alison Seymour emphasized that ChildLine aims to enable children to make their own decisions about action whenever possible.

It is important for the counsellor to maintain a slow pace. Alison Seymour comments on the danger of 'jumping in too quickly: we need to learn to slow things down'. Pace is very difficult to judge, without experience, and is one of the many aspects of counselling with which training engages. For example, after role playing counsellor/child, the 'caller' might report that 'it felt as if you wanted me to get on with my story', responding perhaps to unconscious anxiety in the 'counsellor'.

The high cost of telling

David responded with relief to the absence of pressure, advice and judgement (this account is a compilation by ChildLine staff based on the experience of a real child):

I was really glad when I found out about ChildLine, because otherwise I don't think I could ever have started talking about my problems, not with someone who knew me, or even someone who could look at me while I was talking, or maybe try to stop me if I felt like running away. When I phone ChildLine I don't even have to tell them my first name if I don't want to, and if I felt I didn't want to talk anymore I could just put the phone down. Though I've never done that it's nice to know that I could if I wanted to.

It took a few calls with the same counsellor before I could actually say what the problem was. It's embarrassing, I'm ashamed of it, it still feels like it's my fault. My father's been sexually abusing me. When I was about nine he started coming into my bedroom at night to 'read me a story', but instead he'd make me feel uncomfortable and start touching me. As I got older he made me put his penis in my mouth, and had anal intercourse with me. I picked up those words from a TV programme. It's easier talking about it like someone else would because it makes it seem like it isn't actually happening to me. Most of the time I want to throw up.

I thought for a long time that what was happening was OK because Dad said that it was a game that all fathers played with their sons, a secret game that only the men knew about. But now I know that he's lying. I know that I'm different from other kids of my age.

I know, too, what my choices are. I could tell my mother, or somebody else in my family, but I honestly don't think they'd believe me. Dad's told me they wouldn't, and I believe him. The rest of my family think I'm a trouble-maker anyway, a 'problem-child' – they just don't know what the problem is. And my Dad's a solicitor. I could involve someone else in my family or a social worker but then everyone would know.

I'd have to talk about it over and over again, maybe in court. My little brother and I might end up in care. My dad might end up in prison. That would break my mother's heart. She might have to sell the house, she might stop loving me, and my Dad might too. It might seem odd, but I still love my dad in a way. I just want him to stop doing what he's doing to me.

I'm going to need to keep phoning ChildLine until I can get up the courage to tell someone else, or until I feel ready to let my counsellor there do that for me. I know that nothing will change unless I tell someone, and I know that I need to tell someone soon. Last week was my brother's eighth birthday (ChildLine, 1990, p. 6) (re-paragraphed).

ChildLine counsellors 'are not telling children that they must take action; instead, they help them to come to an informed decision about whether action is what they want. Then we can make contacts on their behalf' (Seymour). This is a protection denied to, for example, teachers or social workers who would have to disclose allegations of abuse or criminal behaviour to the police or social services department. 'ChildLine would only make contact with another agency without the caller's consent if it was believed that their life was immediately at risk' (Seymour).

ChildLine has been able to recognize the cost to the child of telling someone about abuse, and such consequences as the dramatic and often irrevocable destruction of the family by removal of the child/ren, imprisonment of the abusing adult/s and/or ending of parents' partnership. It recognizes too that problems for children do not end with entry into care where there may be many moves and little if any counselling or security. '"One day in court was worse than several years of abuse" a small boy told us' (Howarth, in ChildLine, 1990, p. 6).

Children who have told someone about abuse 'can feel in a worse position than before and may retreat' (Seymour). David knew that he would have 'to tell someone soon', someone who, unlike the ChildLine counsellor, would be obliged to initiate action. ChildLine would hope that, by that time, David would feel that he had been in control and made a good, however painful, decision.

'Most serious situations may take eight or nine calls before children will disclose what is going on. When it is a case of sexual abuse the children will usually think they are to blame, have a poor self-image, and feel dirty. Most of all, they don't want their family to be split up because they have "told"' (Eaton, 1990, p. 21).

Anna, aged 15, telephoned six times before she was able to bring herself to talk to ChildLine. Now she has established a long-term relationship with one counsellor and has been able to tell her mother about the sexual abuse she was suffering at the hands of her step-father. Anna's mother believed and supported her. Anna's step-father has left the home and the counselling work continues to help Anna

212

build a new life. She first called ChildLine more than a year ago (Harrison, in ChildLine, 1989, p. 6).

Although a sense of crisis may have brought the child to the telephone, in situations of continual abuse the child's sense of crisis may be stimulated by, as with David, the need to talk, not to initiate immediate or even eventual action. Valerie Howarth. Executive Director of ChildLine, says '"We are telling our counsellors it's your crisis – not the child's". The crisis comes from the counsellor hearing for the first time about the abuse. For the child, the "crisis" has been going on for months or years' (Eaton, 1990, p. 21).

Cooperation

Ideally, if intervention from, for example, a social services department will be necessary, ChildLine counsellor and social worker may work together during the period when plans are being made, involving the child by sharing information and listening to the child's views. ChildLine, may sometimes be involved in court proceedings:

Antony, aged 13, first rang ChildLine in a very distressed state. He was unhappy at home. He said he was expected to do most of the household chores and was frequently told to look after his two year old brother. Antony said that no matter how hard he tried he was unable to please either his mother or his step-father. In subsequent calls Antony disclosed sexual abuse by his step-father.

With the help of a counsellor he was able to look at ways he could help himself. Antony decided to tell his aunt who understood, believed and supported him.

When care proceedings were taken by social services Antony gave his permission for ChildLine to present details of his calls. He and his young brother became the subject of care orders. Antony's solicitor wrote to ChildLine and said, 'Undoubtedly the existence of evidence provided by ChildLine helped considerably in bringing the matter to a swift conclusion and particularly in minimising the pain for Antony' (Harrison, in ChildLine, 1989, p. 6) (reparagraphed).

It was crucial that details of Antony's calls were revealed only with his permission. He could be confident of confidentiality for as long as he wished.

ChildLine counsellors may also be involved as part of a team:

Mandy, aged 11 years, telephoned ChildLine demanding a social worker and refusing to return home. After discussion, ChildLine referred her to the local social services department and found that she already had an allocated social worker and was also seeing a psychologist. All the agencies agreed that Mandy would be directed to her social worker as a main source of help, to her psychologist for specialist sessions and that ChildLine counsellors would talk to her at set times. The agencies are now working together within a clearly defined plan and Mandy is beginning to deal with her emotional, educational and family difficulties, (p. 6).

Words, silence, listening

For some children the nightmare is so great that they are unable to speak, even when the telephone is answered. 'I always have to put the phone down, I'm scared...someone will tell my parents.' This girl wrote to Esther Rantzen, founder and chairman of ChildLine. 'I'm screaming inside my head, feeling angry and unhappy, I need to talk to someone and I need someone to give me a hug when I cry...There's never anyone' (Rantzen, 1990, p. 2).

The aim of ChildLine counsellors is to fill this gap, whether for a few minutes or a succession of regular, long calls. One conversation may, as with Annie (above) enable the child to take some important decision or the counsellor may act as a bridge to other sources of help, whether leading to support or more intervention. A volunteer counsellor considers that

> The most valuable thing I can offer a caller is to listen to them. This may sound obvious but often children have no-one who can or will listen to them – not just to the things they say but also the things they don't say. I wish I could wave a magic wand and make everything better for them but I accept that I cannot. Instead I am there to listen to them, to support and comfort them, and to help them to find them a way to help themselves (ChildLine, 1990, p. 8).

Telephone counselling may be hampered by its lack of visual contact and cues. For many children, as David mentioned, this may be an advantage: 'I don't think I could ever have started talking about my problems, not with someone who knew me, or even someone who could look at me while I was talking, or maybe try to stop me if I felt like running away' (ChildLine, 1990, p. 6).

Deprived of visual aids, counsellors learn really to listen and to communicate by voice alone – by voice, that is, and silence. Alison Seymour speaks of 'learning to hear different silences' and of responding appropriately. It is crucial not to be perceived by the child as 'hustling' or 'trying to move it on' yet the counsellor may need to communicate to the caller that silence is acceptable, there is no hurry, no need to speak, the counsellor is present, focusing on the unseen, unheard child and able to wait. 'We try to give opportunities for the child to speak and also give reassuring information, for example, about the 24 hour service, confidentiality and that the counsellor understands how difficult it may be to begin talking.' If there was still no spoken response the counsellor 'would tell the child that we were ending this call, encouraging them to ring again'.

Because silence is so rare in most people's repertoire of communication skills and may seem to the child to betoken the counsellor's withdrawal or disapproval, it may be necessary to indicate gently that contact had not been broken: 'It seems as though you're finding it difficult to talk at the moment, just take some time to think and I'll be quiet.'

The counsellor needs to communicate permission to speak, to say anything, however appalling the child fears the words may sound and to be silent, creating an environment of comfort, to hold the girl who wrote of her loneliness, 'I need someone to give me a hug when I cry' (Rantzen, in ChildLine, 1990, p. 2). Encompassing the child with acceptance, regarding with respect, responding with compassion.

This is the basis of response to every call. Alison Seymour says, 'It is important to give a respectful response to every call.' Apparently silly calls may be testing. For example, 'where a group of lads has rung up for a laugh' one may 'ring back with a real problem and admit he was in the group' (Eaton, 1990, p. 21).

Empathy and empowerment

Whatever the call, the counsellor responds with empathy, a slippery concept, defined by Alison Seymour as

> the ability to get alongside somebody in whatever emotional state they're in; you don't have to have experienced it and you may not understand it but you can get into the position where you're trying to understand, being honest about what you don't understand. You and the child are on a shared level and you're suspending judgement about what part the child is playing in the interactions that are being described.

However long or short the call, the counsellor works within the concept of building a relationship as an active but not intrusive presence. One counsellor comments that 'staying calm amidst uncertainty, anxiety, fear, distress and terror is of the essence' and that the work 'means empowering children, not rescuing them:...hearing their needs, accepting them and helping them through growing trust to reach their own choices...allowing them to experience perhaps for the first time that there may be hope.' The children 'may not be responsible for what is happening to them but they can be helped to see that they are able to become responsible for themselves' (ChildLine, 1989, p. 12).

Volunteer care and training

The demands are immense. 'It feels like I have crammed a weeks work into four hours! No complaints though' (ChildLine, 1989, p. 12). This is taken into account in the organization of the agency. Volunteer counsellors work a minimum of one shift (three hours in the Midlands branch) per fortnight. At the end of each shift, every counsellor receives 'debriefing' with a counselling supervisor. There are also regular individual supervision and group training sessions.

Volunteers are recruited for personal qualities rather than background experience or academic qualifications. Every potential volunteer attends a preliminary training course including skills based learning on listening, relationship building and telephone counselling for children and young people.

Volunteers are encouraged to look at their beliefs regarding, for example, race, abuse, marriage, 'looking at what sort of person they are'. Role playing is extensively used and found to be helpful in uncovering such dilemmas as 'response to a 12 year old who is wondering if he is gay or a 10 year old abused but wanting to stay with her parents' (Seymour). It is also important to be able to work with other people and to learn how to give and receive helpful, supportive but not 'bandaging' comment on day-to-day practice.

Of the two thirds of applicants accepted for training about half complete the course and 'go on the phones'. It is essential that volunteers can pace themselves, for example, taking time to make notes immediately after a call, having a break rather than going from call to call. This seems to be especially important in a working environment where several people are in deeply concentrated conversation with callers while a switchboard operator receives new calls. Headsets by no means fully exclude extraneous noise.

ChildLine

ChildLine has a number of advantages, not least of which is a clearly defined purpose and structure, and freedom from statutory obligation or control. While no child is ever refused the attention of a counsellor, the service is self-limiting by the constraints of available telephone lines. A counsellor, weary at the end of a shift, cannot be sent out to investigate alleged abuse and there is no waiting room full of clients.

The personal responsibility of the counsellor is limited. The provision of more lines and counsellors, the use of resources, is not the problem of the counsellor whose time and energy will not be lost in discussion of yet another financial constraint or departmental reorganization.

Expectations and provision of training and support/supervision are integral to the organization. Counsellors, however well aware of their feelings and responses and able to subordinate them to focusing on the child, are expected to feel and respond and to need help themselves.

The burden is heavy but it is recognized and shared. The service so largely staffed by volunteers is organized on a meticulously professional basis at all levels.

A major advantage of ChildLine to the children is that not only is it free (0800 denotes Freefone and there is a Freepost address) but also it invites, indeed depends on, self-referral. Provided that children can get through, attention is assured. They are free to offer their own story and their own valuation of themselves, other people and events. They can expect to be believed.

In most agencies the child is defined as a patient needing help to recover from some 'illness' or manage some disability, or referred because of behaviour regarded by adults as unacceptable and therefore requiring treatment. The child is referred by a succession of adults – parent, teacher, doctor.

Nasreen found her ChildLine counsellor very helpful in dispelling the image that 'it was me, not my experience, that was out of control' (ChildLine, 1990, p. 7). She did not have to present some dramatic crisis or produce disturbing behaviour in order to gain attention from ChildLine. Her need was to keep 'both of the important aspects of her life balanced and intact' (p. 7).

To live more fully

This chapter began with a girl saved from death during several hours of high drama. It ends with another girl, helped through calm attention to gain self-respect and empowerment 'to live more fully' (Egan, 1990, p. 5). Her call 'got through', beginning to dispel the nightmare. (This account is a compilation by ChildLine Staff based on the experience of a real child.) Nasreen

telephoned ChildLine about six months ago, when life at home was getting seriously difficult. I don't know if you can understand what it's like to be Asian and British at the same time. Sometimes I have trouble figuring it out myself, and that makes it hard when you want to define yourself as something. When I was at school I didn't do very well in my exams, and my parents were actually glad about it because it meant that they could just marry me off.

What I wanted was to get a job; in fact, I wanted to have a career, but my parents were set against it. They didn't allow me to go out, or to wear nice clothes or make-up, because they thought that the less attractive I was the safer I would be from boys, and from ruining my family's honour. There were a lot of rows at home. It got to the point where I felt like I didn't want to be there at all, but I wasn't allowed to be anywhere else.

One time my father got so angry that he said he'd send me back to Pakistan to get married. My parents knew some other girls of my age who felt OK about having arranged marriages, and about a strict upbringing generally, so I suppose they were afraid that when I said I didn't want that I might really be saying that I didn't want to be Pakistani.

One of the ways that the counsellor I spoke to was helpful was just by agreeing that my situation at home sounded really difficult. That was a relief, because a lot of the way that I'd been brought up told me that it was me, not my experience, that was out of control.

The woman at ChildLine helped me clarify things a bit by telling me what she heard me saying to her, like that I seemed to have a British self that was really important to me and an Asian self that was equally so. It seems important seems obvious enough now that that's a problem in itself, because the two cultures that shape me are sometimes in conflict, but before I phoned a lot of things like that didn't seem very clear. I appreciated the fact that the counsellor was honest with me and said that in some ways it was difficult for her to help me because she didn't know that much about Pakistani culture.

She was able, though, to give me some information about a face-to-face counselling centre in my area, a place where I could talk with workers who might understand my 'two selves' better. I think I'm really lucky that I live in a part of London where they have counselling for young women from Asian cultures. They've been helping me a lot to work towards compromising with my family, and towards keeping both of the important aspects of my life balanced and intact (ChildLine. 1990, p. 7) (re-paragraphed).

References

ChildLine publications:
ChildLine. (1989). *ChildLine*. London, Harrison, H. How ChildLine helps. pp. 4–5; ChildLine Volunteers Speak, p. 12.
ChildLine. (1990). *ChildLine 1990*. London, Rantzen, E. Chairman's report, pp. 2–3; Howarth, V. Reaching the children, pp. 4–5; Children Talking, pp. 6–7; ChildLine's Volunteer Counsellors, pp. 8–9.
ChildLine leaflet.
For further information write to:
ChildLine, 2nd Floor, Royal Mail Building, Studd Street, London N1 0QW. Tel.: 071 239 1000.
Eaton, L. (1990). At the end of the line. *Social Work Today*, 21,(48), 20–21.
Egan, G. (1990). *The Skilled Helper: A Systematic Approach to Effective Helping*. Brooks/Cole, Pacific Grove, California.

Bibliography

Key to abbreviations used:

Journal titles:
A/F   = *Adoption and Fostering*
BJRE   = *British Journal of Religious Education*
SWT   = *Social Work Today*

Publishers:
BAAF   = British Agencies for Adoption and Fostering.
BBC   = British Broadcasting Corporation.
OUP   = Oxford University Press.
QHS   = Quaker Home Service.
SPCK   = Society for the Propogation of Christian Knowledge.
UP   = University Press.

All titles published in London unless otherwise noted, except Penguin, Harmondsworth.

In...   = for full details see entry under author/editor of main work.
Quoted in... = for full details of text which is cited in main work, see entry under author of main work: primary source not seen by present author.

Abott, L. *Approach to Music.* Quoted in E. Bailey.
Ahmed, S., Cheetham, J. and Small, J. (eds) (1986). *Social Work with Black Children and their Families.* Batsford/BAAF.
Allan, J. (1988). *Inscapes of the Child's World: Jungian Counseling in Schools and Clinics.* Spring Publications, Dallas, Texas.
Allan, J. A. B. and Nairne, J. L. (1984). *Class Discussions for Teachers and Counselors in Elementary School.* Guidance Centre. Faculty of Education, University of Toronto.
Allen, C. (1991). The Inner Light. *Nursing Standard,* 5,(20), 52–3.
Allen, H. M. (1986). Life Story with a Difference. [book review]. *A/F,* 10,(2), 66–7.
Althea, (1982). *When Uncle Bob Died.* Collins.
Alvin, J. (1965). *Music for the Handicapped Child.* Oxford UP.
Alvin, J. (1975). *Music Therapy.* Hutchinson.
Amory, C., Gillespie. A., Halliday, D. and Skaife D'Ingerthorpe, R. (1986). Letter. *Community Care.*
Andersen, H. C. (n/d). *Fairy Tales.* Ward Lock.
Aptekar, H. H. (1955). *The Dynamics of Casework and Counseling.* Houghton Mifflin, Cambridge, Mass.
Aquinas, T. (1274). *Summa Theologica.* Quoted in Moran.
Aries, P. (1973). *Centuries of Childhood.* Penguin.

Amstrong, H. (1991). *Taking Care: a Church Response to Children, Adults and Abuse*. National Children's Bureau.

Arthur, C. J. (1985). Religion, Identity and Maturity: some remarks on Erikson's 'Eight Ages of Man' and religious education. *BJRE*, 7,(2), 48–53.

Asimov, I. (1990). *Nemesis*. Bantam, London.

Asrat-Girma. (1986). Afro-Caribbean children in day-care. In Ahmed, et al., pp. 40–50.

Atwood, M. (1991). Interview in *Bookshelf*. BBC Radio 4, 13.10.91.

Axline, V. (1971). *Dibs: in search of self*. Penguin.

Bach, S. (1969). *Spontaneous Painting of Severely Ill Patients: a contribution to psychosomatic medicine*. *Acta Psychosomatica 8*. Geigy.

Bailey, E. (1958). *Discovering Music with Young Children*. Methuen.

Bailey, P. (1973). *They Can Make Music*. OUP.

Barrett-Aranui, H. (1989). Nga matapihi o te waiora: (windows on Maori well-being). In Munro et al. pp. 97–106.

Bassin, A., Bratter, T. E. and Rachin, R. L. (eds) (1976). *The Reality Therapy Reader: a survey of the work of William Glasser*. Harper and Row, New York.

Bawden, N. (1987). *Circles of Deceit*. Macmillan.

Bayless, K. M. and Ramsey, M. E. (1982). *Music: a Way of Life for the Young Child*. Mosby, St Louis.

Benner, D. G. (1991). *Counselling as a Spiritual Process. Lingdale Paper 17*. Clinical Theology Association. St. Mary's House, Oxford.

Benton Grange School. (1979). What I feel I am due. In Harris and Hyland, pp. 16–18.

Bergethon, B. and Boardman, E. (1979). *Musical Growth in the Elementary School*. Holt, Rinehart and Winston, New York.

Berryman, J. W. (1985). Children's spirituality and religious language. *BJRE*, 7,(3), 120–7.

Bettelheim, B. (1976). *The Uses of Enchantment: the Meaning and Importance of Fairy Tales*. Thames and Hudson.

Bhaduri, R. (1990). Counselling with Karma. *SWT*, 21,(33), 17.

Bhaduri, R. (1991). A sense of Karma. *SWT*, 22,(33), 14–15.

Blake, W. (1927/1757–1827). The schoolboy. *Selected Poems of William Blake*. OUP.

Bluebond-Langner, M. (1978). *The Private Worlds of Dying Children*. Princeton UP, New Jersey.

Bogues, F. (1979). The lost years. In Muldoon, pp. 84–5.

Bohler, J. (1987). The use of storytelling in the practice of pastoral counselling. *Journal of Pastoral Care*, 41,(1), 63–71. (Also in Foskett and Jacobs.)

Boswell, J. (1989). *The Kindness of Strangers: the Abandonment of Children in Western Europe from late Antiquity to the Renaissance*. Lane (Penguin).

Boulding, E. (1989). *One Small Plot of Heaven: Reflections on Family Life by a Quaker Sociologist*. Pendle Hill Publications, Wallingford, Pennsylvania.

Bowen, E. (Wilson, A. (ed.)) (1983). *The Collected Stories of Elizabeth Bowen*. Penguin,
 The return, pp. 28–34;
 Coming home, pp. 95–100;
 The visitor, pp. 124–35;
 The jungle, pp. 231–41;

The dancing-mistress, pp. 253–62;
The little girl's room; pp. 425–34;
The apple tree, pp. 461–70;
Look at all those roses, pp. 512–20;
Ivy gripped the steps, pp. 686–711.

Bowen, E. (1986). The mulberry tree. In Lee, pp. 13–21.

Bradford, J. (1978). *The Spiritual Rights of the Child: a discussion paper.* Church of England Children's Society, London. (Also in Harris and Hyland.)

Bradford, J. (1989). Spiritual rights and religious rights in the 1989 convention. *Children Worldwide.* International Catholic Child Bureau, pp. 41–3.

Bradley, A. and Jamieson, K. (eds). (1980). *Dandelion Clocks.* Penguin.

Brett, R. (1991). Orkney: aberration or symptom? *The Journal of Child Law*, Sept. -Dec. 143–6.

British Association for Counselling. (1984). *Code of Ethics and Practice for Counsellors.* BAC, Rugby. (See also Dryden, Charles–Edwards and Woolfe, pp. 425–36.)

Brontë, C. (1966/1847). *Jane Eyre.* Penguin.

Burton, H. (1968). *In Spite of All the Terror.* OUP.

Byars, B. (1976). *The TV Kid.* The Bodley Head.

Byars, B. (1982). *The Two-thousand Pound Goldfish.* The Bodley Head.

Cairns, K. (1990). Climate for learning. *SWT*, 21, (38), 26–7.

Campbell, B. (1988). *Unofficial Secrets: Child Sexual Abuse – the Cleveland Case.* Virago.

Carpentier, A. (de Onis, H. (trans.)) (1968). *The Lost Steps (Los Pasos Perdidos).* Penguin.

Carroll, L. (1989). *The Complete Illustrated Works of Lewis Carroll.* Chancellor.

Carter, A. (1981). *The Magic Toyshop.* Virago.

Carter, A. (1990). *The Virago Book of Fairy Tales.* Virago.

Casey, J. (1978). Tamed strawberries. In Harwood and King, pp. 37–50.

Chaplin, J. (1988a). *Feminist Counselling in Action.* Sage.

Chaplin, J. (1988b). Feminist therapy. In Rowan and Dryden, pp. 39–60.

Chaplin, J. (1989). Counselling and gender. In Dryden et al., pp. 223–36.

Chardin, T. de, Quoted in Moran.

ChildLine. (1989). *ChildLine.* ChildLine.

ChildLine. (1990). *ChildLine 1990.* ChildLine.

Clarkson, P. (1989). *Gestalt Counselling in Action.* Sage.

Coles, R. (1986). *The Moral Life of Children.* Atlantic Monthly Press. Boston. Quoted in Hoffman.

Comyns, B. (1985). *Sisters by a River.* Virago.

Comyns, B. (1989). *A House of Dolls.* Methuen.

Connor, T., Sclare, I., Dunbar, D, and Elliffe, J. (1984). A residential homefinding unit. *A/F*, 8, (4), 44–6, 72.

Connor, T., Sclare, I., Dunbar, D., and Elliffe, J., (1985). Making a life-story book. *A/F*, 9, (2), 32–5, 46.

Cooley, J. (1990). Searching for a way through: an account of bereavement work with a seven year old boy. Unpublished article. (Subsequently published in *Bereavement Care.* Spring, 1992.)

Crompton, M. (1979). Common needs and shared fears in 'non-natural' mothers. *Community Care*; 4.1.79, pp. 20–22.

Crompton, M. (1980). *Respecting Children: Social Work with Young People.* Edward Arnold.

Crompton, M. (1982). *Adolescents and Social Workers.* Gower/Community Care, Aldershot.

Crompton, M. (1990). *Attending to Children: Direct Work in Social and Health Care.* Edward Arnold, Dunton Green.

Crompton, M. (1991). Invasion by Russian dolls. *A/F*, 15(1), 31–3.

Cupitt, D. (1985). *The Sea of Faith: Christianity in Change.* BBC.

Dorfman, E. (1951). Play therapy. In Rogers, pp. 235–77.

Dryden, W. (ed.) *Counselling in Action* series. Sage.

Dryden, W. (ed.) (1984). *Individual Therapy in Britain.* Harper and Row.

Dryden, W. (1984a). Rational-emotive therapy. In Dryden, pp. 235–63.

Dryden, W. (1984b). *Rational-emotive Therapy: Fundamentals and Innovations.* Croom Helm. Quoted in Murgatroyd.

Dryden, W. (ed.). (1990). *Individual Therapy in Britain: a Handbook.* Open UP, Milton Keynes.

Dryden, W., Charles–Edwards, D. and Woolfe, R. (eds) (1989). *Handbook of Counselling in Britain.* Tavistock/Routledge.

Dunbar, M. (1987). *Catherine: a Tragic Life. The Story of a Young Girl who Died of Anorexia Nervosa.* Penguin.

Durant, D. N. (1978). *Arbella Stuart: a Rival to the Queen.* Weidenfeld and Nicholson.

Eaton, L. (1990). At the end of the line: (ChildLine). *SWT*, 21, (48), 40–41.

Eco, U. trans. Weaver, W. (1989). *Foucault's Pendulum.* Secker and Warburg.

Egan, G. (1990). *The Skilled Helper: a Systematic Approach to Effective Helping.* Brooks/Cole, Pacific Grove, California.

Eisenberg, N. and Strayer, J. (1987). *Empathy and its Development.* Cambridge UP, Cambridge.

Eliade, M. trans. Mairet, P. (1975). *Myths, Dreams and Mysteries: an Encounter Between Contemporary Faiths and Archaic Realities.* Harper and Row, NY.

Eliot, G. (1979/1860). *The Mill on the Floss.* Penguin.

Elkind, D. (1971). The development of religious understanding in children and adolescents. In Strommen, *Research on Religious Development.* Hawthorn. pp. 677–8. Quoted in Greer.

Erikson, E. (1965). Eight ages of man. *Childhood and Society.* Penguin.

Ernst, S. and Maguire, M. (eds) (1987). *Living with the Sphinx: papers from the Women's Therapy Centre.* The Women's Press.

Fahlberg, V. (1981). *Helping Children when they Must Move.* BAAF.

Farmer, P. (1969). *Charlotte Sometimes.* Chatto and Windus.

Fawell, R. (1987). *Courage to Grow.* QHS.

Ferguson, S. (1987). *A Guard Within.* Collins.

Ford, J. K. and Merriman, P. (1990). *The Gentle Art of Listening: Counselling Skills for Volunteers.* Bedford Square Press/National Council of Voluntary Organisations.

Forrester, W. (ed.) (1980). *Great Grandmama's Weekly: a Celebration of the Girl's Own Paper. 1880–1901.* Lutterworth; Guildford.

Foskett, J. and Jacobs, M. (1989), Pastoral Counselling. In Dryden, et al., pp. 252–65.

Foskett, J. and Lyall, D. (1988). *Helping the Helpers*. SPCK. Quoted in Foskett and Jacobs.

Fowler, J. W. (1981). *Stages of Faith: the Psychology of Human Development and the Quest for Meaning*. Harper and Row, San Francisco, Calif.

Gardam, J. (1983/1986). *The Summer after the Funeral*. Penguin/Hamish Hamilton.

Gardam, J. (1987). The weeping child. In Lee.

Gardner, R. (1970). *The Boys and Girls Book about Divorce: with an Introduction for Parents*. Jason Aronson, NY.

Garner, A. (1967). *The Owl Service*. Collins.

Georgeson, V. (1980). Sophie's blues. In Bradley and Jamieson, pp. 156–64.

Gill, B. M. (1986). *Nursery Crimes*. Hodder and Stoughton.

Gillespie, A. (1986). 'Art therapy' at the Familymakers Project. *A/F*, 10, (1), 19–23.

Gillespie, A. (1991). Personal letter to M. Crompton.

Gillman, H. (1988). *A Minority of One: a Journey with Friends*. Swarthmore Lecture. QHS.

Glasser, W. (1975). *Reality Therapy: a New Approach to Psychiatry*. Harper and Row, NY.

Glasser, W. (1976a). A realistic approach to young offenders. In Bassin, et al., pp. 510–24.

Glasser, W. (1976b). What children need. In Bassin. et al., pp. 465–81.

Godden, R. (1989a). *An Episode of Sparrows*. Penguin.

Godden, R. (1989). *A House with Four Rooms: Autobiography; Vol.* 2. Macmillan.

Goldacre, P. (1980). Helping children with bereavement. *A/F*, 4, (2), 37–40.

Golding, V. (1990). Speaking out leads to survival. *SWT*, 21, (38), 18–19.

Goldman, R. (1964). *Religious Thinking from Childhood to Adolescence*. Routledge and Kegan Paul. Quoted in Greer.

Goodall, J. (1984). Foreword to English Edition. In Shelley, pp. 10–11.

Gosse, E. (1949/1907). *Father and Son: a Study of Two Temperaments*. Penguin.

Goudge, E. (1936). *A City of Bells*. Duckworth.

Goudge, E. (1950). *Gentian Hill*. Hodder and Stoughton.

Goudge, E. (1974). *The Joy of the Snow: an Autobiography*. Hodder and Stoughton, Dunton Green.

Goulding, E. (1984). Foreword. In Shelley, pp. 6–9.

Graves, R. (1955). *The Greek Myths' Vols*. 1 and 2. Penguin.

Graves, R. (1961). *The White Goddess*. Faber and Faber.

Greer, J. E. (1980). Stages in the development of religious thinking. *BJRE*, 3, (1), 24–8.

Griffith, P. (1982). Personal communication. In Bayless and Ramsey, pp. 181–4.

Grimm, J. and W. (Marshall, B. (trans.)) (n/d). *Grimms' Fairy Tales for Children and the Household*. Ward, Lock.

Gripe, M. trans. Austin, P. B. (1974). *Hugo and Josephine*. Pan.

Groome, T. H. (1980). *Christian Religious Education: Sharing Our Story and Our Vision*. Harper and Row, San Francisco, Calif.

LeGuin, U. (1971). *A Wizard of Earthsea*. Penguin.

Halmos, P. (1965). *The Faith of the Counsellors*. Constable.

Hamilton, H. A. (1963). *The Religious Needs of Children*. National Children's Homes.

Hargie, O., Saunders, C. and Dickson, D. (1981). *Social Skills in Interpersonal Communication*. Croom Helm.

Harris, D. and Hyland, J. (eds) (1979). *Rights in Residence: a review of the Residential Care Association*. RCA Publications.

Harwood, R. and King, F. (eds) (1978). *New Stories, 3: an Arts Council Anthology*. Hutchinson in association with The Arts Council of Great Britain and PEN.

Hawes, B. (1979). Rights in retrospect. In Harris and Hyland, pp. 63–4.

Hawking, S. (1988). *A Brief History of Time: from the Big Bang to Black Holes*. Bantam.

Heffers. (1991). *Choices* (Catalogue). Cambridge.

Her Majesty's Stationery Office. (1989). *Children Act*.

Hillman, J. (1988). Foreword. In Allan, pp. xiii–xx.

Hodgson-Burnett, F. (1951/1911). *The Secret Garden*. Penguin.

Hoffman, M. L. (1987). The contribution of empathy to justice and moral judgement. In Eisenberg and Strayer, pp. 47–80.

Holgate, E. (1972). Introduction to *Communicating with Children*. Longman.

Homer. (Rieu, E. V. (trans.)) (1946). *The Odyssey*. Penguin.

Houghton, C. J. (1976). On the day when mother died. In Mirror Group Newspapers, pp. 104–106.

Houston, G. (1990). *The Red Book of Gestalt*. The Rochester Foundation.

Hoy, L. (1987). *Your Friend, Rebecca*. Century Hutchinson.

Hoy, L. (1989). *Kiss File JC 110*. Walker.

Hughes, D. (1985). The importance of music. *Music in Action*. '85. UK Council for Music Education and Training in association with Able Children. Pullen, Knebworth.

Hull, J. (1981). *God-talk with Young Children: Notes for Parents and Teachers*. Birmingham Papers in Religious Education No. 2. The University of Birmingham and the Christian Education Movement.

Hunt, N. (1982). *The World of Nigel Hunt: the Diary of a Mongoloid Youth*. Asset Recycling, Norwich.

Hunter, M. (1987). Julia: a 'frozen' child. *A/F*, 11, (3), 26–30.

Inskipp, F. with Johns, H. (1984). Developmental electicism: Egan's model of helping. In Dryden. pp. 364–88.

Isaacs, S. and Hickman, S. (1987). Communicating with children after a murder. *A/F*, 11, (4),. 32–35.

Ivey, A. and M. B. (1990). Assessment and facilitating children's cognitive development: developmental counseling and therapy in a case of child abuse. *Journal of Counseling and Development*, 68, (2), 299–305.

Jacobs, M. (1984). Psychodynamic therapy: the Freudian approach. In Dryden, pp. 23–46.

Jacobs, M. (1988). *Psychodynamic Counselling in Action*. Sage.

James, W. (1902). *The Varieties of Religious Experience*. Random House. Quoted in Berryman, p. 58.

Jansson, T. trans. Warburton, T. (1973). The invisible child. *Tales from Moomin Valley*. Penguin.

Jersild, A. T. (1963). *The Psychology of Adolescence*. NY. Quoted in Arthur, p. 5.

Jewett, C. (1984). *Helping Children Cope with Separation and Loss*. Batsford/ BAAF. Quoted in Cooley.

Johnson, S. P. (ed.). (1965). *A Book of Princesses*. Penguin.

Jolly, H. (1982). In Althea, p. 25.

Jolly, J. (1981). *The Other Side of Paediatrics: a Guide to the Everyday Care of Sick Children*. Macmillan, Basingstoke.

Jones, A. (1984). *Counselling Adolescents: School and After*. Kogan Page.

Jones, G. and Jones, T. (trans.) (1949). *The Mabinogion*. Dent.

Jung, C. G. (1933). *Modern Man in Search of a Soul*. Quoted in Eliade.

Kadushin, A. (1972). *The Social Work Interview*. Columbia UP, NY.

Kibble, D., Parker, S. and Price, C. (1981). The Age of Uncertainty: religious belief amongst adolescents. *BJRE*, 4, (1), 31–5.

King, A. and Clifford, S. (eds) (1989) *Trees be Company: an Anthology of Poetry*. Bristol Classical Press. Bristol.

King, C. (1963). *Stig of the Dump*. Penguin.

Klingberg, G. (Boulding, E. (trans.)) (1959). A study of the religious experience in children from 9–13 years of age. *Religious Education*, 54, (May 1959), 211–16, Quoted in Boulding.

Klink, J. L. (Wilson, R. A. (trans.)) (1972). *Your Child and Religion. (Kind en Geloof)*. SCM. (Uitgeverij Ambo. n.v. Bilthoven, NL.).

Küber-Ross, E. (1983). *On Children and Death*. Macmillan, NY.

Lambert, K. (1984). Psychodynamic therapy: the Jungian approach. In Dryden, pp. 76–101.

Lane, D. (ed.). (1991). *Child and Adolescent Therapy: a Handbook*. Open UP, Milton Keynes.

Lee, H. (ed.) (1986). *The Mulberry Tree*. Virago.

Lee, H. (ed.) (1987). *The Secret Self, 2: Short Stories by Women*. Dent.

Lessing, D. (1979). *Shikasta*. Jonathan Cape.

Lewis, C. S. (1950). *The Lion, the Witch and the Wardrobe*. Geoffrey Bles.

Lightbown, C. (1979). Life story books. *A/F*, nu. 3, 9–15.

Lowe, P. (1988). *Special Needs in Ordinary Schools. Responding to Adolescent Needs: a Pastoral Care Approach*. Cassell.

Lowry, S. P. (1982). *Familiar Mysteries: the Truth in Myth*. OUP.

McDowell, N. (1976). God and heaven. In Mirror Group Newspapers p. 3.

McMaster, J.(ed.). (1982). *Methods in Social and Educational Caring*. Gower, Aldershot.

Macaulay, R. (1965). *Told by an Idiot*. Collins.

Macaulay, R. (1983). *The World my Wilderness*. Virago.

Macdonald, G. (1965/1863). The light princess. In Johnson, pp. 147–76.

Magee, B. (1987). *The Great Philosophers: an Introduction to Western Philosophy*. OUP.

Mallon, B. (1987). *An Introduction to Counselling Skills for Special Educational Needs: Participants Manual*. Manchester UP.

Marshall, M. R. (1975). *Libraries and Literature for Teenagers*. Deutsch.

Marshall, M. R. (1981). *Libraries and the Handicapped Child*. Deutsch.

Mascaro, J. (trans.). *The Bhagavad Gita*. Penguin.

Mearns, D. and Thorne, B. (1988). *Person-centred Counselling in Action*. Sage.

Mennell, M. (1986). The experience of Bradford Social Services Department. In Ahmed, et al. pp. 120–31.

Meredith. G. (1912). Enter these enchanted woods. In King and Clifford, pp. 52–3.
Meyer, N. and Martin, D. (1991). *Don Quixote*. (After Cervantes.) BBC Radio 3.
Mirror Group Newspapers (1976). *Children as Writers, 3*. Heinemann.
Moran, M. (1968). *Pastoral Counselling for the Deviant Girl*. Chapman.
Morgan, S. (1986). Practice in a community nursery for black children. In Ahmed et al. pp. 69–74.
Morris, M. (1986). Communicating with adolescents. *A/F*, 10,(4). 54–5, 71.
Morrison, D. W. (1977). *Personal Problem-solving in the Classroom: the Reality Technique*. Wiley, NY.
Muldoon, P. (1979). *The Scrake of Dawn: Poems by Young People from Northern Ireland*. Blackstaff Press/The Arts Council of NI, Belfast.
Munro, A., Manthei, B. and Small, J. (1989). *Counselling: Skills of Problem-solving*. Routledge.
Murdoch, I. (1963). *The Unicorn*. Chatto and Windus.
Murgatroyd, S. (1985). *Counselling and Helping*. British Psychological Society/Methuen.
Natten, M. (1979). Childhood. In Smith, p. 6.
Newbould, B. (1981). *Music to an Unpurged Ear: Inaugural Lecture*. University of Hull.
Nicolson, O. (1989). More than a playground problem. *SWT*, 7.12.89, 18–19.
Noonan, E. (1983). *Counselling Young People*. Methuen.
Nordoff, P and Robbins, C. (1971a). *Therapy in Music for Handicapped Children*. Gollancz.
Nordoff, P. and Robbins, C. (1971b). The Children's Tune. *Individual Music Therapy*. British Society for Music Therapy.
Nordoff, P. and Robbins, C. (1975). *Music Therapy in Special Education*. Macdonald and Evans.
Norman, B. (1991). Barry Norman on...*Radio Times*. BBC.
Oaklander, V. (1978). *Windows to our Children: a Gestalt Therapy Approach to Children and Adolescents*. Real People Press, Moab, Utah.
O'Connor, D. (1982). Assessment in practice. In McMaster. pp. 28–42.
Onion, N. (1991). Nordoff-Robbins Music Therapy Centre. *Music Journal*, Incorporated Society of Musicians. July 1991, 51.
Page, F. (1984). Gestalt therapy. In Dryden, pp. 180–204.
Penman, C. (1986). The Quaker idea. In Quaker Social Responsibility and Education, pp. 76–7.
Plath, S. (1963). *The Bell Jar*. Heinemann.
Pluckrose, H. (1974). in *Every Side of the Picture*. The Save the Children Fund.
Prestage, R. (1972). Life for Kim. In Holgate, pp. 97–107.
Priestley, J. B. (1929). *The Good Companions*. Heinemann.
Prys-Williams, B. (1986). Jerusalem again! Lovely. In Quaker Social Responsibility and Education, pp. 68–9.
Quaker Social Responsibility and Education. (1986). *Learners All: Quaker Experiences in Education*, QHS.
Rabuzzi, K. A. (1988). *Motherself: a mythic analysis of motherhood*. Indiana UP, Bloomington.
Randell, K. (1989). The luxury of knowing who you are. *SWT*, 21,(10), p. 22.

Redfern, K. (1991). How do we treat our children? *The Friend*, 149,(27), 853–4.

Renault, M. (1970). *Fire from Heaven*. Longman.

Reps, P. (compiler). With Senzaki, N. (transcribers) (1971) *Zen Flesh, Zen Bones*. Penguin.

Richards, J. (1991). *Childhood in the Middle Ages*. BBC Radio 3.

Rickford, F. (1991). On record: child sexual abuse. *SWT*, 21.3.91, 26.

Rinehart, C. A. (1980). The state of the art. Music: a basic for the 1980s. *Childhood Education*, 36,(3), 140–5. Quoted in Bayless and Ramsey, p. 179.

Robinson, E. (ed.) (1978). *Living the Question*. The Religious Experience Research Unit. Manchester College, Oxford.

Robinson, J. G. (1971). *Charley*. Collins.

Rodgers, J. L. (1984). Is God a teddy bear? Images of God. In Shelley, pp. 91–9.

Rogers, C. R. (1951). *Client-centered Therapy: its Current Practice, Implications and Theory*. Constable.

Rogers, C. R. (1961). *On Becoming a Person: a Therapist's view of Psychotherapy*. Constable.

Rowan, J. and Dryden, W. (eds). (1988). *Innovative Therapy in Britain*. Open UP.

Rowe, D. (1987). *Beyond Fear*. Collins.

Royal College of Nursing. (1978). *Counselling in Nursing. The Report of a Working Party held under the Auspices of the RCN Institute of Advanced Nursing Education*. RCN.

Rutter, M. (1983). *A Measure of our Values. Swarthmore Lecture*. QHS.

Ryburn, M. (1991). The myth of assessment. *A/F*, 15,(1), 20–27.

de Saint-Exupéry, A. (Woods, K. (trans.)) (1974). *The Little Prince*. Pan.

Salisbury, E. (1991). The ten words. *The Friend*, 149,(42), 1346.

Sartre, J. P. (1944). *Huis Clos*.

Sawbridge, P. (1990). Post-adoption counselling: what do we actually do? *A/F*, 14,(1), 31–3.

Schuurman. S. (1987). *Tristan: Physically and Mentally Handicapped – Socially and Spiritually Gifted*. George Ronald. Oxford.

Sereny, G. (1972). *The Case of Mary Bell*. Evre Methuan.

Seymour, C. (1990). *Counselling Children*. Unpublished thesis. University of Durham.

Shahar, S. (1990). *Childhood in the Middle Ages*. Routledge.

Shapiro, L. E. (1984). *The New Short-term Therapies for Children: a Guide for the Helping Professions and Parents*. Prentice-Hall. New Jersey.

Shelley, J. A. and others. (1984). *Spiritual Needs of Children*. Scripture Union.

Shelley, P. B. (circa 1820). *Music, when Soft Voices Die*.

Smith, W. H. (1979). Children's Literary Competition, 1978. *Children as Writers: 20th Year*. Heinemann.

Spender, D. (1980). *Man Made Language*. Routledge and Kegan Paul.

Sophocles (Watling, E. F. (trans.)) (1947). *The Theban Plays*. Penguin.

Stevens, J. (1971). *Awareness; exploring, experimenting and experiencing*. Real People Press, Moab, Utah. Quoted in Seymour.

Stevenson, R. L. (1886). *Kidnapped*.

Stevenson, Y. (1976). *The Hot-house Plant: an Autobiography of a Young Girl.* Elek/Pemberton.

Storr, C. (1964). *Marianne Dreams.* Penguin.

Storr, C. (1974). *Thursday.* Penguin.

Strayer, J. and Eisenberg, N. (1987). Empathy viewed in context. In Eisenberg and Strayer, pp. 389–98.

Streich, H. (1970). Unpublished paper read at the Institute for Analytical Psychology, Zurich, August 1970. Quoted in Alvin, 1975.

Strommen, M. P. (ed.) *Research on Religious Development.* Hawthorn. Summary of Elkind. pp. 677–8. Reference in Greer, p 28.

Swift, G. (1978). Learning to swim. In Harwood and King, pp. 323–41.

Sworder, G. (1977). Problems for the counsellor in his task. In Watts, pp. 79–83.

Sykes, J. B. (1982). *The Concise Oxford Dictionary.* Clarendon. Oxford.

Tate, T. (1991). *Children for the Devil: Ritual Abuse and Satanic Crime.* Methuen.

Taylor, E. (1967). *Mossy Trotter.* Chatto and Windus.

Taylor, E. (1985). *Palladian.* Virago.

Taylor, E. (1988). *At Mrs Lippincote's.* Virago.

Tennyson, A. (1832). *The Lady of Shalott.*

Thorne, B. (1984). Person-centred therapy. In Dryden, pp. 102–28.

Thompson, C. L. and Rudolph, L. B. (1988) *Counselling Children.* Brooks/ Cole, Pacific Grove, California.

Thurber, J. (1965). Many moons. In Johnson, pp. 177–88.

Timms, N. (1964). *Social Casework: Principles and Practice.* Routledge and Kegan Paul.

Timperley, R. (1980). *The House of Mad Children.* Robert Hale.

Toynbee, P. (1985). *Lost Children: the Story of Adopted Children Searching for Their Mothers.* Hutchinson.

Wardle, M. (1975). Hippopotamus or cow? on not communicating *about* children. *SWT*, 6, (14), 428–32.

Watts, A. G. (ed.) (1977). *Counselling at Work. Papers prepared by a Working Party of the Standing Conference for the Advancement of Counselling.* Bedford Square Press of the NCSS.

West. J. (1990). Children in 'Limbo'. *A/F* 14, (2), 11–14.

Westerhoff, J. H., III. (1980). *Bringing up Children in the Christian Faith.* Winston Press. Minneopolis.

Wheeler, J. (born Sippel, D.) (1990). The secret is out. *A/F*, 14, (3), 22–7.

Wilson, K., Kendrick, P and Ryan, V. (1992). *Play Therapy: a Non-directive Approach with Children and Adolescents.* Baillière Tindall.

Winnicott, D. W. (1971). *Therapeutic Consultations in Child Psychiatry.* Hogarth.

Winterson, J. (1985). *Oranges are not the Only Fruit.* Unwin Hyman.

Wispé, L. (1987). History of the concept of empathy. In Eisenberg and Strayer, pp 17–37.

Wittgenstein, L. (1921). *Tractatus Logico-philosophicus.* Quoted in Magee.

Subject Index
(excluding main Bibliography)

Abortion 100
Abuse/Assault 6, 19, 20, 25, 27, 38, 45, 49, 50, 51, 58, 59, 63, 66, 75, 76, 77, 84, 97, 105-7, 111, 115, 116, 117, 119, 125, 131, 134, 141, 147, 161, 173, 177, 183, 207, 208-17
Spiritual abuse: See Spirit
Act/Acting/Actor 1, 12, 29, 30, 130, 187, 203
Actors mentioned in text:
Allen, Woody 77
Cleese, John 205
Reid, Beryl 30
Temple, Shirley 29
(See also Drama, Plays)
Adolescence/Adolescents 14, 17, 25, 26, 27, 30, 43, 53, 67, 68, 87, 88, 89, 91, 93, 94, 97, 118, 122, 127, 128, 129, 130, 131, 133, 138, 141, 150, 161, 180, 203
Adoption 65, 68, 83, 84, 126, 144, 148, 152, 159, 160, 161, 178, 185
Adoption And Fostering 14, 43, 54, 67, 68, 141, 161, 162, 180, 201, 207
Adoptive Mother 65, 159
Advice 15, 16, 20, 24, 90, 101, 111, 177, 209, 210
Advisor 182
Aesthetics 29
Africa 22, 125
Afro-Caribbean: See Caribbean
Aggression/Aggressive 72, 128, 150, 168, 171, 199
Aladdin: See Story
Aleksandar: See Children
Aleksandar of Ohrid: See Hero
Alexander The Great: See Hero
Alice (Lewis Carroll): See Story

Allen, Woody: See Act
Alopaecia: See Ill
America/USA 9, 22, 29, 34, 37, 78, 86, 88, 102, 122, 136, 139, 160, 192, 196
Analysis/Analytic 3, 35, 37, 87, 175, 177
Ananse: See Story
Anger/Angry 2, 33, 34, 38, 41, 48, 59, 72, 75, 79, 99, 112, 127, 145, 158, 168, 169, 179, 190, 213
Anglican: See Religion
Anorexia Nervosa: See Ill
Antigone: See Hero
Anxiety 2, 33, 36, 57, 62, 66, 70, 73, 74, 76, 77, 78, 109, 112, 113, 129, 135, 138, 152, 153, 159, 168, 178, 181, 186, 187, 188, 190, 198, 200, 209, 210, 214
Approaches to counselling 9-10, 21-3, 144
Approval 27, 76, 174
Disapproval 174, 214
Arjuna: See Hero
Art/Artist viii, 5, 63, 71, 88, 110, 117, 133, 134, 163-80, 181, 206
Art therapy/therapist 67, 163-80
(See also Draw, Model, Paint, Sculpture)
Artemis: See God
Asian 6, 9, 216-7
India/Indian 82, 112, 125
Pakistan 216-7
Vietnam 34, 192
Assault: See Abuse
Assessment 25, 49, 66, 68, 84, 85, 102, 143-4, 160
Assessment centre 179, 186
Athena: See God

Author *viii, xi, xii,* 11, 28, 33, 114, 120, 121, 138, 148, 149, 151, 152, 160, 166, 169, 200
Authors mentioned but not listed in Bibliography or Author Index:
  Baldwin, James (1924-87) 91
  Camus, Albert (1913-60) 83
  Cervantes, Miguel de (1547-1616) 127, 142
  Cocteau, Jean (1891-1963) 121
  Dostoievsky, Fyodor (1821-81) 91
  Doyle, Arthur Conan (1859-1930) 131
  Ransome, Arthur (1884-1967) 55
  Shakespeare, William (1564-1616) 49, 182, 190
  Solzhenitsyn, Aleksandr (b1918) 83
  Thackeray, William (1811-63) 49
Authority 6, 9, 11, 13, 15, 86, 133, 135, 172
  Local authority 10, 186
Autism: *See* Handicap
Autobiography/Biography *vii*, 6, 23, 28, 67, 90, 93, 106, 118, 119, 135, 138, 143-162
  Stuart, Arbella (1575-1615) 28

Baby 7, 45, 66, 83, 125, 132, 148, 149, 154, 171, 182, 190
Bach, Johann Sebastian (1685-1750): *See* Music
Ba'hai *See* Religion
Baldwin, James: *See* Author
Baptist: *See* Religion
Barney: *See* Children
Bartholamaeus Anglicus 132
Beams (Phoebe): *See* Children
Bee: *See* Children
Belfast: *See* British
Bereaved/Bereavement 1, 18, 71, 78, 83, 97, 102, 113, 128, 136-7, 141, 148, 166-8, 180, 200
  Mourning 128, 182
  (*See also* Grief)
Bhagavad Gita 112, 113, 119, 136, 137, 141
  Arjuna: *See* Hero
  Karma 113, 117, 140
  Krishna: *See* God

Bible 15, 84, 95, 97, 98, 105, 106, 125, 190
  Deuteronomy 95
  Epistle To The Hebrews 105-6
  Genesis 95
  Isaiah 15
  Job 98
  Old Testament 91, 125
  Revelation 106
  I Samuel 190
Bibliotherapy 137-9, 140, 141
  (*See also* Book)
Biography: *See* Autobiography
Birth/Born 8, 95, 115, 125, 148, 157, 159, 197
  Birth family 65, 160, 198
  Unborn 100
Black Beauty: *See* Story
Black Orpheus: *See* Film
Blind: *See* Handicap
Body-Mind-Spirit unity 1, 110
Book/Books *vii, viii,* 2, 6, 9, 12, 13, 15, 23, 33, 39, 63, 64, 74, 79, 82, 85, 86, 91, 93, 95, 108, 116, 127, 128, 130, 133, 138, 139, 141, 143-162, 173, 181, 184, 188, 203
  Book about me 152-3
  Life story book 47, 124, 150, 152-61, 199, 206
  Text book *vii*, 11, 67, 74, 110, 133
  (*See also* Story)
British Association of Counselling (BAC) 61, 62, 67
British/British Isles/Great Britain 3, 7, 17, 43, 118, 125, 133, 197, 216-7
  Belfast 106
  England/English 3, 6, 22, 29, 73, 94, 102, 122, 140, 166, 181, 184, 192
  Cleveland 10
  Leeds 147
  London 6, 56, 94, 183, 204, 217
  Orkney 10, 13
  Scotland 10
  Welsh 56, 102, 127, 203
Buchanan, Michael: *See* Doctor

Café 57, 58, 70, 130, 173
Calvinism: *See* Religion
Camus, Albert: *See* Author

Canada/Canadian 29, 108, 169
Cancer: *See* Ill
Care 6, 10, 18, 46, 47, 59, 64, 75, 76,
    78, 82, 84, 85, 86, 87, 90, 115,
    117, 118, 129, 133, 137, 144,
    150, 152, 155, 156, 157, 159,
    160, 171, 173-4, 176, 197, 211
Care order 157
Intensive care unit 86
Reception into care 56
Residential care: *See* Resident
Caribbean/West Indian 6, 7, 13, 121,
    125
Case *vii*, 60, 152
Case notes 59
Case study 124, 150
Casework/Caseworker *vii*, 6, 17,
    18, 24, 61, 114, 119, 153
Cervantes, Miguel de: *See* Author
Chapel/Chaplain: *See* Religion
Child and adolescent unit 27
Child and family unit 16, 18, 71, 165
Child care officer 49
Child-centred approach 3
Child guidance 16, 19, 66, 72
Childhood 5, 7, 8, 9, 131, 132 (*See
    also* Poem)
Childist *v*, 1-14, 205, 206
Childlessness 83
ChildLine *v, viii, xi,* 15, 79, 150,
    208-17
Rantzen, Esther 213, 214, 217
Seymour, Alison 208-15
Children Act 1989 3, 10, 13, 84
Children's Society 82, 107, 117
Children known to author appearing
    in more than one chapter:
Aleksandar 22, 140
Dorna 64, 150
Luke *ix*, 153-6, 158
Mark *ix*, 38, 52, 56, 57, 61
Vlado 122, 198
Children in literature (fact or fiction)
    appearing in more than one
    chapter:
Barney 55, 73
Beams (Phoebe) 63, 195
Bee 36, 39, 55
Henrietta 46-7, 185
Jeanette 95-6, 148
Julia 12, 51-2, 137, 203

Lennie 1-2, 12, 203
Myra 77-8, 145
Princess Lenore 134-5, 139, 186
Roger (Bowen) 53-4, 64-5, 74-5
Christianity: *See* Religion
Church: *See* Religion
Church of England: *See* Religion
Church of England Children's
    Society: *See* Children's Society
Cinderella: *See* Story
Cleese, John: *See* Act
Cleveland: *See* British
Clinic 7, 16, 24, 43, 62, 110, 117,
    161, 180, 183
Clown 103, 167
Cocteau, Jean: *See* Author
College 16, 19, 94, 150, 182
Comfort/Comfortable/Comforting
    16, 21, 27, 33, 34, 36, 39, 42, 52,
    63, 65, 70, 78, 79, 86, 89, 98, 99,
    120, 213, 214
Community 14, 29, 84, 91, 100-2,
    116, 123, 132, 151
    Community Care 141, 175, 180
Compassion 27, 42, 63, 87
Comic 6, 130, 183
Confidential/Confidentiality 58-61,
    66, 145, 208, 212, 213
Consultant/Consultation 59, 63, 73,
    86, 168
Control 15, 47, 53, 58, 73, 79, 113,
    131, 159, 176, 186, 194, 196,
    209, 211, 216, 217
Convent: *See* Religion
Copleston, Frederick 11
Cordelia 127-8, 138, 139, 190
Court 38, 49, 124, 131, 134, 157,
    204, 211, 212
Crime/Criminal/Offending 38, 65,
    119, 182, 204, 211
Critic 139, 148, 164
Croatia: *See* Europe
Cruse 167-8

Dance/Dancing 4, 41, 43, 63, 111,
    185, 187, 188
Deafness: *See* Handicap
Dead/Death/Die/Dying 1, 12, 23,
    29, 34, 36, 39, 46, 49, 50, 52, 53,
    54, 55, 56, 64, 68, 74, 76, 81, 83,
    85, 86, 88, 93, 94, 96, 97,

98-100, 103, 112, 116, 118, 120, 122, 123, 124, 125, 126, 127, 129, 132, 135, 136-7, 138, 148, 149, 166-70, 178, 180, 184, 189, 191, 192, 194, 209, 216
Black Death 132
Kill/Killing 41, 51, 74, 112, 125, 127, 170
Murder/Murdered 28, 40, 43, 65, 125, 126, 127, 139, 146-7, 165, 166, 180
Suicide 40, 49, 50, 88, 111, 125, 138, 145, 167, 209
(*See also* Bereavement)
Delinquent/Deviant 15, 25, 70
Depression: *See* Ill
Deuteronomy: *See* Bible
Developmental Eclecticism (Egan) 19, 22, 25
Devil/Satan 84, 105, 119, 161, 179, 203, 207
Diary 52, 63, 148, 184
Disability: *See* Handicap
Disapproval: *See* Approval
Disco 6
Divorce 2, 14, 18, 40
Doctor/General Practitioner/ Physician 19, 45, 63, 66, 73, 77, 85, 86, 112, 113, 144, 147, 149, 150, 195, 216
Buchanan, Michael 147
Don Quixote 127, 139, 142
Dorna: *See* Children
Dostoievsky, Fyodor: *See* Author
Down's Syndrome: *See* Handicap
Doyle, Arthur Conan: *See* Author
Dragon: *See* Monster
Drama/Dramatic 1, 2, 10, 55, 124, 127, 136, 138, 139, 145, 181, 216
(*See also* Act)
Draw/Drawing 39, 40, 58, 63, 153-4, 156, 158, 163-180
(*See also* Art)
Dream/Nightmare 39, 40, 42, 44, 47, 50, 52, 55, 69, 77, 78, 96, 121, 126, 141, 151, 167, 194, 206, 208, 213, 216
Dvorak, Antonin: *See* Music

Earth 15, 41, 55, 57, 58, 96, 103, 123
Eden 103

Education *vii, viii,* 1, 6, 16, 18, 20, 22, 23, 24, 68, 85, 87, 88, 105, 108, 110, 117, 120, 125, 131, 132, 181, 182, 185, 192, 197, 204, 205, 213
Educational psychologist 19, 48, 49
Education welfare officer 46
(*See also* School)
Einstein, Albert (1879-1955) 189
Elephant 175-7
"Elephant Song Of Thuy Dang" 192-3
Elijah 54
Ellis, Albert 22, 136, 205
Ellis, Ruth 65
Elvidge, John 115
Empathy *v, viii, xi,* 24, 27-44, 138, 203, 206, 214
Employment/Work 6, 40, 80, 83, 93, 113, 115, 121, 131, 136, 154, 170, 172, 174, 205, 215
Empowerment 130, 136, 160, 214, 216
Enchantment *v,* 36, 51, 117, 120-142, 201
Epictetus 136
Epistle to The Hebrews: *See* Bible
Ethic 9, 61, 67, 94, 136
Europe/European
Britain: *See* British
Croatia 122
France/French 121, 127, 160
German/Germany 9, 22, 29, 160
Greece/Hellenic 3, 22, 47, 121, 122, 124, 125, 189
Macedonia 122, 140
Norse/Scandinavian/Swedish 55, 101, 121, 125
Poland *i,* 160, 163, 193
Serbia 122
Swiss/Switzerland 22, 160, 169, 180
Vienna 22, 124
Yugoslavia 122

Faith *vii, ix,* 14, 25, 48, 84, 87, 88, 93, 94, 95, 98, 99, 108-16, 118, 119, 126, 176, 206, 207
(*See also* Religion)
Family centre 170-1

Family guidance 79
Family Makers Homefinding Unit/
Project 67, 164, 171-3
Family placement unit 83
Family therapy 19
Fancies/Fantasy 1, 23, 39, 53, 74, 76,
134, 135, 164, 167, 172, 177,
179, 204
Rosebush fantasy 177-8
Fear/Fright *viii, xi,* 1, 2, 4, 29, 32,
33, 35, 40, 41, 44, 48, 50, 52, 57,
65, 73, 74, 75, 76, 78, 79, 86, 87,
92, 115, 116, 132, 145, 158, 159,
161, 168, 169, 174, 175, 176,
177, 179, 183, 186, 187, 206,
208, 214
Feminine/Feminist 3, 4, 5, 13, 22,
25, 31, 43, 81, 117, 124, 136,
141, 205
Film 28, 121, 167, 174, 183
Cinema 6, 96, 130
Black Orpheus 121
Ghandi 205
Orphée 121
The Ten Commandments 96
Forgiveness 99, 116
Foster/Fostering/Foster parents/
Foster home 47, 50, 51, 52, 57,
58, 75, 83, 84, 86, 125, 153-5,
158, 173, 183, 190, 198
Foster mother 47, 52
Adoption and Fostering: See
Adoption
France: *See* Europe
Freud, Sigmund (1856-1939)/
Freudian 19, 22, 25, 88, 118,
123
Friend/Friendship 15, 16, 17, 24, 32,
34, 36, 41, 52, 53, 57, 60, 61, 70,
73, 77, 78, 85, 92, 96, 100, 101,
108, 128, 130, 141, 145, 150,
153, 159, 168, 172, 188, 193,
200, 205
The Friend viii, 14, 26
Frozen 2, 14, 52, 68, 78, 126, 129,
137, 141, 153, 161, 166, 185, 207
Fun/Funny 63, 73, 128, 130, 155,
178, 199, 203
Funeral 67, 98, 165, 167, 191, 201
(*See also* Death)

Game/Games 1, 63, 146, 168, 172,
182
Squiggle game 168, 171-2
Garden/Gardener *vii,* 38, 39, 40, 52,
56, 68, 70, 74, 77, 110, 111, 129,
204
Genesis: *See* Bible
Germany: *See* Europe
Gestalt (Perls) 13, 18, 19, 22, 25, 26,
112, 118, 127, 161, 180
Ghandi: See Film
Girls Own Paper: See Magazine
God/Goddess 15, 35, 40, 52, 82, 84,
85, 87, 88, 89, 91, 92, 93, 94, 96,
97, 98, 99, 101, 103, 105, 109,
114, 115, 116, 117, 118, 119,
125, 126, 130, 132, 136, 140,
141, 146, 190
Artemis 136
Athena 126
Hanuman 125
Innana 136
Krishna 136
Goldilocks: *See* Story
Good enough being 115, 144, 171,
200, 203-6
Good enough counselling 206
Governess 148
Government 15, 131
Grandfather 70, 73, 74
Grandmother 53, 70, 73, 94, 129,
137, 157, 158
Great grandmother 167
Nana 36, 103
Greece: *See* Europe
Grief/Grieving 34, 38, 52, 53, 56, 95,
113, 136, 182, 190, 191
Group *vii,* 9, 16, 22, 37, 50, 52, 59,
97, 101, 105, 214
Gryphon: *See* Monster
Guardian 15
Guidance 10, 24, 61, 66, 72, 79, 109,
112, 173
Guidelines 10, 60, 66, 131, 170
(*See also* Child guidance)

Handicap/Disability *xi,* 40, 70, 77,
83, 108, 119, 121, 141, 181, 188,
196, 198, 200, 216
Autism 111
Blind 77, 125, 196

Deafness 183
Downs Syndrome/Mongol 184-5, 201
Mute 34, 35, 72, 75
Hate/Hatred 37, 41, 48, 54, 85, 105, 136, 179
Haunt/Haunting 39, 56, 77, 78, 145, 146
Headache: *See* Ill
Heal/Healing 6, 16, 19, 20, 24, 66, 97, 190-2, 200
Health/Healthy 1, 4, 5, 6, 8, 10, 13, 18, 33, 37, 42, 50, 52, 60, 66, 76, 77, 80, 85, 87, 93, 100, 102, 103, 104, 107, 111, 131, 133, 143, 159, 170, 177, 194, 201, 206
Health visitor 45
Heaven 35, 53, 74, 85, 103, 104, 105, 117, 119, 130, 132
Helen of Troy: *See* Hero
Hell 96, 103, 104, 105
Henrietta: *See* Children
Hephaistion: *See* Hero
Hero/Heroine/Heroic 120, 122, 123, 124, 126, 128, 154, 155, 189, 194
Aleksandar of Ohrid 122
Alexander the Great (356-322BC) 28, 122, 149
Antigone 125, 141
Arjuna 136
Helen of Troy 126
Hephaistion 28, 149
Joan of Arc (1412-31) 92, 93, 158
Lancelot 50, 51, 77, 78
Odysseus/Ulysses 126, 139
Oedipus 124-5, 136, 140, 141
Orpheus 121, 140
Penelope 126
Telemachus 126, 140
Heuvel, Albert van den: *See* Theologian
Hippopotamus: *See* Toy
History *vii*, 6, 8, 9, 16, 35, 39, 47, 83, 109, 111, 122, 131, 133, 135, 136, 141, 143-62, 178, 183, 184
Holistic/Wholeness 5, 13, 20, 85, 103, 110, 112, 115
Holman, Robert *viii*, 100, 116
Homosexual: *See* Sex
Honest/Honesty 12, 34, 66, 69, 74, 114, 127, 148, 150, 189, 210, 217

Hospital 16, 45, 50, 58, 59, 60, 71, 85, 86, 98, 99, 112, 113, 116, 120, 137, 157, 165, 167, 169, 195, 197, 209
Hughes, Carl 203
Humiliation 31, 39, 48, 58, 59, 176
Ill/Illness/Sickness 2, 20, 32, 39, 45, 71, 76, 77, 85, 86, 90, 92, 97, 98, 99, 100, 102, 110, 112, 148, 149, 169, 180, 187, 189, 190, 197, 198, 216
Alopaecia 71
Anorexia nervosa 52, 151
Cancer 12, 169
Depression 5, 33, 34, 39, 50, 71, 72, 96, 109, 111, 121, 138
Headache 71
Leukaemia/Leukemia 98, 99, 169
Migraine 77, 167
Schizophrenia 32, 33
Image/Images 8, 22, 27, 56, 71, 74, 77, 90, 98, 99, 103, 111, 115, 132, 134, 135, 136, 157, 164, 165, 169, 172, 173, 178, 179, 183, 203, 208, 216
Imaginary/Imagination 53, 73, 110, 134, 135, 158, 168, 174, 176
Incest: *See* Sex
India: *See* Asian
Injustice: *See* Justice
Innana: *See* God
Inscape/Inscapes *xi*, 43, 117, 161, 169, 180
Intensive Care Unit: *See* Care
Interpretation/Interpreting 23, 40, 41, 66, 123, 124, 125, 127, 137, 140, 143, 165, 170, 175, 176, 177
Interview 61-2, 79, 81, 83, 96
Intrusion 61, 62, 65, 66, 67, 83, 153
Inward migration 183
Inwardness *viii*, 10, 12, 80, 82
Isaiah: *See* Bible

Jack And The Bean Stalk: *See* Story
James I: *See* King
Jeanette: *See* Children
Jester 134-5, 186
Jesus: *See* Religion
Jew/Semitic: *See* Religion
Joan of Arc: *See* Hero

Job: *See* Bible
Judaism: *See* Religion
Julia: *See* Children
Jung, Carl Gustav (1875-1951)/
    Jungian 7, 13, 22, 24, 25, 39, 42,
    43, 110, 111, 117, 136, 151, 161,
    180
Justice 38, 43, 174, 204
    Injustice 37, 38

Karma: *See Baghavad Gita*
Kill: *See* Death
King 28, 124, 125, 134-5
    David 190
    James I 28
    Lear 127-8, 138, 139, 140, 190
    Lonely King (Samotny Król)
        Frontispiece
    Red King 206
Krishna: *See* God

Lady of Shalott 50, 51, 68
Lancelot: *See* Hero
Language 4, 14, 36, 70, 73, 82, 86,
    89, 95, 98, 99, 113, 115, 116,
    121, 122, 147, 149, 151, 154,
    166, 169, 176, 181, 182, 188
Law/Legal/Legalistic/Legislation 3,
    6, 10, 23, 60, 61, 106, 107, 113,
    186, 204, 209
Lear: *See* King
Lecturer *viii*, 22, 48, 114, 143
Leeds: *See* Britain
Lennie: *See* Children
Legal: *See* Law
    Legalistic: *See* Law
Legend 6, 120-142
    (*See also* Story)
Legislation: *See* Law
Leukaemia: *See* Ill
Librarian/Library *ix*, 77, 130, 131,
    137, 141, 181, 203
Lie/Lying 42, 45, 65, 77, 79, 146,
    147, 210
Life story: *See* Autobiography
Limbo 52-5, 57, 66, 68, 126
Listen/Listening 6, 16, 27, 31, 32, 33,
    34, 36, 42, 66, 67, 80, 86, 90, 95,
    99, 101, 103, 109, 115, 135, 139,
    140, 143, 145, 154, 160, 168,
    191, 208, 213, 215

Literature *vii, ix*, 5, 9, 17, 42, 54, 82,
    90, 108, 110, 112, 122, 130, 131,
    133, 138, 140, 141, 150, 163,
    175, 181, 208
    (*See also* Story)
London: *See* Britain
Loneliness 42, 46, 53, 91, 168, 194,
    214
Lonely King: *See* King
Loss 56, 88, 97, 104, 123, 148, 156,
    180, 188
Lost 29, 58, 68, 81, 106, 128, 186
Love *vii, viii, ix*, 3, 9, 12, 16, 27, 35,
    36, 37, 48, 50, 52, 55, 58, 63, 74,
    78, 82, 87, 92, 96, 97, 100, 103,
    104, 105, 111, 115, 120, 121,
    130, 132, 137, 154, 155, 156,
    160, 170, 182, 190, 205, 211
    Lovers 50-1
    Unlovedness 56
Luke: *See* Children
Lying: *See* Lie

Mabinogion: *See* Myth
Macedonia: *See* Europe
Magazine 6, 15, 121, 122, 131, 183
    Girls Own Paper 15, 25
    Woman 121
    (*See also Adoption and Fostering,
        Community Care, The
        Friend, Social Work Today*)
Magic 20, 56, 67, 73, 130, 134, 171,
    178, 213
Mark: *See* Children
Maori 197, 210
Masculine 4, 124, 126
Medical/Medicine 16, 19, 59, 85,
    109, 132, 133, 144, 160, 170
Meeting (Quaker): *See* Religion
Memory 77, 129, 145, 147-9, 158,
    164, 184, 185, 197, 200, 204
Menstruation 32, 50, 52, 129
    Menopause 122
Middle Ages/ Mediaeval 9, 14, 132,
    133, 141, 161
Midwife 110
Migraine: *See* Ill
Minister: *See* Religion
Minotaur: *See* Monster
Mirror/Looking glass 49, 50, 53, 57,
    80, 121, 126, 137, 138, 164, 206

Mission: *See* Religion
Model/Modelling 40, 163-80
Mongol: *See* Handicap
Monster 40, 154, 169-70, 172, 174,
    178-9, 186
  Dragon 128
  Gryphon 143
  Minotaur 40
Montessori, Maria (1870-1952) 88
Moral/Morality 43, 90, 105, 107,
    114, 121
Mosque: *See* Religion
Mother in law 63, 159
Mourn/Mourning: *See* Bereavement
Mozart: *See* Music
Murder: *See* Death
Music *viii, xi,* 69, 110, 117, 122, 123,
    163, 179, 181-202, 206
  Music therapy 181-202
  Composers referred to:
  Bach, Johann Sebastian
    (1685-1750) 182
  Dvorak, Antonin (1841-1904) 195
  Handel, George Frederick
    (1685-1759) 15
  Mozart, Wolfgang Amadeus
    (1756-91) 189
  Schumann, Robert (1810-56) 189
  Tchaikovsky, Piotr Ilyitch
    (1840-93) 194
Muslim: *See* Religion
Mute: *See* Handicap
Myra: *See* Children
Mystery 134, 141, 176
Mystical 109
Myth *viii,* 3, 51, 88, 110, 111, 117,
    120-42, 157, 161, 206
  Mabinogion 127
  (*See also* Story)

Narnia: *See* Wonderland
National Children's Bureau 115, 117
Neglect 85, 86, 107, 116, 133, 178
Newspaper 65, 130
Nightmare: *See* Dream
Norse: *See* Europe
Novel/Novelist 23, 41, 47, 63, 90,
    120, 138, 146, 148, 149, 160,
    177, 179 (*See also* Author)
Nurse/Nursing *vii,* 16, 18, 19, 26, 27,
    45, 46, 53, 71, 78, 84, 85, 86, 89,
    107, 117, 133, 144, 165, 197

Nursery 6, 7, 14, 45, 94, 161, 193
Nursery nurse 6, 152, 170-1
Nancy Mint 152, 170-1, 176
(Psychiatric nurse) Kay 27, 71

Odysseus: *See* Hero
Oedipus: *See* Hero
Offending: *See* Crime
Old Testament: *See* Bible
Orkney: *See* Britain
Orphan/Orphanage 46, 56, 185
Orphée: See Film
Owl/Owls 127, 139, 141, 163-81,
    175-8, 191

Paediatric/Paediatrician 46, 86, 201
Paint/Painting 55, 132, 136, 163-81
Picture 6, 9, 39, 63, 65, 94, 127,
    128, 130, 132, 154-8, 168-81
  Portrait 138, 155, 173-4
  (*See also* Art)
Pakistan: *See* Asian
Panic 48, 71, 135
Pastor/Pastoral 15, 22, 25, 43, 85,
    110, 118, 119, 136, 140
Patient 27, 28, 32, 73, 85, 86, 180,
    200, 216
Peace 69, 70, 71, 73, 75, 77, 80, 101,
    113, 149, 157, 171, 177
Penelope: *See* Hero
Perls, Fritz 22, 151
Person Centred (Rogers) 19, 20, 22,
    26, 43, 44, 81, 113, 114, 119,
    161
Philosopher/philosophy 3, 4, 6, 8, 9,
    11, 12, 22, 23, 62, 70, 98, 136,
    155
Photograph 45, 65, 122, 152, 153,
    154, 156, 158, 166-7
Piaget, Jean (1896-1980) 86, 87
Pinochio: *See* Story
Pity 27
Platonic 133
Play 6, 7, 19, 21, 25, 46, 63, 72, 100,
    132, 146, 155, 157, 165, 193
  Playground 6, 80, 81
  Playleader 45
  Playmate 15
  Playroom 31, 53, 57, 58, 151, 176,
    197, 198
  Play therapy 7, 26, 53, 57, 81

Role play 210, 215
Play (Music) 134, 186, 188, 194, 198
Plays (*See also* Act) 29, 127
Poem/Poet/Poetry 6, 23, 51, 103, 104, 106, 119, 182, 199
    Poems quoted in text:
    "Childhood" 103-4, 119
    "Enter These Enchanted Woods" 120, 141
    "Music When Soft Voices Die" 184, 202
    "Spring" 53
    "The Lady of Shalott" 50, 51, 68
    "The Lost Years" 106-7
    "The Schoolboy" 104
Poland: *See* Europe
Police 50, 59, 60, 134, 150, 170, 211
Politics 5, 6, 123, 140, 183
Postcards 157-8
Power 5, 8, 11, 15, 38, 40, 62, 70, 89, 115, 134, 136, 137, 139, 140, 144, 157, 165, 176, 186-8, 200
    Empower: *See* Empowerment
Priest: *See* Religion
Prince 78, 128, 131, 180, 187
Princess 78, 128, 131, 141, 187, 201
    Princess Lenore: *See* Children
Prison/Prisoner/Gaol 32, 39, 40, 47, 48, 50, 122, 166, 211
Privacy/Private *v*, 21, 42, 43, 45-68, 97, 115, 125, 139, 157, 173, 180, 199, 201, 206
Probation 49
Professor 9, 102, 108, 131, 182
Protestant: *See* Religion
Psyche 35, 110
Psychiatrist/Psychiatry 16, 19, 23, 25, 27, 40, 41, 43, 46, 71, 102, 144, 150, 151, 166-8, 180
Psychoanalysis 22, 94, 124, 136, 189
Psychodynamic 19, 25, 27, 43
Psychologist/Psychology *vii*, 4, 16, 19, 22, 26, 28, 29, 33, 34, 42, 46, 48, 49, 57, 63, 70, 108, 109, 110, 111, 112, 123, 130, 133, 140, 170, 182, 195-7, 212-3
Psycho-spiritual 108

Psychotherapist/Psychotherapy 16, 17, 24, 26, 29, 44, 51, 68, 108, 109, 110, 137
Punishment/Punitive 51, 79, 87, 125, 131, 205
Pupil 32, 41, 73, 90, 102
Puppets: *See* Toy

Quaker: *See* Religion
Queen 43, 124, 128, 129, 130, 137, 178
    Snow Queen: *See* Story
Question/Questioning 62-4, 66, 86, 87, 90, 96, 114, 115, 116, 119, 126, 135, 144, 152, 164, 170, 176, 177

Rabbi: *See* Religion
Radio 6, 10, 14, 43, 131, 139, 141, 147, 161
Ransome, Arthur: *See* Author
Rantzen, Esther: *See* ChildLine
Rapunzel: *See* Story
Rational Emotive Therapy (Ellis) 22, 136, 205
Rationalist Press Association 94
Realistic/Reality 11, 12, 24, 29, 31, 50, 55, 82, 84, 88, 113, 122, 127, 134, 140, 143, 144, 156, 203, 204, 205
Reality Therapy (Glasser) *xi*, 22, 25, 43
Reception into care: *See* Care
Record 34, 35, 60, 156, 173, 186, 197, 198
Red Riding Hood: *See* Story
Reid, Beryl: *See* Act
Religion 3, 5, 6, 9, 19, 22, 23, 82-119, 124, 134, 136, 140, 205, 206
    Ba'hai 99-100
    Christianity 14, 22, 25, 82, 84, 87, 90, 92, 93, 94, 95, 97, 98, 99, 105, 119, 121, 125, 132
    Anglican 92, 121
    Baptist 98
    Bible: *See* Bible
    Calvinism 105
    Chapel 69, 83, 96
    Chaplain 82, 85, 86, 94, 98, 99

Church 83, 84, 94, 95, 96, 97, · 98, 105, 107, 113, 115, 121, 140
Church Of England 96
Communion 91, 99
Convent 106
Jesus 54, 89, 92, 94, 97, 123, 130, 132, 134
Jesuit 22
Meeting (Quaker) 34, 69, 91, 107
Minister/Ministry 7, 19, 22, 102, 105
Mission/Missioner 82, 129
Nun 15
Priest 19, 85, 146, 205
Protestant 22, 87
Quaker/Religious Society of Friends 69, 82, 90, 91, 93, 97, 101, 102, 117, 119, 134
Roman Catholic 87, 114, 117, 134, 164
Vicar 130
Judaism/Jew 22, 87, 90, 91, 106, 113, 121, 124, 125
Rabbi 85
Synagogue 83, 91, 107
Torah 125
Muslim 113
Mosque 83, 107
Zen 112, 119
(*See also Baghavad Gita*, Devil, Faith, God, Heaven, Hell, Ritual, Worship)
Reporter 124, 131, 143, 150, 160, 194
Resident/Residential *vii*, 10, 47, 51, 67, 90, 107, 115, 145, 166, 171, 178, 186, 193,
(*See also* Orphan)
Respect *viii*, 4, 6, 7, 31, 38, 43, 51, 59, 64, 66, 73, 81, 99, 101, 108, 126, 136, 143, 149, 150, 161, 163, 170, 176, 179, 180, 193, 195, 196, 201, 206, 214, 216
Revelation: *See* Bible
Rhythm/Rhythmic 4, 5, 111, 190, 194, 196, 200
Right/Rights 61, 67, 82, 89, 107-8, 117, 174

United Nations Declaration of the Rights of The Child (1959) 107
Ritual 82, 105, 119, 134, 147, 161, 182, 183, 203, 207
Roger: *See* Children
Rogers, Carl (1902-87)/Rogerian 3, 19, 22, 29, 31, 113, 135, 151
Roman Catholic: *See* Religion
Rose *v*, 81, 129, 160, 163-80
Rosebush fantasy 177-8

Sad/Sadness 2, 3, 32, 34, 35, 40, 53, 83, 156, 158, 163-80, 184, 187, 198
Saga: *See* Story
I Samuel: *See* Bible
Satan: *See* Devil
Scandinavia: *See* Europe
Schizophrenia: *See* Ill
School *xi*, 1, 6, 7, 18, 19, 20, 24, 25, 33, 36, 43, 46, 49, 50, 51, 52, 53, 57, 59, 61, 64, 67, 72, 73, 76, 79, 85, 89, 90, 94, 95, 101, 102, 104, 108, 110, 117, 122, 125, 128, 131, 144, 145, 147, 154, 157, 161, 167, 170, 173, 180, 182, 193, 194, 198, 201, 202, 203, 204, 208, 209, 216
Boarding school 46, 53, 75, 77, 93, 102, 148
Sunday school 6, 83, 85, 111
School counsellor/counselling 19, 57
"The Schoolboy": *See* Poem
(*See also* College, Education, Governess, Pupil, Student, Teacher, Tutor, University)
Schumann, Robert: *See* Music
Scotland: *See* Britain
Sculpture/Statues 9, 163
(*See also* Art)
Secrecy/Secret *vii*, 48, 49, 50, 52, 53, 56, 60, 65, 68, 78, 94, 105, 145, 158, 161, 162, 178, 186-90, 195, 200, 210
Self-Esteem 2, 36, 173, 175, 176, 183, 187, 198, 200
Semitic: *See* Jew
Serbia: *See* Europe
Sex/Sexual 3, 4, 18, 19, 31, 50, 59, 60, 65, 66, 77, 78, 83, 85, 109,

111, 115, 122, 128, 129, 130, 135, 141, 147, 161, 173, 177, 189, 205, 209, 210, 211, 212
Homosexual/Gay 129, 215
Incest 125
Sexual abuse: *See* Abuse
Seymour, Alison: *See* ChildLine
Shakespeare, William: *See* Author
Sheriff Kelbie 10
Sickness: See Ill
Silence/Quiet *v, viii*, 21, 23, 33, 45, 50, 64, 66, 67, 68-81, 101, 115, 126, 129, 134, 182, 183, 186, 193, 206, 213, 214
Sleeping Beauty: *See* Story
Snow Queen: *See* Story
Snow White: *See* Story
Society 37, 38, 121, 126, 131, 133
Social care 5, 18
Social services/department 7, 17, 173, 211, 212
Social studies 110
Social Work Today 81, 117, 140, 161, 162, 208, 217
Social Worker *vii*, 6, 13, 16, 17, 18, 19, 38, 41, 46, 49, 50, 51, 56, 59, 60, 64, 67, 70, 72, 75, 78, 81, 83, 85, 86, 97, 107, 112, 113, 114, 120, 125, 133, 134, 136, 143, 144, 150, 152, 153, 154, 156, 158, 159, 161, 165, 166, 173-4, 175-6, 180, 181, 183, 190, 201, 209, 210, 211, 212
Sociologist 117
Solicitor 12, 60, 210, 212
Solzhenitsyn, Aleksandr: *See* Author
Song/Sing 1, 63, 122, 181-202, 203
Sorrow 38, 143
Soul 83, 100, 105, 110, 111, 114, 121, 169, 179
(*See also* Spirit)
Space 20, 31, 46, 53, 57, 66, 67, 100, 120, 131, 140, 164, 165, 171, 173, 175, 179, 190, 210
Spirit/Spiritual *viii, xi*, 1, 3, 5, 7, 10, 15, 16, 18, 19, 20, 33, 48, 63, 76, 77, 78, 80, 89-119, 123, 126, 131, 137, 146, 181, 182, 190, 206
Spiritual abuse 105-7, 108, 115
Squiggle game: *See* Game

Stepdaughter 45
Stepfather 50, 66, 155, 173, 211, 212
Stepmother 129, 137, 171
Story/Tales *v, vii, viii, xi*, 23, 38, 41, 43, 48, 49, 58, 59, 67, 68, 70, 74, 77, 78, 81, 106, 109, 110, 116, 117, 120, 123, 124, 120-142, 143-162, 163, 173, 174, 179, 187, 188, 189, 193, 194, 195, 199, 200, 201, 203, 205, 206, 210, 216
Aladdin 139
Alice 55, 143, 183, 206
Ananse 125
Black Beauty 92
Cinderella 139
Goldilocks 58, 139
Jack And The Bean Stalk 139
Pinochio 137, 143
Rapunzel 137, 139, 189, 199
Red Riding Hood 139
Sleeping Beauty 45-52, 56, 77
Snow Queen 52, 128
Snow White 52, 129, 137, 139
(*See also* Author, Autobiography, Bibliotherapy, Book, Drama, Legend, Literature, Myth, Poem, Saga)
Stuart, Arbella: *See* Autobiography
Student 11, 29, 32, 59, 84, 121, 151-2
Student counselling/welfare 16, 19, 31, 32, 76, 163
Suicide: *See* Death
Surgery 144
Swedish: *See* Europe
Swimming 48, 173
Swiss: *See* Europe
Symbol/Symbolism 46, 104, 111, 124, 126, 128, 129, 158, 164, 165, 168, 170, 176, 182, 205
Sympathy 27, 28, 29, 31, 32, 34, 42, 77, 159, 177
Synagogue: *See* Religion

Tales: *See* Story
Talk/Talking 36, 46, 56, 60, 69, 71, 72, 73, 74, 75, 78, 79, 80, 90-8, 100, 103, 106, 172, 173, 175, 176, 181, 209, 210, 214, 217
Taoism 112
Tchaikovsky, Piotr Ilyitch: *See* Music

Teacher/Teaching 1, 7, 15, 16, 18, 23, 24, 35, 41, 46, 49, 50, 59, 64, 70, 72, 75, 80, 85, 93, 96, 110, 118, 120, 121, 133, 139, 150, 151, 164, 169, 170, 173, 181, 182, 185, 188, 192, 194, 195, 196, 198, 200, 205, 208, 211, 216
Headmistress 94
(*See also* School)
Teddy bear: *See* Toy
Telemachus: *See* Hero
Telephone 4, 19, 24, 46, 47, 57, 60, 65, 79, 115, 157, 170, 171, 208-17
Answerphone 147
(*See also* ChildLine)
Television/TV 1, 2, 6, 13, 80, 130, 203, 206, 210
Temple, Shirley: *See* Act
Thackeray, William Makepeace: *See* Author
The Ten Commandments: See Film
Theologian/Theological 4, 24, 105, 110, 116, 133, 136
Heuvel, A van den 4, 24
Torah: See Religion
Touch 21, 34, 35, 38, 114, 178, 210
Toy 56, 67, 155, 195
Hippopotamus 155, 162
Puppets 168
Teddy bear 98, 99, 119, 153-6
Train/Training 10, 16, 17, 19, 20, 39, 79, 86, 110, 112, 116, 131, 133, 165, 176, 177, 182, 210, 214-5
Trust *viii*, 45, 51, 64, 87, 113, 115, 132, 150, 152, 159, 167, 176, 214
Truth *viii*, 2, 12, 42, 56, 65, 74, 76, 78, 89, 90, 91, 95, 105, 114, 115, 121, 125, 130, 141, 144, 146, 148, 149, 152, 159, 160, 175, 186, 188, 189, 194
Turtle 122, 143-4, 173-4
Mock Turtle 143
Teenage Mutant Ninja Turtle 139, 174
Tutee/Tutor *ix,* 84, 138, 151-2, 174

Ulysses: *See* Hero
United Nation: *See* Rights
University 14, 25, 29, 30, 32, 33, 34, 43, 69, 93, 94, 96, 121, 122, 133, 150, 181

University of Hull *viii, ix*, 182, 201
USA: *See* America

Verma, Jatinder 124
Vicar: *See* Religion
Victim 2, 16, 19, 36, 41, 51, 106, 138
Victim support group 16
Video 6, 60, 147
Vienna: *See* Europe
Vietnam: *See* Asian
Violence 39, 54, 91, 94, 106, 108, 150, 157, 167, 174, 177
Vision 47, 94, 103, 110, 111, 113, 133, 136, 163, 177
Vlado: *See* Children
Voluntary/Volunteer 16, 18, 67, 72, 77, 150, 167-8, 183, 213-7
Voluntary counselling service 19
Vulnerable/Vulnerability 4, 35, 114, 115, 129, 160

Waitress 57, 173
Walk/Walking 21, 58, 59, 100, 105, 129, 167, 173
War/Battle 28, 69, 125, 126, 149, 182, 183, 204
War veteran 34
Warmth 31, 34, 52, 87, 101
Welsh: *See* Britain
West Indian: *See* Caribbean
Wholeness: *See* Holistic
Wilderness 45, 53, 54, 55-7, 66-8
Witch 39, 111, 119, 129, 137, 179, 187
Wizard 39, 134, 160, 161
Woman: See Magazine
Work: *See* Employment
Wonder/Wonderland 55, 67, 90, 108, 132, 143, 161
Narnia 110, 111
Worship (*See also* Religion) 22, 82, 84, 85, 89, 94, 102, 111, 113, 117, 134, 182
Wound 42, 45, 104

Youth counsellor 150
Yugoslavia: *See* Europe

Zen: *See* Religion

Author Index
(excluding main Bibliography)

Abbott, Lawrence 187, 200
Ahmed, Shama 13, 200
Allan, John 7, 13, 24, 39, 43, 110, 117, 161, 169–70, 177, 180
Allen, Charlotte 84, 89, 117
Allen, Helena M. 153, 161
Althea 81
Alvin, Juliette 186–7, 189, 190, 194–5, 198, 199, 201
Amory, C. 175–6, 180
Andersen, Hans Christian 52, 67, 128–30, 140, 192, 201
Aptekar, Herbert H. 17–9, 24
Aquinas, Thomas 15, 24
Ariès, Philippe 9, 13, 132, 140
Armstrong, Helen 115–6, 117
Arthur, Chris J. 87, 117
Asimov, Isaac 41–2, 43, 66, 67
Asrat-Girma 6, 13
Atwood, Margaret 23, 24
Axline, Virginia 24, 73, 81

Bach, Susan 169, 180
Bailey, Eunice 183, 185, 187–8, 198, 201
Bailey, Philip 188, 197, 198, 201
Barrett-Aranui, Hinekahukura 197, 201
Bassin, Alexander 25
Bawden, Nina 154, 156, 161
Bayless, K.M. 183, 184, 192–3, 201
Benner, David G. 108–110, 117
Benton Grange School 46, 47, 67
Bergethon, Bjornar 183, 184, 185, 201
Berryman, Jerome W. 88–9, 117
Bettelheim, Bruno 123–4, 125, 128, 137, 139, 140, 189, 199, 201
Bhaduri, Reba 112–3, 117, 136–7, 140

Blackmore, John 130, 140
Blake, William 104, 117
Bluebond-Langner, Myra 169, 180
Boardman, Eunice 183, 184, 185, 201
Bogues, Fionnuala 106–7, 117
Bohler, J. 136, 140
Boswell, John 9, 13, 132, 140
Boulding, Elise 100–1, 117
Bowen, Elizabeth 41, 53–4, 58, 64–5, 67, 70–1, 74–5, 77–8, 80–1, 145–8, 161
Bradford, John 82–3, 89–90, 107–8, 117
Bradley, Alfred 201
Bratter, Thomas E. 25
Brett, Rachel 10, 13
British Association for Counselling 61, 67
Brontë, Charlotte 54, 67, 131
Burton, Hester 67
Byars, Betsy 1, 13, 157–8, 161, 203, 206

Cairns, Kate 90, 117
Campbell, Beatrice 147, 161
Carpentier, Alejo 69, 81
Carroll, Lewis 55, 67, 143, 161, 206
Carter, Angela 67, 128, 141
Casey, Janice 75, 81
Chaplin, Jocelyn vi, 3, 4, 5, 13, 22, 25, 32, 43, 76, 81, 111, 117, 136, 141
Chardin, Teilhard de 116, 117
Charles-Edwards, D. 118
Cheetham, Juliet 13, 200
ChildLine 209–217
Clarkson, Petrūska 11, 13, 18, 20, 25, 111–2, 118
Clifford, Susan 141

Coles, R. 37, 43
Comyns, Barbara 67
Connor, Terry 152–3, 158–9, 161
Cooley, Joan 167–8, 180
Crompton, Margaret 12, 13, 45–7,
  59–60, 62, 64, 67, 74, 79, 81, 133,
  137, 139, 141, 150, 151, 161, 163,
  180, 181, 197, 201
Cupitt, Don 24

Department of Health 13, 84, 118
Dickson, David 63, 67
Dorfman, Elaine 25, 72, 78, 81
Dryden, Windy 14, 25, 43, 118, 135,
  141
Dunbar, David 152–3, 158–9, 161
Dunbar, Maureen 52, 67
Durant, David N. 28, 43
Eaton, Lynn 79, 81, 208–9, 211, 212,
  217
Eco, Umberto 11, 13, 23, 25
Egan, Gerard 19, 22, 25, 27–8, 30,
  43, 216, 217
Eisenberg, Nancy 28–9, 43, 44
Eliade, Mircea 121, 124, 141
Eliot, George 54–5, 67
Elkind, David 87, 118
Elliffe, John 152–3, 158–9, 161
Erikson, Erik 5, 14, 86, 87, 118
Ernst, Sheila 25

Fahlberg, Vera 152, 161
Farmer, Penelope 203–4, 207
Fawell, Ruth 96–7, 118
Ferguson, Sarah 94–5, 118
Ford, Janet K. 59, 67
Forrester, Wendy 15, 25
Foskett, J. 110, 118, 136, 141
Fowler, John W. 88, 118

Gardam, Jane 38–9, 43, 63, 67, 195,
  201
Gardner, Richard A. 2, 14
Garner, Alan 127, 139, 141, 177, 180
Georgeson, Valerie 191–2, 201
Gill, B.M. 146–7, 161
Gillespie, Ann vi, 57, 67, 164–5,
  171–3, 175–6, 177, 180
Gillman, Harvey 90–1, 118
Glasser, William 22, 25, 33, 43, 151
Godden, Rumer 56, 63, 67, 82, 118

Goldacre, Patricia 120, 141
Golding, Vicki 49–50, 66, 67
Goldman, R. 87, 118
Goodall, Janet 86, 90, 118
Gosse, Edmund 105–7, 118
Goudge, Elizabeth 46–7, 63, 67, 73,
  81, 149, 161, 185, 201
Goulding, Erna I. 85–6, 118
Graves, Robert 120, 122, 141
Greer, J.E. 87–8, 118
Griffith, Pamela 192–3, 198, 201
Grimm, Jakob and Wilhelm 129, 141
Gripe, Maria 64, 67
LeGuin, Ursula 21, 160, 161

Halliday, D. 175–6, 180
Halmos, Paul v, vii, 108, 118, 207
Hamilton, H.A. 118
Hargie, Owen 63, 67
Harris, David 67, 118
Harwood, Ronald 68, 81
Hawes, Brenda 47, 68
Hawking, Stephen 120, 141
Heffers 139, 141
Hickman, Sally 40–1, 43, 65, 68,
  166–7, 180
Hillman, James 7, 8, 14, 25, 39, 43,
  110–1, 118
Hodgson-Burnett, Frances 56–7, 68
Hoffman, Martin L. 28, 36–8, 43
Holgate, Eileen 68, 75, 81
Homer 141
Houghton, Catherine J. 46, 56, 68,
  97–8, 118
Houston, Gaie 25
Hoy, Linda 127–8, 138–9, 141
Hughes, Donald 182, 201
Hull, John 118
Hunt, Nigel 184–5, 201
Hunter Margaret 12, 14, 51–2, 68,
  137, 141, 161, 203, 207
Hyland, Jim 67, 118

Inskipp, Francesca 25
Isaacs, Stephen 40–1, 43, 65, 68,
  166–7, 180
Ivey, Allen and Mary Bradford 21,
  25

Jacobs, Michael 25, 27, 43, 110, 118,
  136, 141

James, William 88, 118
Jamieson, Kay 201
Jansson, Tove 75–6, 81
Jersild, Arthur T. 87, 118
Jewett, Claudia 168, 180
Johns, Hazel 25
Johnson, Sally Patrick 141, 142, 201
Jolly, Hugh 74, 81
Jolly, June 197, 201
Jones, Anne 17, 20–1, 25, 27, 43
Jones, Gwyn 127, 141, 180
Jones, Thomas 127, 141, 180
Jung, Carl Gustav 121, 141

Kadushin, Alfred 78–9, 81
Kendrick, P. 26
Kibble, David 89–90, 118
King, Angela 141
King, Clive 55, 68, 73, 81
King, Francis 68, 81
Klingberg, Göte 101, 118
Klink, Johanna L. 118
Kübler-Ross, Elisabeth 169, 180

Lambert, Kenneth 25
Lee, Hermione 43, 161
Lessing, Doris 22–3, 25
Lewis, C.S. 110, 119
Lightbown, Chris 159, 161
Lowe, Polly 25, 30, 43
Lowry, Shirley Park 123, 124, 126
Lyall, D. 136, 141

McDowell, Nicola 35–6, 43, 103, 119
McMaster, John 68
Macaulay, Rose 47, 68
Macdonald, George 128, 141
Magee, Bryan 11, 14
Maguire, M. 25
Mallon, Brenda 20–1, 25, 30, 43, 205, 207
Manthei, Bob 60–1, 114, 119, 201
Marshall, Margaret R. 137–8, 141
Martin, D. 127, 139, 142
Mascaro, Juan 113, 119, 141
Mearns, Dave 25, 27, 29, 31–2, 34–5, 43, 119, 150, 161
Mennell, Mike 183, 198, 201
Meredith, George 120, 141
Merriman, Philippa 59, 67
Meyer, N. 127, 139, 142

Moran, Margaret 15, 17, 25, 114, 116, 117, 119
Morgan, Syble 7, 14
Morris, Mike 12, 14, 60, 68
Morrison, Donald W. 20, 25, 57–9, 68
Muldoon, Paul 119
Munro, Anne 60–1, 68, 114, 119, 210
Murdoch, Iris 120, 142
Murgatroyd, Stephen 26, 27, 29, 43, 205, 207

Nairne, Judith L. 24
Natten, Markus 103–4, 119
Newbould, Brian 182, 201
Nicolson, Olivia 79, 81
Noonan, Ellen 16–7, 26
Nordoff, Paul 198–9, 201
Norman, Barry 28, 43

Oaklander, Violet 26, 161, 175, 177–8, 180
O'Connor, Denis 48–9, 68
Onion, N. 201

Page, F. 26
Parker, Stephen 89–90, 118
Penman, Clive 93, 119
Plath, Sylvia 138, 141
Pluckrose, Henry 163, 180
Prestage, Robina O. 51, 68, 72, 73, 81
Price, Colin 89–90, 118
Priestley, J.B. 120, 142
Prys-Williams, Barbara 102, 119

Quaker Social Responsibility and Education 119

Rabuzzi, Katherine A. 123–4, 142
Rachin, Richard L. 25
Ramsey, M.E. 183, 184, 192–3, 201
Randell, Kathy 158, 161
Redfern, Keith 7–8, 12, 14
Renault, Mary 28, 43
Reps, Paul 112, 119
Richards, Jeffrey 9, 14, 131–3, 141, 161
Rickford, Frankie 134, 142
Rinehart, Carroll A. 183, 201

Robbins, Clive 198, 199, 201
Robinson, E. 119
Robinson, Joan G. 55–6, 68
Rodgers, Jack L. 98–9, 119
Rogers, Carl R. 3, 19, 22, 26, 29, 31, 40, 44, 61–2, 68, 81, 135, 151
Rowan, J. 14
Rowe, Dorothy 33–4, 37, 41, 42, 44, 150, 161
Royal College of Nursing 26
Rudolph, Linda B. 23, 26, 31, 44, 135–6, 142, 151, 162
Rutter, Michael 102, 119
Ryan, Virginia 26
Ryburn, Murray 143–4, 161

de Saint-Exupéry 176–7, 180
Salisbury, Elizabeth 4, 14, 24, 26
Sartre, Jean Paul 83, 104, 119
Saunders, Christine 63, 67
Sawbridge, Philippa 159, 161
Schuurman, Suzanne 99–100, 119
Sclare, Irene 152–3, 158–9, 161
Sereny, Gita 147, 161
Seymour, Claire 177, 180
Shahar, Shulamith 9, 14, 132, 142
Shapiro, Lawrence E. 26, 35, 44, 57, 59, 61, 68, 139, 142, 181, 195–7, 202
Shelley, Judith Allen 85–7, 119
Shelley, Percy B. 184, 202
Skaife D'Ingerthorpe, R. 175–6, 180
Small, John 13, 60–1, 114, 119, 200, 201
Smith, W.H. 119
Spender, Dale 4, 14
Sophocles 125, 142

Stevens, J. 177, 180
Stevenson, Yvonne 91–4, 119
Storr, Catherine 36, 39–40, 44, 55, 68
Strayer, Janet 28–9, 43, 44
Streich, Hildemarie 189, 202
Strommen, M.P. 119
Swift, Graham 48, 57, 68
Sworder, Geoffrey 40, 44

Tate, Tim 84, 119, 147, 161, 203, 207
Taylor, Elizabeth 53, 68, 130–1, 142, 148, 161
Tennyson, Alfred 49–50, 68
Thorne, Brian 25–7, 29, 31–2, 34–5, 40, 44, 113–4, 119, 150, 161
Thompson, Charles L. 23, 26, 31, 44, 135–6, 142, 151, 162
Thurber, James 134–5, 139, 142, 185, 202
Timms, Noel 114, 119
Timperley, Rosemary 178–9, 180
Toynbee, Polly 65, 68

Wardle, Margaret 154, 162
Watts, A. G. 44
West, Janet 53–4, 68
Westerhoff III, John H. 5, 7, 8, 14, 119
Wheeler, Joan 65–6, 68, 159–60, 162
Wilson, Kate 26
Winnicott, D.W. 168, 171, 180, 205
Winterson, Jeanette 90, 95–6, 119, 148, 162
Wispé, Lauren 28–9, 44
Wittgenstein, Ludwig 8, 14
Woolfe, R. 118